*The Rhetoric of Morality and Philosophy*

# The *Rhetoric of Morality and Philosophy*

Plato's *Gorgias* and *Phaedrus*

## Seth Benardete

The University of Chicago Press
Chicago and London

The University of Chicago Press, Chicago 60637
The University of Chicago Press, Ltd., London
© 1991 by The University of Chicago
All rights reserved. Published 1991
Paperback edition 2009
Printed in the United States of America

18 17 16 15 14 13 12 11 10 09     2 3 4 5 6

ISBN-13: 978-0-226-04240-4 (cloth)
ISBN-13: 978-0-226-04241-1 (paper)
ISBN-10: 0-226-04240-5 (cloth)
ISBN-10: 0-226-04241-3 (paper)

Library of Congress Cataloging-in-Publication Data

Benardete, Seth
    The rhetoric of morality and philosophy : Plato's Gorgias and
  Phaedrus / Seth Benardete.
      p.   cm.
    Includes index.
    ISBN-10: 0-226-04240-5
    1. Plato. Gorgias.   2. Plato. Phaedrus.   3. Plato—Ethics.
  4. Plato—Contributions in methodology.   5. Plato—Literary art.
  6. Methodology.   7. Ethics. Ancient.   8. Rhetoric—Philosophy.
  I. Title
    B371.B46   1991
    184—dc20
                                                        90-39379
                                                             CIP

*On ne fait pas attention que l'âne serait par lui-même, et pour nous, le premier, le plus beau, le mieux fait, le plus distingué des animaux, si dans le monde il n'y avait point de cheval.*

Buffon

# Contents

|  | List of Figures | viii |
|---|---|---|
|  | Acknowledgments | ix |
|  | Introduction | 1 |
| I | Gorgias 447a1–461b2 | 5 |
| II | Polus 461b3–481b5 | 31 |
| III | Callicles 1 481b6–499b3 | 61 |
| IV | Callicles 2 499b4–527e7 | 82 |
| V | *Phaedrus* | 103 |
| VI | Phaedrus and Socrates 227a1–230e5 | 106 |
| VII | Lysias 230e6–237a6 | 116 |
| VIII | Socrates 1 237a7–242a2 | 120 |
| IX | Socrates' *Daimonion* 242a3–243e8 | 127 |
| X | Socrates 2 243e9–257b6 | 132 |
| XI | Writing 257b7–258d6 | 155 |
| XII | Horses and Asses 258d7–260d2 | 161 |
| XIII | The Art of Speeches 260d3–262c4 | 169 |
| XIV | Lysias and Socrates Examined 262c5–266c1 | 175 |
| XV | Rhetoric 266c1–274b4 | 182 |
| XVI | An Egyptian Story 274b6–278b6 | 187 |
| XVII | Lysias and Isocrates 278b7–279c8 | 192 |
|  | Epilogue: On Reading Poetry Platonically | 195 |
|  | General Index | 197 |
|  | Index of Platonic Passages Discussed | 203 |

# Figures

| | | |
|---|---|---|
| 1 | Structure of *Gorgias* | 2 |
| 2 | Virtues and vices of body and soul | 35 |
| 3 | Templates of arts and their phantom images | 45 |
| 4 | Makeup of Polus | 45 |
| 5 | Just, beautiful, and good | 52 |
| 6 | Just, beautiful, good, and pleasant | 53 |
| 7 | Punisher, punished, and spectator | 54 |
| 8 | Callicles' makeup | 73 |
| 9 | Partial structure of *Gorgias* | 81 |
| 10 | Just, beautiful, and good | 86 |
| 11 | Justice as punishment, beautiful, and good | 87 |
| 12 | Transformation of good and beautiful into beautiful | 87 |
| 13 | Callicles as Polus and Callicles | 88 |
| 14 | Initial relation of Lysias, Phaedrus, and Socrates | 108 |
| 15 | Subsequent relation of Lysias, Phaedrus, and Socrates | 109 |
| 16 | Lysias experienced | 109 |
| 17 | Lysias as virtual image | 110 |
| 18 | Just, beautiful, good, and pleasant in *Gorgias* | 123 |
| 19 | Opinion and desire in *Phaedrus* | 124 |
| 20 | God, monster, and man | 128 |
| 21 | Three erotic speeches in *Phaedrus* | 129 |
| 22 | Human hubris and divine madness | 130 |
| 23 | Ascent and locomotion | 138 |
| 24 | Beings, souls, and gods | 148 |
| 25 | Lover, beloved, god, and being | 157 |
| 26 | Law, legislator, law-abiding | 158 |
| 27 | Opinion | 172 |
| 28 | Being and likeness | 173 |
| 29 | Being, opinion, and soul-type | 173 |
| 30 | Hubris and madness | 178 |
| 31 | Socrates' two speeches in *Phaedrus* | 180 |

# Acknowledgments

I wish to thank the Earhart Foundation for a fellowship in the summer of 1989 to complete this work.

Ronna Burger, Robert Berman, Michael Davis, and Barbara Witucki read the manuscript with great care and made several suggestions for its improvement. I also wish to thank my daughter Alexandra Emma for designing figure 2.

# Introduction

To put side by side an interpretation of one Platonic dialogue with that of another does not make a book; but although *Gorgias* and *Phaedrus* are not as matched a pair as *Sophist* and *Statesman* are, something can still be said for putting them together. If Socrates in the *Gorgias* were primarily concerned with justice and morality, the *Republic* and not the *Phaedrus* would form a more natural couple with it. An idealistic Socrates and a Socrates fighting mad do go together (*Republic* 536c4), while a lovesick Socrates hardly suits the killjoy of the *Gorgias*. The antihedonism of Socrates, however, is not as strict as it seems (*Gorgias* 458a2–5); and Socrates in the *Gorgias* is not out to defend morality but to understand "so-called rhetoric." The moral fervor of the *Gorgias* is an atmospheric effect of how Gorgias, Polus, and Callicles understand what Socrates is saying. The *Gorgias* exemplifies a thesis of the *Phaedrus*—that it is one thing to know what happens when an argument of a certain kind meets a soul of a certain kind, but quite another to be able to recognize it when it happens right before one (*Phaedrus* 271d5–272a1). In the *Gorgias*, Socrates puts all his cards on the table and still has them all up his sleeve. Socrates is completely consistent throughout the dialogue while his interlocutors diverge further and further from his straight argument. First Gorgias, then Polus, and finally Callicles puts a spin on Socrates' argument that sends each of them progressively more and more off course, while at the same time we are shown that this divergence constitutes rhetoric as the phantom image of justice. The structure of rhetoric is the three-staged difference between what Gorgias, Polus, and Callicles believe Socrates means by justice and what Socrates really means (fig.1).

A structure of this kind is probably unique among Platonic dialogues. Indeed, one may conjecture that each dialogue has its own peculiar structure and is like an animal of a distinct species; so in an important sense no one dialogue offers much help for the taxonomy of any other. The *Phaedrus*, however, in which Socrates compares a perfect writing to an animal (264c2–5), comes closest of any dialogue to having a structure that is a passkey for every other dialogue. The *Phaedrus* does not open up any other dialogue, but it accounts for what

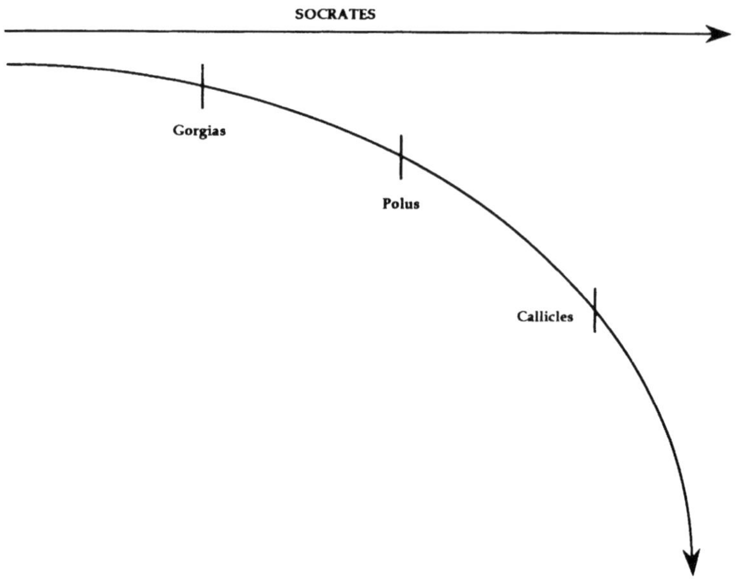

2   Introduction

```
                          SOCRATES
─────────────────────────────────────────────────▶
        ┼
      Gorgias
                       ┼
                      Polus

                                   ┼
                                Callicles
                                          ▼
```

Figure 1

happens in every other dialogue without saying what happens in any of them. The peculiarity of Plato's art consists in his showing the nature of philosophy in general while showing the impossibility of deducing from its nature the nature of a philosophic argument in particular. There is a structure to philosophy but no method of philosophy. Philosophy has a *logos* but no algorithm.

The *Phaedrus*, then, might be thought a suitable partner for any other Platonic dialogue, but the issue of rhetoric binds it closely with the *Gorgias*. Socrates extracts a definition of rhetoric from Gorgias that involves, as we would expect, speech and persuasion (452e1–453a5); and in the *Phaedrus*, Socrates on his own likewise understands rhetoric in the same terms (261a7–b2). In the *Gorgias*, however, Socrates understands rhetoric as a form of flattery that does not involve either speech or persuasion. Spurious rhetoric turns out to be a phantom image of justice; genuine rhetoric is the science of eros. The *Gorgias* and *Phaedrus* between them point to a psychology in which the locus of moral indignation and the love of the beautiful in the human soul are properly understood. This book on these two dialogues is meant to be on the way to the formulation of such a psychology. In a nonscientific way, the gods, as beings from whom men demand justice and to whom men look up as perfect beings, can be said to prefigure the problematic unity of a Platonic psychology. The gods, however, are either the gods of the city or the gods of the poets, and the city is as silent about the nature of the gods as the poets are loquacious. The two gods who are almost the special preserve of Greek poetry are Hades and Eros. Hades involves not only the issue of body and soul but also of divine reward and punishment. Socrates arranges for a confrontation with the Hades of the poets by picturing the setting of the *Protagoras* as the Homeric Hades in which he (Socrates) is another Odysseus who first sees Hippias as another phantom Heracles who was himself a god and then sees Prodicus as another Tantalus who was punished forever (*Protagoras* 315b9, c8). Piety, one may add, is as conspicuously a virtue in the *Protagoras* as is its absence elsewhere. The companion dialogue to the *Protagoras* is the *Symposium*, where all the main speakers except Aristophanes were present in the *Protagoras*, and the topic is the praise of the god Eros. The *Gorgias* and *Phaedrus*, then, pick up as their theological counterparts the *Protagoras* and *Symposium* respectively. I propose to treat the latter pair in another book, *The Gods of the Poets*, which will explicate the theological dimension of the *Gorgias* and *Phaedrus*.

# I
# Gorgias

(447a1–461b2)

The issue in the background of the *Gorgias* is very simple. If Gorgianic rhetoric has the power Gorgias claims for it, it would necessarily follow that the best city in speech of the *Republic* could be realized anywhere on earth and at any time. Either the philosopher could learn this all-powerful rhetoric, or he could hire the all-powerful rhetorician to speak on his behalf and to persuade any political gathering that the philosopher ought to be king. Whether rhetoric was just or morally neutral, it would have this power regardless; but it could not be enlisted into the service of philosophy if it were necessarily unjust and therefore strove to gain for its practitioners a position that was not rightly theirs. Gorgianic rhetoric, then, must either be essentially unjust if it is powerful or, if it is either just or neutral, be too weak to undertake such a salvation of political life. Socrates' interest in conversing with Gorgias, which Callicles finds perplexing, could thus be explained. Gorgias is a potential ally of Socrates insofar as we conceive of Socrates' turn to political philosophy as having its political aim in reform and revolution. Any hope of this kind, however, which Socrates might have cherished, is surely shattered by the end of the Gorgias section of the dialogue. Since neither Polus nor Callicles can ever have been considered suitable partners in a Socratic enterprise— each in his own way is in favor of injustice—Socrates' interest in Gorgias, Polus, and Callicles remains puzzling. Why should there be so long a dialogue with such recalcitrant opponents? Socrates silences all three, but he seems to persuade none of them. He proves before us that his rhetoric is not powerful enough to go public and make up for Gorgias' failure. Socrates, in asserting that he is the true politician, admits that in appearance, that is, in the element of opinion, he is powerless.

This initial puzzle of the *Gorgias*, which must occur to anyone who looks at it from the perspective of the *Republic,* is deepened when one asks while reading it what keeps together the themes of rhetoric and morality. If the Gorgias section were an aporetic dialogue by itself (cf. 461a7–b2), would anyone miss the rest? Polus and Callicles are spokesmen for injustice, but they are weak. Neither can represent the possibility that rhetoric can be all-powerful and establish tyranny everywhere on earth. Rhetoric seems to be the opening wedge into the larger issue of justice and two Socratic paradoxes—that it is better to suffer injustice than to do it, and it is better to submit to punishment if one is unjust than to get off scot-free. In light of these paradoxes, rhetoric seems to be in itself no more than one of several ways of gaining power in any city in which things are not wholly decided by either brute force or established law. The issue thus seems to be tyranny, and whether Archelaus ever spoke to the Macedonians and persuaded them of his right to rule seems irrelevant. Polus, who cites Archelaus as a contemporary witness to the union of happiness and injustice, does not mention any instance of Archelaus' persuasiveness. Indeed, the noun "persuasion" (*peithō*) occurs nineteen times in the Gorgias section and not once afterward. That "persuasion" should vanish when it does, despite the effort Socrates put into discovering Gorgias' belief that to persuade by means of speeches in any political gathering is the greatest human good, is all the more surprising because Socrates does not present his double fourfold scheme of which rhetoric is a part until the Polus section, where he outlines his understanding of rhetoric. Socrates' scheme elicits very little interest, even though "sophistry" and "politics" are left wholly undefined, to say nothing of "justice," which, Socrates says, is the genuine art of which rhetoric is the phantom image. That justice is an art initiates the argument of the *Republic*, but Socrates devotes a good part of the *Republic* to its explication. In the *Gorgias*, however, no definition of justice is offered, even though Socrates denies that it is possible to speak of anything as good or bad before it is determined what it is. Socrates thus admits that the *Gorgias* as a whole is rhetorical. He apparently adopts the way of artless rhetoric in order to defend justice as an art.

Even if for the sake of argument such a conclusion should be granted, it cannot be regarded as very satisfactory if Socrates adopts the weapons of a sham practice and wields them to so little effect that he convinces no one. To be rhetorically effective is to bring about a change not in utterance but in behavior, and it is as hard to imagine that Gorgias and Polus abandoned their profession as to imagine that we know nothing of Callicles from any other source because Socrates convinced him to give up politics. Rather than to convict Socrates of so senseless a ploy, of exposing the powerlessness of Gorgianic rhetoric by showing himself to be incompetent in its use, it is safer to begin by asking whether the themes of rhetoric and morality are not two but one, and whether the dialogue as a whole is, as its title suggests, an exposition of Gorgianic rhetoric with as tight an argument as we have learned to expect from Socrates. Such a reorientation in our approach to the *Gorgias* would entail that the absence in it of a definition of justice belongs to the argument and is not an egregious oversight on Socrates' part. Justice is necessarily undefined; otherwise, Socrates' claim about the nature of rhetoric would be false. Not only does Gorgias not teach justice when he teaches rhetoric but he cannot teach it. Neither he nor his disciple Polus knows what it is. They are as irrational as Callicles, who despises the vulgar whose desires he extols. The three interlocutors of the *Gorgias* exhibit rhetoric. They are the *logos* of Socrates' geometrical schemes. They prove that Socrates was right about rhetoric. The *Gorgias* is the presentation of a Socratic experiment in which Socrates comes to test an hypothesis. Only if Gorgias, Polus, and Callicles were not to say what they do say would Socrates' test falsify his hypothesis. The mistakes in the reasoning of the *Gorgias* are not Socrates' mistakes but the very mistakes of rhetoric that demonstrate its spuriousness. The *Gorgias* is the positive print of an etiolated negative. It captures forever the ghost of justice.

No other Platonic dialogue is as saturated with allusions to events that span the Peloponnesian War (431–404 B.C.) as the *Gorgias*. Pericles died in 429 (503c2–3); Gorgias came to Athens in 427;[1] Demos is known as beautiful in 423 and stupid by 422 (481d5);[2] Alcibiades became prominent about 420 (519a8); Archelaus (470d) began his rule in the same year in which Nicias died, 413; Aristocrates died in 406 (472a7); and Socrates performed his one political act in the trial of the generals at Arginousae in 406 (473e6).[3] Since it is impossible to square "the recent death of Pericles," as Callicles puts it, with the *Gorgias* occurring one year after Socrates' tribe presided at the trial of the generals, we have to say that Plato situates the *Gorgias* in wartime Athens but in such a way that we are enjoined to believe that the conversation never occurred. The *Gorgias* is of a time but not in time. Callicles, who is not known from elsewhere, would thus represent the time without being anyone of the time. He begins the dialogue, and his first words are, "Of war and battle." These words certainly suit one who scorns what he takes to be the moralizing of Socrates and who wants to bring Socrates face to face with reality; it is only slightly absurd if the spokesman for reality either is not real himself or at least

---

1. In light of what turns out to be the nerve of the *Gorgias*, it seems to be more than a coincidence that Cleon's speech in Thucydides, decked out as it is with more than the usual number of Gorgianic flourishes, and which recommends the execution of the entire male population of Mytilene, should be delivered in the same year as Gorgias' arrival in Athens as part of the embassy from Leontini. Thucydides says that Cleon was the most violent of the citizens and the one most persuasive to the demos (3.36.6)

2. J. K. Davies, *Athenian Propertied Families 600–300 B.C.* (Oxford 1971), 330.

3. E. R. Dodds, *Plato's Gorgias* (Oxford 1953), 473e6.

is set in a time frame that cannot be. But what are we to make of the total absence of any mention of the Peloponnesian War in the discussion? Socrates speaks of the paraphernalia of Athens' empire—ships, walls, dockyards, and tribute (517c2, 519a3)—but not of the empire itself (cf. 514a2); and Callicles chooses to illustrate the inexorable drive of acquisitiveness with Darius' invasion of Scythia, which failed, rather than with the expansion of Athens ever since it got rid of the Pisistratids (Herodotus 5.78). Is Callicles as squeamish about Athenian imperialism as he is about catamites (494a7)? Gorgias speaks of the rule rhetoric obtains for its artisans each in his own city (452d5–8), but he is as silent about war as he is about the competition among rival rhetoricians in a single city. Whether the best rhetorician in such cases comes out on top is not clear, but Gorgias' silence seems to grant at least that not all foreign relations are a matter of diplomacy. It is perhaps too easy to conclude from all this that rhetoric knows nothing about anything other than words, and for all its hardheadedness it is lost in dreams. But even if this conclusion is unwarranted, one would still have to ask after the significance of Socrates at his most moral fighting under illusory circumstances against those who claim first prize in the contest of no illusions. Is Socrates the moralist as impossible as the reality of the setting in which he is most moral?

At the beginning of the *Gorgias* Callicles and Socrates exchange proverbial expressions. Callicles speaks of war and battle, Socrates of a feast. Courage in the service of pleasure comes close to being the formula for what Callicles proposes. Callicles seems to be accusing Socrates of cowardice; Socrates lets others do the fighting and comes later for the celebration. Socrates understands at once that there was no fighting and that he came too late to a feast. Callicles' talk of war and battle was a cover for the pleasure he took in listening to talk. Perhaps there is nothing really remarkable about the ease with which Socrates guesses at Callicles' meaning; but coming as it does at the beginning of a dialogue about rhetoric, it warns us of the risks of interpretation, especially if rhetoric is not an art and aims at gratification in the guise of the sternest morality. Gorgias will urge on his own the execution of any rhetorician who uses his art unjustly (457c3). At the moment, Socrates' exposure of Callicles' meaning suggests that Socrates came at the right time if he wanted to learn from Gorgias about the power of his art. Had he come earlier, Gorgias would have been displaying his power, and it would perhaps not have been as easy with Gorgias as it is with Callicles to figure out the truth of his display. Socrates will later apologize for the extreme caution with which he approaches the meaning of Gorgias' answers, so as to make sure that neither he anticipates what Gorgias has in mind nor Gorgias in turn indulges Socrates in his inferences. Socrates has a way of irritating his interlocutors while gratifying the audience which witnesses their discomfiture (458d1–4). Battle and feast thus seem to be a formula that embraces Socrates' way no less than Callicles' fantasy of case-hardened softness (cf. *Philebus* 21c6–8). Callicles' fantasy, then, might just be one of the several masks that rhetoric assumes in trying to guess at the true art of Socratic politics.

Socrates blames his late arrival on Chaerephon; Chaerephon compelled him to linger in the marketplace. Socrates is a pushover for distractions. His comrade can do with him as he wishes. Chaerephon says their delay is no problem; he will be no less the cure than the cause of the injury. Chaerephon seems to allude to the story of Telephus, whom Achilles' spear wounded and later healed when Telephus agreed to show the Greeks the way to Troy. Chaerephon claims that Gorgias is his friend and will make another display either now if Socrates so decides (*dokei*) or later if Socrates so wants (*boulei*). Chaerophon claims to control Gorgias as easily as he controls Socrates. The big men are extraordinarily accommodating to their hangers-on. Callicles too offers to arrange for Gorgias' display; Gorgias is staying at his house and will perform whenever Socrates and Chaerephon want to come. Not only, then, does the dialogue continue its riddling start with the banter of violence and accommodation, but Chaerephon casually introduces, without making any obvious distinction between them, two words, *dokein* and *boulesthai*, to which Socrates later assigns the difference respectively between the arbitrariness of the will and the rationality of ends. This difference is now of no importance; nothing now resists the achievement of whatever Socrates wants. Between the time of Callicles' suggestion that Socrates ask Gorgias himself about whether he is willing to converse and Socrates' telling Chaerephon to ask Gorgias who he is, Socrates, Chaerephon, and Callicles have passed from outside to inside the hall where Gorgias had just finished his display. Nowhere else in Plato does anyone walk without its being noted in some way, but here they proceed as if to will was to act and walls vanish at one's pleasure. The easy atmosphere with which the *Gorgias* opens seems to show something comparable to the effect of Gorgianic rhetoric without its showing in action the power of Gorgianic rhetoric so that we could judge its power. Plato thus seems to imply that Gorgianic rhetoric is powerless, and whatever effect it appears to achieve is due to the effect having already been achieved. The rhetorician comes after the feast.

Socrates allows us to make a preliminary comparison of Gorgias' way with his own by getting Chaerephon to question Gorgias. A substitute Socrates prompts Polus to come forward as a substitute

Gorgias. We get to watch an exhibition round before the main event. Gorgias' way shows up in Polus' claim that he, like Gorgias, can answer any question; and Socrates' way shows up in Chaerephon proceeding by way of examples to question Polus. Chaerephon seems less skilled at Socratic questioning than Polus is at rhetorical answers. Is rhetoric more teachable than dialectic? The very form of the word "rhetoric" implies that it is an art, but Socrates in the *Gorgias* never speaks of dialectic. Perhaps the ability to answer any question has no counterpart in the ability to ask any question. The formulaic answers of rhetoric assume the absence of novelty in the questions, but Socratic questioning seems to be grounded in novelty. One comes to know what one does not know in a previously unknown way. Chaerephon, who did not know when he detained Socrates in the marketplace that Socrates did not want to hear Gorgias' display oratory, must improvise a question without knowing what Socrates does not know. Socrates' interest is in the power of Gorgias' art. He wants to find out, without experiencing the power, what power rhetoric has. He effectively arranges for this by putting off any display on Gorgias' part and having Polus discharge all the flourishes of rhetoric in a minor skirmish. Socrates can thus illustrate before Gorgias the difference between rhetoric and conversation and establish as a principle that rhetoric is not to interfere in the discussion of rhetoric; and once Gorgias agrees that he can teach rhetoric and therefore that it is taught like any other art, Socrates can anticipate his later distinction between persuasion and instruction and establish that rhetoric is not used in the teaching of rhetoric. The apparent inferiority of Chaerephon to Polus makes it possible to strip Gorgias of all his rhetorical power and have him raise his sights and so lay claim to a higher rank for his rhetoric than the "so-called rhetoric" of Polus (448d9). Gorgias in fact will accept as a matter of course that knowledge is virtue.

The strung-out form in which Socrates expresses his interest in Gorgias—he wants to know about "the power of the art of the man"—suggests that Socrates has to ask three questions: Who is Gorgias? What is his art? What is its power? Socrates lets Chaerephon ask the first of these questions. Ask him, he tells him, who he is. Socrates tells Chaerephon to model his question on the following: "If he were in fact a maker of shoes, his answer to you would surely have been a shoemaker." Socrates contrasts "maker of shoes"(*hupodēmatōn dēmiourgos*) with "shoemaker" (*skutotomos*), a two-word phrase with a compound word, which if decompounded would be more literally translated as a cutter of leather. "Rhetorician" (*rhētōr*) is not a compound word, and its literal meaning is "speaker." It could designate not a professional but man as the speaking animal; indeed, if anyone were to be singled out among human speakers as the speaker, Socrates would be everyone's choice, especially since Socrates seems to have claimed for his own private use the verb *dialegesthai*, the ordinary word for the speaking of one human being with another. Despite Gorgias having been denied the use of rhetoric in his conversation with Socrates, he is very reluctant to restrict the range of rhetoric; and in the course of his gradual admission of its limits he lets us entertain the question of whether there could be a global science of speech that dealt no less with the form of any sentence in any art or science than with the gossiping of neighbors and public addresses to any kind of audience. Insofar as Socrates certainly practices something that ranges over all of this field, Socrates' question about Gorgias, if turned against himself, would demand that we first ask Who is Socrates? before we ask about his power and his art.

Socrates' example of the shoemaker involved no proper names. Chaerephon therefore departs from this example in trying to keep to it and still preserve the individuality implied in the question of who Gorgias is. His first example is Gorgias' brother Herodicus and his second example two brothers, the painters Aristophon and Polygnotus, of whom Polygnotus is so famous that Chaerephon does not have to give his name. The three examples seem to mark out the way in which rhetoric is going to be understood. Medicine is the genuine art for the body and rhetoric its spurious counterpart for the soul. Callicles will urge Socrates to learn rhetoric as a necessary form of self-protection, and perhaps Socrates' indifference to this feature of rhetoric does not differ from his practice of not wearing shoes (*Phaedrus* 229a3–4; *Symposium* 174a4). If, moreover, we ask about the possible unity of the arts of medicine and painting, which Chaerephon allows Gorgias hypothetically to have, we are asking, in complying with Socrates' geometrical proportions, whether there could be a single art that handles the health of soul and the representation of its health. Could there be an art that induces both real justice and its simulacrum? Socrates' question to Gorgias, whether in teaching rhetoric he also teaches justice, seems to be a variant of this question. When Glaucon poses the issue of justice in the *Republic*, he imagines that the presence of real justice cannot come to light except as injustice (360e1–361d3). So if only spurious justice can appear, the medicine and painting of soul cannot but be themselves a spurious unity. We of course could say in reply to Glaucon that Plato is the discoverer of this art, for he represents the justice of philosophy while inducing in us philosophy; but Plato's induction and representation of philosophy do not bring about in the individual the show and the reality of justice. We try to emulate and not imitate Socrates.

12   Gorgias

Polus' rhetorical answer to Chaerephon's question about what art Gorgias knows is that it is the best and most beautiful of the arts, and since experience makes human life proceed artfully and inexperience randomly, Gorgias knows how to make human life be least subject to chance and proceed as rationally as possible. If the greatest threat to leading a rational life comes from other men and not from storms at sea and other natural catastrophes, Polus' answer is not very different from that which Sorates extracts from Gorgias, that rhetoric is the cause of human freedom and of ruling others politically. It is not obvious why Polus could not have given Gorgias' answer and chose to praise rhetoric before he defined it. Socrates implies, in criticizing Polus' answer for its rhetorical shape, that so-called rhetoric is essentially epideictic and praises whatever has been faulted. Socrates suggests that Polus emulates Gorgias' *Praise of Helen,* in which Gorgias excused or defended Helen against her detractors. The gist of his encomium was that any action can be understood as a submission to compulsion, and whether Helen fell in love, was persuaded by speech, seized by force, or compelled by divine necessity, she cannot be blamed. Socrates, then, would imply that rhetoric can regularize the randomness of life only after the event and rectify in retrospect its irrationality. Rhetoric makes up stories that put the sheen of reason on what was experienced at the time as senseless. Polus' defense of rhetoric prior to any attack on it would thus be necessary for rhetoric. Rhetoric must always react and never initiate. It can get one off but cannot start one off. It cannot be a ruling art.

The distinction Socrates draws between quiddity and quality is followed by a distinction between brachylogy and macrology. The latter distinction is known to Gorgias, and one of his selling points is that no one can say the same thing as briefly as he can. Socrates implies, in the first of many proportions of the *Gorgias,* that brachylogy stands to macrology as the inquiry into what something is stands to speeches of praise and blame. Socrates thus relegates rhetoric to the sidelines in the discussion of rhetoric and keeps himself as questioner in control of the discussion. Although Gorgias lodges a weak protest against the arbitrariness of the measure of length, he does not realize that Socrates is laying down the rule that an answer is to be relative to the length of the question, and however long the question is the answer must be shorter. This rule is strictly maintained throughout the Gorgias section until Gorgias praises at length the power of rhetoric and ruins his case (456a7–457c3). However well Gorgias illustrates the difference between long and short speeches, we cannot but be uneasy at the license Socrates grants himself as questioner to be as long as he wants. It is true that the three branches of rhetoric (forensic, deliberative, and epideictic) all go in for long speeches and have as their aim persuasion, but it is not obvious that short speeches are rhetorically neutral and bring about instruction (cf. Thucydides 5.85–86). The model for brachylogy that Socrates seems to have in mind is a mathematical proof which is at its most elegant when it draws its conclusion in the clearest and most concise way. Every step in a mathematical proof can be phrased as a question, and the shortest possible answer to each will be yes or no. Yes and no seem to be rhetorically neutral, but what they gain in brevity they lose in concealing the degree of conviction behind the answer. Gorgias answers yes to Socrates' first two questions, and Socrates praises him for his brevity. Socrates' praise takes the form of an oath, "By Hera!" His oath seems to be the kind of expression rhetoric wants to provoke in the auditor, since Gorgias' answer may express his indifferent politeness to Socrates' questions no less than a genuine assent to the propositions. Socrates' attempt to provoke Gorgias by praising him so extravagantly does not meet with any success. Gorgias comes forward as more reasonable than Socrates. He seems to be the model of rationality.

To the extent, then, that brevity represents the rationality of the speaker and disguises the state of his soul, Socrates has not only let Gorgias become opaque to him and to us but has introduced into the discussion a distinction between mind and soul that might be fatal to any psychology. Rhetoric could be a science only if it can understand the causes of the express assents and dissents of those who listen to speeches, for otherwise it must take the form of the response for the truth about the degree and kind of conviction. Rhetoric would then not know whether there has been any persuasion and, more fatally perhaps, what in the speeches has been persuasive and what not. A tightly reasoned argument might turn out to be for argument's sake and of no significance to the interlocutor. Polus first and then Callicles more elaborately make this point on behalf of Gorgias and themselves. Nothing they say to Socrates has anything to do with their true sentiments. The triumphs of Socratic reasoning only go to show the impotence of reason. We thus seem forced to choose between a dialectic that alters no one's convictions and a rhetoric that is effective but knows neither how it is effective nor what it effects. Rationality is empty; rhetoric is blind.

Socrates asks Gorgias about what of the beings rhetoric is. Socrates' two examples—weaving and music, one of which deals with the making of cloaks and the other with the making of songs—imply that Socrates expects a two-part answer: rhetoric deals with the making of speeches. Gorgias, however, disregards the examples and assumes

Socrates is asking of which of the beings is rhetoric the science. His bare answer, "about speeches," certainly admits the interpretation that rhetoric deals with the speeches of the beings, everything in short that anyone says about anything; but Gorgias seems to mean that speech is one of the beings and rhetoric is the science of speech. Aristotle's *Organon* would be part of such a science. Gorgias, however, does not want rhetoric to be comprehensive if it thereby has to be instrumental. In order to narrow the scope of rhetoric, Socrates gives the example of medicine. Medicine has its own speeches through which it teaches medicine, makes manifest the sick, and explains how they are to become well. Medicine is both diagnostic and therapeutic. If rhetoric were comparable, it would diagnose and cure the sick of soul through the same kind of speeches it used in transmitting its teaching. Such a rhetoric fits the Eleatic stranger's idealized description of Socrates' soul-cathartics in the *Sophist* (230b4–d5). Socrates surely must have an interest in a science that seems to set the standard for his own practice. As long as Gorgias, in the interest of brevity, remains cryptic, he could pass for Socrates. At the heart of Gorgianic rhetoric is Socratic dialectic. In its macrological expansion of that core it becomes "so-called rhetoric."

Rhetoric is unlike any other art, Gorgias says, because it does not deal with the manufacture and actions of the hand; the entirety of its actions and ratification is through speeches (*dia logōn*). "Through speeches" decompounds *dialegesthai*, the word Socrates had used first in opposition to display oratory and then to Polus' rhetorical training.[4] Gorgias, however, does not decompound "manufacture" (*kheirourgia*), so that the strict contrary of "work of the hands" would not be "through speeches" but "through the mouth." Yet gesture and posture are not a small part of oratory, and it is not clear why Gorgias wants to present rhetoric as without a corporeal element. Socrates seems to go along with Gorgias' distinction while objecting that other arts also accomplish everything through speeches. In covering the range from silence to speech, Socrates groups arts together at several places along the way and ends up with a total paradox. At one end are arts that could work in total silence (painting and sculpture); some need little speech; some have their speeches equal to their actions (acting, for example, or singing to the lyre); others are mostly speeches and need little or no deed (arithmetic, logistic, geometry, checkers). The indispensable need for action in geometrical constructions makes

---

4. Theaetetus makes a serious error when he fails to see that speeches are the instrument through which the soul examines being, same, other, etc. (*Theaetetus* 185c4–e2).

Socrates' divisions suspect (*Republic* 527a6–b1); but even without geometry one does not see why the number theoretician cannot proceed in as total a silence as the painter. It looks as if "through speeches" meant at first "through spoken speeches" and then slid over into the meaning "through reasonings." Socrates' articulation could be saved if one said that sculpture cannot do what it does through speeches and that arithmetic can do everything it does through speeches. Rhetoric would then be unique among the nonmanufacturing arts because it can only do what it does through spoken speeches. Gorgianic rhetoric, then, would once more be a rival to Socrates', and he too seems to deny that writing can replace the living voice. At the moment, however, it is not the very discussion Socrates and Gorgias are having that must be distinguished from Gorgianic rhetoric. Mathematics is its rival. Mathematics, it seems, is less disputably an art than dialectic.

Socrates distinguishes between what Gorgias wants (*boulesthai*) to say and what he literally (*tōi rhēmati*) says. Gorgias' literal meaning identifies mathematics with rhetoric. Mathematical speech seems to be speech that must be literally understood; it must say precisely what it means and leave no room for a further question. Rhetoric, however, seems necessarily to be nonliteral speech; its persuasiveness might well consist in never saying what it means. Gorgias of course as a teacher of rhetoric would have to speak literally about how to speak nonliterally. He would, as Aristotle does, explain one kind of metaphor in terms of a proportion and say that since bowl is to Dionysus as shield is to Ares, one can call the bowl the shield of Dionysus and the shield the bowl of Ares (*Poetics* 1457b16–22). In a sense, Socrates is now making Gorgias conform to the speeches of rhetoric if rhetoric is an art. He is teaching Gorgias how to teach rhetoric. If his teaching is a success, he will have shown that rhetoric is an art and can possibly be put in the service of philosophy to make the philosopher-king. Socrates, then, must show either that there is a certain point beyond which his teaching of Gorgias cannot go or that his teaching can be carried through to the point that rhetoric emerges as an art but is not all-powerful. It is impossible to say until the very end of the dialogue whether Socrates demonstrates either point.

As Socrates goes through the definitions of various mathematical sciences, he becomes more and more careless in his use of *logos*. He first speaks of "in speeches," then of "through speech" in the case of arithmetic, and of "by speech" in the case of logistic and astronomy (451a6, b1,6,c6); by the time he defines astronomy, whose speeches are about the motion of the stars, sun, and moon in their relative speed to one another, *logos* seems to be a superfluous term, or else it simply means that these arts are only theoretical. Gorgias at least seems to look at it in this way, for when he states the beings with which rhetoric deals, he says they are the greatest and best of human things. He stakes the claim of rhetoric not so much on its exclusive use of spoken speech as on its concern with the most important and chief good of man. Gorgias now has other competitors—medicine, gymnastic, and chrematistic—none of which works primarily through speeches. Rhetoric, then, is fairly unique, since it sits high on one scale whose criterion is the degree to which *logos* is involved in the practice of an art, and high on another scale whose criterion is the human good. Rhetoric's chief rival would now be sophistry. Socrates says as much in his account of rhetoric; but when Socrates says it again to Callicles, Callicles expresses nothing but loathing for sophistry. Callicles believes the chief rival to rhetoric is philosophy.

Socrates cites a drinking song to show that others dispute with rhetoric the claim Gorgias makes for it. A drinking song does not carry much weight; but if rhetoric is an art that can persuade any crowd, Gorgias has his work cut out for him if he believes he can manage to get himself heard in a drinking party. In only one respect does Socrates pay any attention to the ranking in the song of health, beauty, and wealth; he imagines that the three artisans of each of these goods speak in the order in which the song places them but on his own behalf as the agent of the highest good. According to Socrates' own scheme, health is as inferior to beauty as medicine to gymnastic and justice to the art of legislation. However that may be, none of Socrates' imaginary spokesmen offers an argument for his counterclaim. The doctor rests his case on a rhetorical question: "What greater good do men have than health?" The trainer does not rank himself over against the doctor and the moneymaker; he merely expresses surprise if Gorgias could show a greater good of his art than of his own. He too then uses a rhetorical device. The moneymaker leaves it up to Socrates to decide between him and Gorgias. He takes wealth to be indisputably the greatest good, but he alone wants to know what Gorgias will say to be greater. By representing each of the artisans as more or less self-satisfied, Socrates suggests to Gorgias that rhetoric could have as its task to supply each art with catchy phrases and persuasive copy in order to expand its share in the market of goods. There would be no conflict of interest if one agency handled all three accounts. If rhetoric, then, is to be more than the art of advertising, it would have to evaluate the various goods and rank them in an authoritative manner. The dispute for first place among them shows the need for a ruling art.

Gorgias seems to understand very well what Socrates' argument requires him to say. He is the maker of "what is in truth the greatest good and the cause no less of freedom for men themselves than of ruling others, each in his own city" (452d5–8). Gorgias' phrase "in truth," which Socrates distantly echoes in saying that he is probably alone in his use of the "truly political art" (521d7), implies that Gorgias cannot openly contradict received opinion about the ranking of the goods. He is not going to try to replace the drinking song. Rhetoric is a greater good than that of which it is the cause, freedom and rule; but neither Polus nor Callicles seems to agree with Gorgias. Gorgias himself keeps a foothold in the "logistical" sciences, but there is hardly a trace of this theoretical dimension in his two disciples. Rhetoric is the capacity to persuade by speeches in any political gathering. Rhetoric brings freedom and slavery; it is the craftsman of willing slavery or unforced tyranny. Rhetoric dissolves the need for the use of force within the city. The speaker who persuades effects in the auditor who is persuaded a state of obedience. The present passive of the verb "to persuade" (*peithesthai*) is indistinguishable from the present middle, which means "to obey." Socrates makes two alterations in summarizing what Gorgias says, without meeting with any objections. He drops Gorgias' restriction to persuasion in a multitude and specifies instead the place in which the persuasion is induced, "in the soul." If Plato is letting Socrates allude to his elaborate comparison in the *Republic* of the class structure of the city to the soul's structure, it is safe to say that so compressed a brachylogy can hardly be matched anywhere else. Gorgias, in any case, finds no difficulty with the substitution. We can only wonder at this point whether Gorgias believes in the equivalence of city and soul. Could their possible equivalency have something to do with the coincidence of obedience and persuasion in *peithesthai*?

Before Socrates begins the next round of questions, which are designed to narrow the range of rhetoric still further, Socrates interpolates the first of several cautionary remarks about how Gorgias is to understand who Socrates is and what he is doing. Socrates' first statement involves an anacoluthon: "Listen, Gorgias, I, know well, that, as I persuade myself, if anyone in conversing with another wants to know that very thing about which the *logos* is, me too to be one of them; and I claim you are too." "Me too to be one of them" has no construction in the sentence; it started out to be "Know well that I too am one of them," but the parenthetical remark "as I persuade myself" ceased to be a phrase that was independent of the main sentence and took over its construction. The main sentence was either a simple one to begin with—"I am one of those who want to know," with an inserted plea—"know well that it is so"—or these two phrases were meant to be combined. In either case, Socrates began by saying that he wanted Gorgias to know who he is and ended up by saying that he persuaded himself that he was of a certain sort. A sentence with a grammatical incoherence, however idiomatic, introduces Socrates' account of why he does not want to suspect but wants to know what Gorgias means by rhetorical persuasion. Socrates makes a threefold distinction. There are possibly some who in a conversation want to know what is that about which the speech is; there is Socrates who wants Gorgias to know that he does not know what Gorgias is saying; and again there is Socrates who persuades himself that he is one of the first group. Socrates distinguishes between his knowledge of ignorance, which is of two kinds—what rhetoric is and what Gorgias says it is—and his lack of knowledge about his wanting to know. I know I am ignorant, Socrates says; I want to know, but I do not know that I want to know. Socrates' self-persuasion suggests that there might be a kind of rhetoric that would bring about conviction about one's own sincerity with regard to one's wishes. This type of persuasion would be concerned with the will and not knowledge. In the case of moral action, the agent would say: "I know what is right; I want to do what is right; but I do not know whether I want to do what is right for the sake of what is right." A rhetoric that altered the agent's doubt into certainty about the morality of acting morally might not be a good thing; but a rhetoric that managed to restrain the certainty of the will for right seems to be exactly what is needed to check the righteous from self-righteousness.

It is not at all obvious whether there can be such a rhetoric. "I persuade myself" is a phrase that suggests a state which is immune to outside tampering. Could Gorgias persuade Socrates that he had not persuaded himself? Could anyone bring Socrates to replace "I persuade myself" with "I know myself"? Did Socrates persuade himself with a refutable argument? These difficulties call attention to Socrates' telling Gorgias twice, "Know well." This expression does not have anything to do with knowledge; it is just a way of saying, "Be persuaded." Gorgias is to be persuaded that Socrates is one who either wants to know or is persuaded that he does; and since Socrates wants to include Gorgias, Gorgias either wants to know or is persuaded that he does. Gorgias, then, does not know in either case what rhetorical persuasion is. Socrates does not want to guess at what Gorgias does not know; he wants Gorgias to bring out into the open his ignorance.

Socrates complicates his speech still further. He tells Gorgias: "Know well that I don't know clearly; however, I do suspect what I believe you say the persuasion from rhetoric to be and about what." Here again Socrates has let a parenthetical expression of politeness, "I believe," determine the construction so that, instead of saying he suspects what Gorgias means, Socrates says he suspects what he believes Gorgias means. He is guessing at his own belief. If we were to simplify Socrates' speech and let both his "I suspect" and "I believe" stand for "I don't know," then Socrates tells Gorgias that he does not know he does not know what Gorgias means. An expression of uncertainty, when inserted parenthetically, disguises the conviction that lies behind it, so that whereas it seems to express one's willingness to be rid of what one acknowledges to be no more than a suspicion, it is in fact a statement of the invincibility of one's belief. Socrates, then, on the one hand, by incorporating "as I persuade myself" into his main sentence, tells Gorgias he does not know whether he wants to know, and, on the other, by incorporating "I believe" into a clause that "I suspect" already governs, tells Gorgias he does not know whether he is as suspicious of his suspicion about what Gorgias means as he ought to be. Gorgias, then, is confronted with two puzzles about persuasion. In the first case, he seems to be incapable of changing Socrates' doubt about his own sincerity, and in the second, he must try to dislodge the stubbornness with which Socrates might hold onto a tentatively expressed conviction. Socrates, however, is not being so scrupulous for the sake of Gorgias but for the sake of the *logos*, in order that it make as manifest as possible that about which there is a *logos*. Socrates' main concern is with rhetoric; what serves that concern is full clarity about what Gorgias means. Socrates does not explain what the connection might be between the two things he does not know. One is tempted, however, to guess that what Gorgias says is what rhetoric is (cf. 454c1–5), and rhetoric will come to light in and through Gorgias without Gorgias being any the wiser. The *logos* will on its own make rhetoric plain independently of the will and intention of Gorgias.

In order to lead up to showing Gorgias that rhetoric is not the only art of persuasion, and therefore that his definition is too general, Socrates cites Zeuxis. If Gorgias had said that the painter Zeuxis was he who painted pictures, Socrates would have rightly asked what kind of pictures and where. Only if Zeuxis were the only painter would Gorgias' answer have been adequate. Zeuxis was famous for painting pictures without character (Aristotle *Poetics* 1450a27–29). His pictures showed such beauty of face and form that nothing betrayed the presence of choice. Why, however, should Socrates choose Zeuxis? Socrates' decompounding of the word for painter (*zōgraphos*) yields "he who paints the *zōa*." *Zōa* is ambiguous. It means either living beings or images of living beings and everything else. The painter's task is to persuade the viewer that the image he sees is that of which the image is. *Zōa* are *zōa*. The rhetorician too can be said to put images in the soul and have them pass for the real thing. That *zōa* are *zōa* could be the model for rhetorical persuasion (cf. *Phaedrus* 275d4–9). Socrates, however, does not exploit his own example, even though his question, where does Zeuxis paint his pictures, points directly back to the presumed equivalence of "in the city" and "in the soul."

Socrates asks Gorgias whether anyone who teaches anything persuades what he teaches, and Gorgias says it could not be more certain that he persuades. It becomes clear from the turn the discussion takes that Socrates is distinguishing between the teaching of an art and the product of an art, so that it can be said of the painter too that as a teacher of painting he teaches what he persuades. Whether the painter must teach what is along with what appears to be, or whether he can keep to the teaching of appearances, has its counterpart in rhetoric (cf. *Phaedrus* 259e4–260d2); but Socrates does not raise this question with Gorgias, nor does Gorgias ask for any clarification. Socrates skirts this issue by taking as his example arithmetic, where what arithmetic teaches on the level of instruction is the same as what it does on the level of performance. The problems of arithmetic are of the same order as its theorems. Socrates underlines this point by speaking of instructional persuasion (453e6). It is unclear therefore whether persuasion supervenes on instruction, and to teach is also to persuade, or whether persuasion and instruction can coincide, and then to teach is to persuade. Socrates gets Gorgias to accept the latter possibility. Persuasion is the comprehensive class of which there are two species, trust and knowledge. It would seem, then, that rhetoric, like painting, induces knowledge when it teaches and trust when it exhibits, but arithmetic and other theoretical sciences never induce trust.

After Gorgias says that rhetoric is the art of persuasion in law courts and before all other crowds and about those things which are just and unjust, Socrates interpolates another remark on the way of the conversation. He tells Gorgias that he has confirmed his suspicion. Whatever may be true of instruction and persuasion, it is impossible to say that Socrates still suspects what he now knows. Suspicion is not the comprehensive class of which guesswork and knowledge are its two species. Knowledge replaces suspicion. Socrates then asks Gorgias whether it seems to him that learning and trust are the same or different; Gorgias says he believes they are different; and Socrates praises him for his belief and tells him he will know they are different once he realizes that there is true and false trust but no false and true knowledge. Gorgias, then, began with true trust without knowledge; Socrates supplied the proof and Gorgias now knows. It is impossible to say either that Gorgias now has true trust and knowledge, or that when Socrates taught Gorgias he persuaded him, for he was truly persuaded before Socrates' instruction that trust and knowledge were different. Gorgias, therefore, was mistaken to say that the arithmetician persuades what he teaches, for otherwise the pupil must gain simultaneously true trust and knowledge. So even when Socrates establishes the two species of persuasion and designates one as that which supplies trust without knowledge, he does not designate the other as supplying knowledge with trust but simply knowledge (cf. 454e7–8).

What has happened? Gorgias asserted that the power to persuade was in truth the greatest good. If persuasion comprehended all knowledge and belief, Gorgias would have a very strong case. Socrates, then, has worked out before Gorgias, without any restriction to forensic rhetoric, the consequences of his claim. He has let Gorgias bring his *logos* to its conclusion strictly in conformity with Gorgias' own hypothesis, and yet Gorgias does not get it. He does not see that Socrates has inserted a correct proof between a false hypothesis and a false conclusion, and that he himself is in a state of false trust with regard to rhetorical persuasion. On the basis of that false trust, Socrates can argue and Gorgias must accept the view that whoever knows justice is just, for if one knows what is just one has been persuaded (454e1), and to be persuaded of what is just has no meaning unless one does what one is persuaded it is just to do. Rhetoric stands or falls by its claim to effective power; and once knowledge is a kind of persuasion, Gorgias cannot claim to teach his pupils justice without claiming to make his pupils just. Gorgias of course would be no better off if he withdrew the claim and asserted instead that he persuaded his pupils to be just, for then, even without his peculiar hypothesis, he would be shown to be a fraud if any pupil of his failed to be just. A man of principle is a man who acts on his convictions, and Gorgias cannot afford to say that his pupils are without the right sort of convictions unless he admits that his rhetoric does not persuade or persuades what is wrong. It is necessary to conclude, then, that the so-called Socratic thesis that virtue is knowledge is not the hypothesis Gorgias unwittingly accepts, but it is Gorgias' own hypothesis, which is directly linked with the twofold genus of persuasion, and it only looks like Socrates' thesis. For the first time we begin to get an inkling of what Socrates means when he says that rhetoric is the phantom image of justice.

Gorgias grants tacitly that there could be instructional persuasion about justice, and explicitly that rhetoric practices convictional persuasion in law courts and before other crowds. He accepts further Socrates' three reasons why rhetoric cannot be instructional: the crowd is too large, the time too short, and the matter too big. Gorgias is certainly aware that he and Socrates are not speaking in isolation. At what point a group becomes too large a crowd, the time too short, and the matter too big would surely be nice questions for rhetoric to determine (cf. *Phaedrus* 271d7–272a4). We know that Socrates thought that the one-day capital cases prevalent at Athens prevented him from gaining an acquittal at his own trial (*Apology of Socrates* 37a5–b2). The *Gorgias* is long enough to make something clear. If it is rhetoric, perhaps rhetoric is not too big a matter to be handled before a large audience, but to account for that of which it is a phantom image might require more time and a smaller audience.

Socrates admits that he cannot yet grasp what he is saying. The difficulty he has in mind probably concerns the shift between the instructional and convictional levels of rhetoric. If the experts should but cannot advise in the Athenian assembly about harbors and walls, it would seem that the instructional persuasion they have is not and cannot be persuasive before a crowd, and the rhetorician should have the knowledge of how to adapt the knowledge of others into a form that wins the trust of assemblies. Why, however, cannot the experts themselves do the necessary adaptation? Something more must be involved in popularization than simplification. The dilution of knowledge into trust must essentially alter the knowledge. Gorgias does not object to Socrates' examples that the proposals Themistocles and Pericles carried were superficially technical but essentially political, and the expert shipwright and master builder have no more knowledge of the political than the people at large. If, moreover, one thinks of the military matters Socrates mentions along with his first example, the election of physicians, one cannot but think of the plague, whose effects were so disastrous because Pericles' policy led to the overcrowding of Athens. In the chapters of Thucydides devoted to the plague, Thucydides speaks as a diagnostician, but he offers no advice for a people to follow; and in Pericles' speech, which is designed in part to divert the thoughts of the Athenians away from their suffering, there is nothing scientific (2.47–64). Socrates can hardly be suggesting that a physician's speech under the circumstances would be superior to Pericles'. Would the physician as physician have to recommend surrender on any terms in order to reduce the rate of contagion? Gorgias, however, neither denies to the sciences the competence to handle everything which nonetheless must be dealt with nor assigns to politics as a science its own area of expertise. If rhetoric is just Gorgias' name for politics, then Gorgias has to state the things about which rhetoric gives advice and about which it would have to know. As Socrates has rigged the argument, Gorgias could plausibly suggest that rhetoricians should select the ambassadors the city sends abroad;

but Gorgias ignores a function he himself has often filled and argues for the quasi-universal power of rhetoric. He gives up competence from knowledge for power from trust. He prepares the basis for Socrates' proof to Polus that irrational power is powerless.

Gorgias' speech falls into two main parts. They are hardly consistent with one another. The first praises the power of rhetoric; the second defends it. The first part concerns the practice, the second the teaching of rhetoric. Both parts fall into two subsections. In the first subsection Gorgias gives evidence; in the second he indulges his imagination; and in the third and fourth subsections he offers a defense of himself. Aware somewhat of the inconsistency between the second and fourth subsections, between the power of rhetoric and its just use, Gorgias has to grant that Socrates could only come to know the power of rhetoric if it was used unjustly. Only if the rhetorician should want to run the risk of execution—a penalty Gorgias himself proposes—would rhetoric have more than imaginary power. Gorgias, at any rate, does not complete his introductory sentence and hence leaves it open as to what effect it would have on Socrates once he knew that rhetoric comprehends almost all powers and keeps them subject to itself. Gorgias is himself enchanted by rhetoric's power; he is tongue-tied when he has to convince another of it. Rhetoric really does seem to be powerless.

The link between the first and second subsections of Gorgias' speech is medicine. Gorgias says that often when his brother and other physicians failed to persuade a patient to take his medicine, whether it was a drug to be drunk, or surgery or cautery to be submitted to, he succeeded in persuading by no other art than rhetoric. Gorgias first presents himself in the service of another art and capable of overcoming the resistance the fear of either real or imaginary pain induces in the patient. Next he has a physician and a rhetorician, on their arrival at any city Socrates might wish to name, compete by speech in an assembly for election to the office of physician. The physician, he says, would not even show. Gorgias, then, goes from real cases where the rhetorician and the physician are distinct to an imaginary case where the rhetorician comes forward as a quack. It is possible, of course, that Gorgias, in the presence of his brother, pretended to be a physician, but it was not necessary; in the second case, however, the rhetorician must pretend to be what he is not. Without the juxtaposition of these two cases, we would have been inclined to say that Gorgias' effectiveness as rhetorician consisted in his power to allay the fears and expand the hopes of the patient, and his patter lowered the rate of failure and exaggerated the chances for a complete recovery. If Gorgias contradicted his brother to his face, he was believed not because the patient took him as more of an expert, but because he told him what he wanted to believe. Gorgias, then, does not distinguish between a fraudulent appeal to the passions and a fraudulent claim to expertise. He thereby reveals that he does not know what causes him to be effective. He believes that because the assembly would elect him as a doctor, they would be electing him because he was a doctor and not on account of his extravagant promises. The failure of the assembly to state what really moves them deceives Gorgias into believing that what they say moves them moves them. Gorgias is taken in by labels. He looks into the mirror of his own rhetoric and believes it to be true.

Gorgias introduces his defense of rhetoric by an elaborate comparison of it with boxing and other gymnastic exercises. Gorgias thus prepares the way for Socrates' use of medicine and gymnastic as the two corporeal arts of which legislation and justice are the psychic counterparts; but in his speech Gorgias does not use medicine and gymnastic in the same way. The physician is someone Gorgias both helps and injures; the trainer is someone Gorgias wants to be thought of as his model. Gorgias argues that the trainer cannot be hated or exiled if his pupil learns to box and then beats up his mother and father. That a son hardly needs to take a single boxing lesson in order to have the skill to strike his parents does not occur to Gorgias; but we know from Aristophanes' *Clouds* that Phidippides, after he had been to Socrates' "reflectory," argued for his right to beat his father and his mother (1321–1446). If Gorgias' case is going to gain any support from gymnastic competition, he should propose that rhetoricians meet at festivals and fight it out among themselves. What we call accidental homicide and the Greeks just murder (*dikaios phonos*) can easily happen in an athletic contest; but the rhetorician is not needed to defend an action that the law does not condemn. In the rhetorical counterpart, the humiliation of the losing rhetorician, however brutally the victor might have inflicted it, would be part of the agony of defeat and no one's responsibility except the victim's: he should not have weighed in against so superior an opponent. Gorgias, then, can fully justify rhetoric if he deprives it of all political power. Rhetoric cannot be just unless it is toothless.

When Gorgias comes to apply the notion of the trained father-beater to the trained rhetorician, who could but ought not strip the doctor of his reputation (*doxa*), Gorgias becomes most moral and recommends the execution of rhetoric's unjust users. He is so eager to save his own neck that he volunteers to be the chief prosecutor of everyone else. His moral stance makes him absurd. If the rhetorician has the power Gorgias says he has, it is impossible that the unjust rhetorician could ever be found unjust by any jury before whom he would be permitted to plead. Gorgias makes the rhetorician powerful when he is proving that the physician is an impostor, and he makes the rhetorician weak when he is defending himself against the charge of falsely convicting the physician of imposture. Gorgias cannot put together justice and power in rhetoric. They are as far apart in it as the coincidence of philosophy and power is remote.

When Gorgias' art is just it urges the submission to pain; when it is unjust its aim is to shame. Socrates prefaces his argument with a presentation of his practice, in which there is pleasure for him as refuter and refuted, and either indignation or shame for whomever he refutes and deprives of his *doxa*. *Doxa* now means not only reputation but also opinion, and Socrates admits that it is impossible to remove a false opinion without removing a false reputation as well. His preface amounts to his asking Gorgias whether he is willing to submit to this twofold removal. The difficulty Gorgias might have in submitting consists in the suspicion that Socrates is out to get him and, resentful of his position in the world, speaks not to the matter at hand but *ad Gorgiam*. Socrates does not deny that the suspicion of malice cannot be removed entirely. Whatever Socrates may say, appearances are against him. Only if Gorgias is the same sort as himself would Socrates continue questioning him with any pleasure. Socrates had previously said that he persuaded himself that he was one of those who want to know about whatever the *logos* is. Now he does not qualify his self-characterization in any way. He is one of those who takes equal pleasure in being refuted if he himself says something untrue and in refuting another if he says something untrue. Socrates thus implies that if he took no pleasure in either being refuted or refuting, but he still wanted to talk, he could replace "as I persuade myself" with "I know." The obstacle to self-knowledge is pleasure. The gratification that rhetoric exploits in the auditor has its Socratic counterpart in self-indulgence, which makes it impossible for Socrates to know the sincerity of his desire to know. Rhetoric and dialectic would be equally pleasure-oriented, and whether Gorgias the crowd-pleaser or Socrates the self-indulgent was preferable would depend on who one was—Socrates' associate or part of Gorgias' crowd. Socrates, however, says he prefers to be refuted than to refute, for it is a greater good for oneself to be freed from the greatest evil than to free another. Socrates puts his own good before another's. He is not exceptionally just. Socrates' justice, in freeing Gorgias from false opinion, is not grounded in his will to do Gorgias good but in his own pleasure; and Socrates hopes that the same holds for Gorgias. Gorgias can be just to Socrates while gaining pleasure for himself, or Gorgias can be no less pleased and gain a greater good if Socrates refutes him. If one refutes another, justice goes along with pleasure; if one is refuted, pleasure goes along with good.

Socrates identifies the greatest evil with a false opinion about that which he and Gorgias are discussing; but he does not tell Gorgias what opinion Gorgias has of which he proposes to relieve him, and whose removal would benefit him and delight Socrates. Gorgias has told Socrates nothing so far about rhetoric except that it makes speeches about justice and can be used unjustly (460e7). Since philosophy too makes speeches about justice, Gorgias implies that philosophy can be unjust. That it is unjust to ask what justice is, is a false opinion constituting the greatest evil a human being can have. Socrates has just shown that if Gorgias holds the same opinion as he does about refutation, Gorgias cannot maintain that philosophy can be unjust; but by the same token Socrates grants that philosophy will appear unjust if Gorgias takes his losing hard and carries the audience with him. Socrates can benefit Gorgias in either case, but he cannot remove the bad reputation of philosophy under all circumstances. Socrates proposes that the conversation go on if Gorgias says he is a Socratic type; Gorgias says he is; more precisely he says, "I say that I too am one of the sort you describe." He obliges himself, regardless of how he feels, to behave throughout the refutation as if he were not angry and certainly to hold off from saying anything nasty about Socrates. Gorgias promises not to denounce Socrates and make an issue of his justice.

Although Gorgias is willing to mouth an emulation of Socrates, he seems unwilling to be refuted in private. They ought to have first consulted, he says, the wishes of the audience before their own. Socrates had offered the audience to Gorgias as full of prospective pupils, but Gorgias seems to be more just in being so solicitous of them apart from his own advantage. It is of course not to occur to us that Gorgias' solicitude might be a cover for his graceful withdrawal, and that he could then say with perfect justice that it was not his fault if he could not prove in deed what he said he was in speech. However this may be, Chaerephon the democrat speaks for everyone else as well as himself, and Callicles is equally enthusiastic. Chaerephon speaks of his own advantage, Callicles of his pleasure. They split apart what Socrates had kept together. There is no one in the audience, it seems, who finds any good in pleasure or any pleasure in his good. To be a spectator to a refutation is not of the same order as to be a participant.

Gorgias will soon put himself in the position of choosing to maintain his reputation for justice—it would be disgraceful for him to bow out now when he had promised to answer anyone's question—rather than to let anyone know whether he will have become any better after Socrates has refuted him. His reputation as a rhetorician means less to him than either his reputation for justice or his own improvement. Gorgias' opacity to us is matched by the opacity of the audience to him. He agrees with Socrates' conclusion that since the rhetorician is more persuasive before a crowd of nonknowers than the knower is, the rhetorician appears to the nonknowers as one who knows. By Socrates' own account, the physician will say that health is the greatest good, and all the rhetorician will have to do, in order to appear to know more than the physician about the good without appearing to know what the physician knows about health, is argue plausibly that a combination of other goods is greater than health alone. Gorgias does not reckon with this possibility. Perhaps he knows that he cannot persuade before a crowd of nonknowers that the power to persuade before a crowd of nonknowers is in truth the greatest good. Gorgias' failure, at any rate, to distinguish between what makes the nonknower convincing to nonknowers and what appears to make him convincing keeps him from understanding both his own rhetoric and the reason Socrates did not know about his own sincerity. Gorgias neither knows himself nor knows why Socrates does not know himself. The ground of his ignorance is the same in both cases. In his ignorance of pleasure Gorgias appears perfectly moral.

Gorgias had implied in his praise and defense of rhetoric that rhetoric was essentially agonistic; he now asks Socrates whether rhetoric is not overwhelmingly easy if without one learning all the other arts one does not come off as inferior to the other craftsmen. Rhetoric is the art of self-enhancement, which, Gorgias believes, means to appear to know. The sole title to superiority is knowledge, and the highest title is to know how to appear to know. Socrates postpones the issue of superiority and asks instead whether the rhetorician is as ignorant of the just and unjust, the ugly and the beautiful, and good and bad as he is about whatever each of the other arts deals with. Gorgias accepts the view that there is a knower of these things. Indeed, Polus could hardly have said that rhetoric was the most beautiful of the arts and Gorgias that it was in truth the greatest good unless they counted themselves among the knowers; otherwise, it is hard to explain why Gorgias assumes that the knower of the beautiful, the good, and the just speaks before the crowd of nonknowers (459e1). Since Socrates shifts so quickly from public speaking to private teaching, he scarcely gives us time to ask what difference it would make whether the rhetorician knew or not the just and the unjust. If the knower of justice matches the physician, his knowledge will make him appear to be a nonknower before the nonknowers; and the rhetorician, regardless of whether he knows what the knower of justice knows, will falsely appear to know by rhetoric. We would have expected, then, that Socrates' question was going to be whether Gorgias teaches his pupil how to persuade nonknowers that what he knows to be just is just. Instead, Socrates asks the apparently simpler question whether Gorgias' pupil has to know "the truth about these things," or does Gorgias make him appear to know among the many though he does not know and appear to be good though he is not. Prior to the subsequent argument, in which Gorgias grants that one is what one knows, "good" can only mean "a good rhetorician" (449a7). Socrates, then, is asking whether Gorgias makes the good rhetorician appear to be a good rhetorician. If Gorgias says he does, then the rhetorician will not appear as anything else; if Gorgias says he does not but the rhetorician disappears entirely into what he claims to be, what imposture does the rhetorician put over when he is speaking about the beautiful, the just, and the good? Had Gorgias understood Socrates' question, he would have had to designate the political as the field of the beautiful, the just, and the good, and claimed that the rhetorician looks like the true statesman, or he would have had to say that these things are a concern of philosophy, and that the rhetorician is the sophist when he is trying to pass himself off as the philosopher.

Gorgias is faced with the following difficulty. If the rhetorician, in using his rhetoric unjustly, must be punished, the city, on the one hand, must have decided that he was acting unjustly, and the rhetorician, on the other, cannot have persuaded the city that he knows justice, or rather that he is just. The city must believe that he knows what is just and is not acting accordingly; but Gorgias says the rhetorician practices what he knows, and what he knows is how to seem to be just. Gorgias, then, must have been speaking of the rhetorician's injustice against the standard of nonseeming justice. This standard, then, must be fully known to the city, otherwise Gorgias cannot recommend the punishment of unjust rhetoricians. Gorgias could of course say that the rhetorician who knows justice is not always successful in translating his knowledge into seeming knowledge, and when the city convicts him it is only for a seeming injustice. The many would then be the same nonknowers they were in the case of any art, but Gorgianic rhetoric would cease to be the art of seeming. If the rhetorician gets caught, either the city must know what the rhetorician does not, or the rhetorician does not have a genuine art. There is one further possibility. The city no more knows justice than the rhetorician knows an art, and in their mutual ignorance the rhetorician sometimes fails to guess what the city is going to decide is unjust.

Socrates' argument does not begin well for Socrates. He lets Gorgias' pupil know before or learn later the just and the unjust things (460a5–7). If his argument were sound, the pupil would be both just and unjust; if Socrates' argument is to be saved, "just" must be of the same order as "physician," and as the latter is not healthy through his knowledge, so the former is not just through his. To be just, then, has a new meaning, to know the truth about justice and injustice (459e8), and knowledge is not virtue but virtue is nothing but knowledge and vice nothing but ignorance (*Sophist* 228d6–11). Socrates needs, then, for Gorgias to accept more than the so-called Socratic thesis if the rhetorician is never to come to light as unjust (460d6–e2). Socrates' first step is that he who has learned something is of the same sort as the knowledge makes him. This must entail for Gorgias, since he granted that persuasion comprehended learning and trust, that the knower has been persuaded to be of the same sort as his knowledge. Socrates then proceeds as follows:

1. He who has learned the just things is just.
2. The just does just things.
3. It is a necessity for the rhetorician to be just, and the just to want to do just things.
4. The just will never want to act unjustly (be unjust).
5. It is a necessity for the rhetorician to be just on the basis of the argument.
6. The rhetorician will never want to act unjustly (be unjust).

Steps 4 and 5 certainly seem superfluous, but they are superfluous only if the rhetorician and the just man of step 3 are one and the same. Step 3 offers two characterizations—one of the rhetorician who is just by his knowledge, and one of the just man who is just by his will to act justly. The just man acts justly by his wanting to act justly, and regardless of whether he is just or unjust in his actions he is nonetheless just. He therefore will never want to be unjust or act unjustly. The rhetorician, however, is just by knowledge and conviction. He will never want to be unjust or act unjustly because, unlike the just man, he cannot be unjust and still be just. Without steps 4 and 5, it would not have been clear that the rhetorician and the just man in step 3 are different; with their insertion it is clear that Socrates handles the just man in step 4 and the rhetorician in step 5. For the rhetorician, step 6 is a weakening of what Gorgias alone has to maintain, that knowledge and conviction coincide; but for the just man, step 4 is the essential definition without which he could never fail to be as just in action as in will (cf. *Laws* 864a1–8).

Socrates' argument questions the coherence of the two parts of Gorgias' speech. If the first part were true, that the rhetorician can beat anyone politically, "if he should want to" (456c2), the circumstances of the second part can never arise, where the rhetorician is to be punished for his injustice. Polus' starting point is to accept the truth of Gorgias' first part and drop the second in conformity with Socrates' argument. Socrates has shown Gorgias how he could keep the second part, so that the rhetorician would always be just and still be punished for his injustice, if he were willing to give up the first part and deny the rhetorician the omnicompetence of rhetoric. If Gorgias were to go further and abandon rhetoric entirely, Gorgias' position would reduce to Socrates', and his justice would consist in his making speeches about justice. He would then be just neither in his will to be just nor in his knowledge of justice, but in the pleasure he takes and the benefit he receives in making speeches about justice in order to discover the truth about justice. Socrates will later have Polus agree that the beautiful can consist in the union of pleasure and benefit. It is the union Socrates offered Gorgias if he were a Socratic type.

# II
# Polus

(461b3–481b5)

Socrates will not say until later what he thinks went on in his conversation with Gorgias, but Polus believes he knows and blames Socrates not for Gorgias' self-contradiction but for exploiting Gorgias' shame, which he admits is not peculiar to Gorgias but universal among rhetoricians. He ignores entirely Socrates' effort to make sure he did not put a single word in Gorgias' mouth. Polus certainly fails to see the root difficulty in Gorgias' position—the teacher of persuasion is respectable, but whoever imbibes his teaching is incapable of persuading the city of his respectability—and believes it can be salvaged if he denies that Gorgias knows or teaches the beautiful, the just, and the good. Polus drops the knowledge of their opposites. Socrates, Polus implies, does not believe what he says: everyone knows that rhetoric has the power to be used unjustly. Socrates' lack of urbanity consists in trying to force Gorgias to admit to his injustice or indifference to injustice. Socrates ought to be ashamed to cause Gorgias shame. It is just to do to another only what one has already done to oneself. Polus' intervention on behalf of Gorgias must be grounded in the morality of Polus. Only his justice, as Socrates acknowledges (461d2), could explain why he wants to help out Gorgias and correct Socrates. Polus wants to benefit them without even the possibility of benefiting himself.

Socrates agrees to submit to Polus' correction under one condition. In Athens, where there is the greatest license (not complete license) to say whatever one wants, Polus cannot say all that he wants. Polus must give up macrology. If he does not, Socrates reserves the right to leave and not listen to Polus. Whatever, then, may hold for medical treatment or punishment, whether of a corporal or psychic kind, the patient of conversational correction, though he does not know what is best for him—he does not know after all the truth—knows what he can stand, and he does not have to endure a correction by every available means. When the issue between Socrates and Polus later turns on the advisability of the unjust man submitting to corrective punishment, no quantitative restriction is ever mentioned; and when Callicles refuses to take any more of Socrates' benefaction, in experiencing that of which the discussion is—punishment—Socrates has no mercy (505c1–4). The severity of Socrates' moral earnestness seems to increase as the dialogue goes on and he himself is no longer the target of reformers. In the story with which the *Gorgias* ends, the incurable are punished forever.

It takes some time before Polus settles down enough for Socrates to define rhetoric, and even the full exposition requires Gorgias to intervene and briefly carry on again as interlocutor. Socrates and Gorgias between them control Polus' impatience: Socrates by getting Polus to indulge him; Gorgias by wanting to know, regardless of Polus, what Socrates means. Gorgias conforms with the guidelines Socrates laid down in their conversation; Socrates draws into the dialogic situation his characterization of rhetoric. Gorgias wants to be rational; Socrates wants the favors of rhetoric. Socrates denies that rhetoric is an art and says it is an experienced way of producing a kind of favor and pleasure; Polus wants to know whether he thinks it is a beautiful thing to be able to favor or gratify human beings. Socrates then wants Polus to grant him a favor. The favor consists in Polus asking Socrates about cookery. Cookery turns out to be the corresponding corporeal part in Socrates' scheme to rhetoric. Polus' indulgence of Socrates has the advantage of advancing the argument and gaining Gorgias' permission for Socrates to make fun of rhetoric without making fun of Gorgias. Polus, then, is used by Socrates to get over a possible awkwardness. Polus, the practiced indulger, forestalls a breach between Socrates and Gorgias. He sweetens Socrates' truth-telling and gets Gorgias to listen to reason. Polus is certainly not performing this task by art, and perhaps there is nothing beautiful in it, but it does seem to be as useful as it is just and necessary to draw off indignation and clear the air of possible misunderstandings. A workman on a scaffold leaves a tool on the ground and asks someone to do him a favor and fetch it; someone has an itch at a place that is not easy of access and asks another to do him a favor and scratch it for him; or, in the absence of a mirror, a tie may have to be straightened or a smudge removed as a favor. The soul too may have an irritation that is inconvenient to get at and someone else must stroke it: forgiveness might be of this kind. If men were always providential and never made mistakes, or things were so arranged as to adjust on each occasion to our contemporary capacities, there would be no need of indulgence. Socrates' radical separation between art and experience thus seems overstrict. Pain, he is going to suggest, is in accordance with rationality; pleasure is not. Dialogically, he has already cast doubt on this suggestion.

Two elements are conspicuously missing from Socrates' analysis of rhetoric. Neither persuasion nor speech has anything essentially to do with rhetoric. Flattery, one can say, replaces persuasion, and speech, now that it appears as characteristic of any art in its ability to give an account (*didonai logon*), does not lend itself to being split between a rational and an irrational element. Socrates' rival definition of rhetoric does more than set aside Gorgias' claim that rhetoric is an art; it strips rhetoric of even the speech that is built into its name and of the notion that it is at times effective. Polus seems quite willing to sacrifice the rationality of rhetoric if he can retain its power, and he knows that flatterers are despised and live from hand to mouth. Polus believes that this is the weak point in Socrates' presentation; but there are far greater obscurities in it of which neither he nor Gorgias seems to be aware. The brachylogy of Socrates' proportions seems to forbid their expansion to a proper length; but that proper length turns out to be the *Gorgias* itself, which may be said to be the macrological account of Socrates' continuous ratios. The interlocutors of the *Gorgias* speak the speeches of Socrates' account of rhetoric. However distant they seem to be from rhetoric, they are conforming to the Socratic pattern. The interlocutors of the *Gorgias* are willful and yet fulfill the strict requirements of its plot.

Socrates' account of rhetoric is in two parts. The first is short and gives the four parts of flattery; the second is longer and requires that Gorgias accept a separation of body and soul and a difference between seeming and being. The short account suffices, at the risk of unintelligibility, for Socrates to answer Polus' question whether rhetoric is beautiful or not, once Polus asks and Socrates answers what part of flattery it is. As a phantom image of a part of politics, it seems to follow from the definition itself that rhetoric cannot be good. Merely by knowing what it is, one knows what sort it is. Quiddity and quality do not make for two answers but one. That these two answers coincide in the case of rhetoric suggests that such a coincidence would not hold for any genuine art and science. The rank of politics is not determined by the necessary baseness of sophistry and rhetoric. The art of punishment may unavoidably be ugly (*Laws* 860b1–8).

The four parts of flattery Socrates names do not include flattery itself. Apparently they do not exhaust flattery; sacrifices and prayers to the gods could in their spurious forms fall under flattery. Flattery in any case might be too amorphous to articulate as if it were a whole; but Socrates does not assign a single name to the fourfold field of the genuine arts either. Socrates has a name for the arts of legislation and justice, but he has no name for gymnastics and medicine. The absence of a name for the comprehensive art of soul and body puts into doubt the apparent theme of the *Republic,* that the true city, in which the arts are geared to satisfy the needs of the body, can be put together seamlessly with the city in which the philosopher is king. Socrates' continuous ratios tend to conceal the issue of wholeness. Parts are matched against parts without the prior constitution of any whole. Gorgias is partly responsible for this. He accepts from Socrates not only that body and soul are each something, but that there is a good condition (*euexia*) of each; but he fails to ask and Socrates fails to say whether there is a good condition of the individual (cf.464c1). Socrates later says that were not soul in charge of body, health and sweets would be all jumbled together; but he does not say whether, when soul rules body, the two arts of soul rule the two arts of body, and if they do, whether there is a single art that comprehends all four and arranges for the happiness of man collectively or individually. In the face of Socrates' silence it will be hard to make out Socrates' teaching about the misery that goes along with injustice.

Gorgias accepts the difference between the seeming good condition of body and of soul and the corresponding reality of their good condition; but he does not ask whether there is likewise a seeming bad condition of body and soul and the corresponding reality of their good condition. Figure 2 represents all possible states of body and soul, in which a state is any combination of "real" or "seeming" with "health" or "sickness" or with "beauty" or "ugliness" of either body or soul. The perfect human being may be considered to be the union of real and seeming beauty and health, and the most defective human being the union of real and seeming ugliness and illness. It may be that not every combination is possible, for example, a seeming beauty of body with everything else both ugly and sick in appearance and reality. Socrates himself, if we simply call to mind the variety of things said about him, seems to combine the reality of the soul's beauty and ugliness with the seeming of the soul's ugliness and health along with the reality and the seeming of bodily health (cf. Cicero *Tusculan Disputations* 54.37.80). A diagnostic science of soul that was capable of such fine discriminations would in itself be quite extraordinary, but a diagnostic science that was also therapeutic does not seem possible. A science of psychic health, which according to Socrates is justice, could not treat the illness of soul unless it were guided by the science of the beauty and strength of soul, for otherwise it could bring about the reality of justice in soul along with the reality of its ugliness and weakness and in such a way that the gymnastics of soul could not correct it. If virtue were all of a piece, a conflict of this kind could not arise; but if virtue were all of a piece, Socrates could not have distinguished in the first place between health and beauty of soul.

Socrates leaves the content of soul-gymnastic completely blank, and no one questions him about it (cf. 470e6–471a3). No one questions

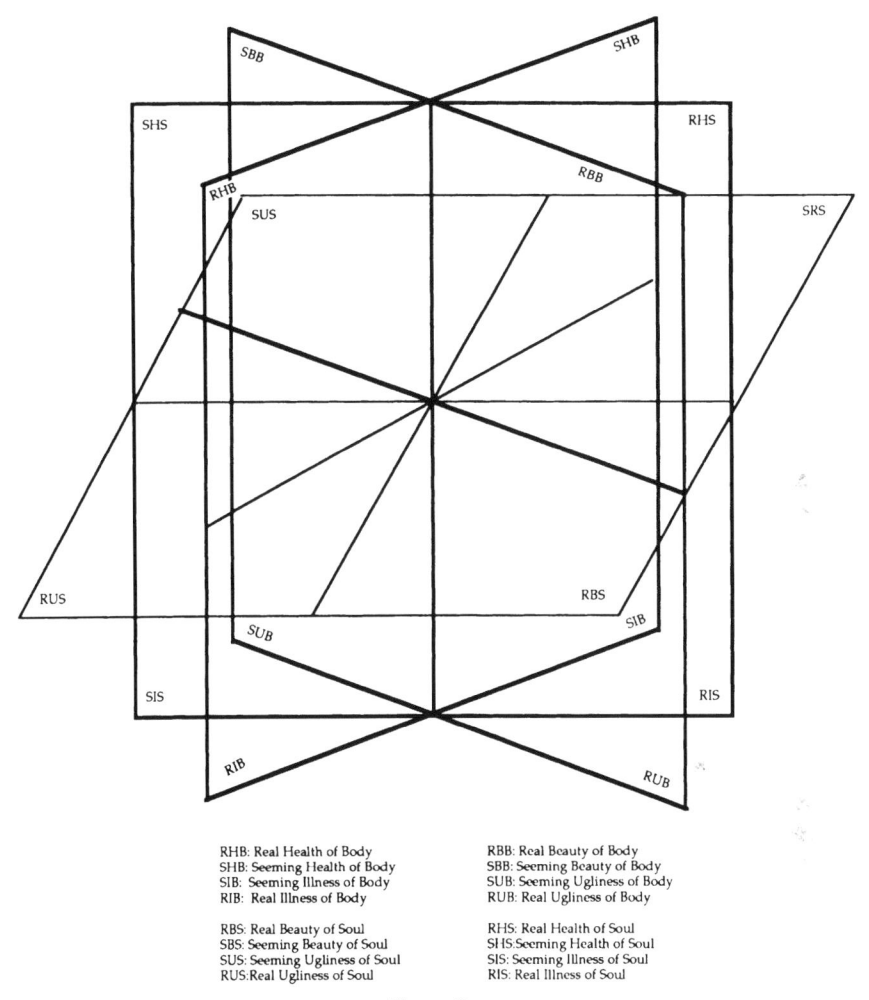

Figure 2

RHB: Real Health of Body
SHB: Seeming Health of Body
SIB: Seeming Illness of Body
RIB: Real Illness of Body

RBB: Real Beauty of Body
SBB: Seeming Beauty of Body
SUB: Seeming Ugliness of Body
RUB: Real Ugliness of Body

RBS: Real Beauty of Soul
SBS: Seeming Beauty of Soul
SUS: Seeming Ugliness of Soul
RUS: Real Ugliness of Soul

RHS: Real Health of Soul
SHS: Seeming Health of Soul
SIS: Seeming Illness of Soul
RIS: Real Illness of Soul

Socrates about the existence on either the diagnostic or therapeutic level of either the science of politics or its two parts, legislation and justice. Socrates presents his own discovery of political philosophy or some version of it as if it were completely in place and universally acknowledged. Since rhetoric is the phantom image of justice, rhetoric must pretend to be justice. It must guess at justice and take on the seeming of justice. Gorgias, in his conversation with Socrates, has just done that, and Polus has objected. Gorgias, without knowing anything about Socrates' political art, has been led by Socrates into speaking the words of an illusory double of Socrates. On his own, he allowed rhetoric to be unjust; through Socrates rhetoric is justice. "Justice" (*dikaiosunē*) is a surprising word in the context of Socrates' ratios, and part of the tradition has the expected *dikastikē*, the art of justice or punishment. It seems to be essential, however, in order to set Gorgias and Polus apart, that justice as knowledge and virtue together be the form in which Socrates first accounts for rhetoric and tells Gorgias what he has experienced. Socrates' first description of rhetorical practice, that it is not artful but characterizes a soul good at guesswork, which is manly and naturally adept at human associations, is nothing else than a sketch of Gorgias as he shows himself in assuming the guise of Socrates. Socrates says of himself that he is a certain kind of man; Gorgias says of himself that he says so too.

Socrates implies that art is to experience as knowledge is to perception (464c5–6). Flattery perceives the fourfold scheme of the two corporeal and the two psychic arts and distributes itself into four parts as well. Since flattery is only guessing when it slips into its four roles, there should be an overlap among the four, so that not only would sophistry and rhetoric, as Socrates admits, be confused themselves and confuse others (465c3–7), but body would intrude into the spurious versions of legislation and justice and soul into cookery and cosmetics. If the means flattery deploys for its pretensions is always pleasure, the soul cannot be kept out, since "bodily pleasure" is a misnomer (*Republic* 442a8). How the body shows up in rhetoric can be said to be a major theme of the *Gorgias.* At the moment, however, it is more important to insist on the difference between the best as the end of the genuine arts and the pleasant as the means of their spurious look-alikes. In the first account, flattery does not come forward with the claim that the good is the pleasant; it speaks the language of good while it entices through pleasure. Flattery is hedonistic; it is not hedonism. The contest between cook and physician is about good and bad foods. In an open contest between health and pleasure, it might not be only children who would choose pleasure if the price were too high for the restoration of health. It is unclear, then, whether cookery, in offering sweets, ever says it is doing good. Cookery might well induce this belief without ever opening its mouth. Cosmetics is an even more difficult case. Cosmetics offers to enhance one's looks; it does not have to say that the beauty it offers is really one's own. It is equally unclear whether its sweeteners are ever experienced by the one who uses them. What it does do is to persuade one that it is far easier to appear than to be beautiful. Its results are faster and in a way more impressive than anything gymnastics can do. In this sense cosmetics indulges one; but it is still uncertain whether one puts on makeup out of shamelessness or shame. Perhaps it is a social grace not to offend one's neighbor and have him say, "It's a pleasure to look at you." Someone, whether Plato or another, wrote that there are no writings of Plato, but those said to be his are of a Socrates who has become young and beautiful *(Epistle 2:314c1–4)*. Is Plato a makeup artist who has had the good sense or the bad taste not to give us Socrates straight? However astringent Socrates may be presented as being, Socrates in his representation cannot but delight. The interlocutors may be raked over the coals; we look on and enjoy the show.

The opposition between art and experience is between the good and the pleasant; but no one asks Socrates whether experience, which Polus said makes for art, can be dispensed with entirely and art achieve rationality by rationality alone. The severity of reason seems to precede and make way for the severity of morality; but the separation of the good and the pleasant, which Socrates' self-portrait had already overcome when he was talking with Gorgias, is as doubtful as the separation of body and soul and of experience and art. Socrates first criticizes flattery for its aiming at pleasure; but he says it is irrational because it does not have an account of the natures it applies and hence cannot speak of the cause of each thing. An art, then, is constituted by its therapeutic aim and its knowledge of cause. It understands the causal relation between the means it employs and the end it pursues. Such a distinction would certainly allow for there to be arts that aimed at pleasure provided they knew the causes of pleasure. Socrates says as much later (501a3–b1). He had already implied through his "as I persuade myself" that pleasure puts a limit on the possibility of self-knowledge; but there might still be a mean between therapy and flattery that would not disgrace the cause of reason.

To know the cause of something seems to be the equivalent of knowing what something is, and to know what sort it is, to know whether it is good. In setting up his ratios, Socrates seems to have proceeded rhetorically. Justice is a good before justice is given an account, and justice is an art before one knows what the art knows and whether it is productive of justice or simply its detector. One cannot but suspect that Socrates' analogues are dictating out of themselves the very structure of the unknown arts of legislation and justice. Socrates' account, then, of justice would be infected with the corporeality of what its counterpart handles and would thus betray the presence of rhetoric in its makeup. The degree to which justice is colored with the rhetoric that apes it determines exactly the degree to which rhetoric can be successful at pulling off its masquerade. Polus at any rate falls for it completely. He comes out in favor of Socratic theses that are in him nothing but the speeches of rhetoric itself.

38  Polus

The confusion in which sophistry and rhetoric are involved, and which was first hinted at in Socrates' dividing persuasion into instruction and trust, does not hold for their genuine counterparts. The legislative art is separate and distinct from justice. That there is no need of justice if the law is effective can be said to be a thesis of the *Republic:* if the class structure works, justice is not needed to make it work, and if the soul structure is in order, justice vanishes into wisdom. If justice, however, is nothing but corrective punishment, it is not obvious whether it too disappears. Gymnastic does not dispense with medicine but will always need it as a supplement. Cookery and cosmetics, on the other hand, cannot readily be seen as a pair. Whatever may be true of the greater rank of sophistry over rhetoric, cosmetics seems both less damaging and more trivial than cookery. Whereas beauty and strength are impossible without health, the pleasure the show of beauty gives to others is apart from the pleasure the show of health gives to oneself. Cookery and cosmetics seem to disassociate inside and outside to such an extent that they operate not only independently of one another but generate in their subjects a split between private experience and a public self that nothing can bridge. On the inside one gorges; on the outside one charms. Whether rhetoric and sophistry contribute to a comparable disjunction is not clear; but if, as Socrates says, there is some confusion between them, one could expect that rhetoric effects on the outside something quite different from the way it is experienced. The speeches of Polus and Callicles should put up a front that expresses and does not express what they mean. Gorgias' followers should lose the identity of saying and meaning that Socrates exacted from Gorgias himself.

In the argument between Polus and Socrates, the issue slides quickly from the prestige of rhetoricians to their power; and once power is the issue, tyrants take over from rhetoricians; but regardless of whether tyrannical power is spurious or not, it does not issue from the mouth. Polus begins as a spokesman for his own profession and ends up as the mouthpiece for criminals who have not hired his services. He mentions tyrants at first by way of example: "Don't rhetoricians," he begins, "just as tyrants do, kill whomever they want?" But Polus gets so caught up in the example that tyrants cease to illustrate his thesis but become it. Tyrants seem to supply so much more powerful a proof than rhetoricians do of the power and prestige of rhetoricians that they overwhelm the rhetoricians and show up their weakness. Polus identifies prestige with power, and power with killing, robbing, and exiling. He does not add, as Glaucon does, the power of sleeping with whomever one wants (*Republic* 360c1). There are only the austere political pleasures for Polus. To be powerful is to have power over another, but not, as one would expect a rhetorician to say and Gorgias had said, for him to do one's bidding but rather to get rid of him. Polus should say that real power shows itself in getting others, the city itself, to condemn and kill whomever one decides on; but killing should be for him an extreme case, as to ruin a physicians's reputation was for Gorgias, and not something a rhetorician would normally have to do, since in itself it delimits the power of persuasion. The rhetorician wants to bring a fellow citizen over to his side; he has him killed because he cannot get him to do what he wants. Killing, under these circumstances, may be necessary; it is hard to see how it can be good. Had Polus mentioned sexual gratification as among the rhetorician's perquisites, he might have cited the pleasure of killing among the goods of power; but Polus seems committed to rationality in defending rhetoric from the charge of flattery. Polus lost himself in the example of tyranny, but he cannot imagine tyranny except from the outside, and his heart is not in it. At the beginning of the argument with Polus, Socrates asks him whether he is starting a speech or asking a question (466b1), and shortly afterward he is in doubt whether Polus is speaking on his own and declaring his opinion or asking him (466c3–5). Socrates does not just thereby force Polus to recognize the difference between bluster and question, but he points to the possibility that the speeches of Polus are not his own convictions but the speeches of rhetorical flattery, and were Polus aware that what he is saying are scraps from the handbook of rhetoric, then rhetoric would be an art that Polus had thoroughly mastered. Socrates has to establish that the rhetorician cannot be using rhetoric as a means that is under the control of reason or another art. Only if rhetoric absorbs the rhetorician completely does the irrationality of rhetorical devices rub off on the rhetorician himself. Every time Polus tries to refute Socrates by a rhetorical appeal (and Socrates chides him for it), we are reminded that if Polus were a rhetorician by art, then no matter how badly the argument went for Polus, Socrates would not be proving his main contention about rhetoric. Polus would then be shown to be a poor rhetorician, or perhaps Socrates is too resistant to its wiles, but Polus would not have refuted rhetoric in himself. Socrates challenges Polus to establish the great power of tyrants and rhetoricians or else to admit they have been deprived of it. Words are to make or break the tyrant. For a rhetorician to decline such a challenge is impossible; for him to accept it is senseless.

The discussion about the difference between rationality and whimsicality prefaces the discussion about justice and happiness. Socrates has Polus agree that power is something good for whoever has it, and it cannot be good if one senselessly does what one wills. Implicit in these admissions is Socrates' former characterization of art, that it acts in light of the good and knows the cause of whatever it effects; but the union of rationality and good in art does not make for power, since no art except moneymaking perhaps seems to be concerned with the interest of its artisans (*Republic* 341c4–342c7). Socrates is now speaking about actions of the patients of the arts and not their agents. He is thus speaking of rationality freed from the control of some particular knowledge. Rationality, in this discussion, puts no limit on any means as long as it serves some good. Although it is not true initially, as soon as Socrates mentions good, bad, and the neutral as among the things that are, ends are designated by nouns and the indifferent by verbs or nouns. The goods Polus accepts are wisdom, health, and wealth. Wisdom replaces beauty in the drinking song, apparently on the basis of Socrates' soul-gymnastics or the art of legislation, but certainly because Polus is insensitive to beauty and the actions men take to get it in their possession. Pleasure, in any case, is not among the goods. The actions Socrates mentions are either troublesome and painful or neutral; sailing shows up as either (467d1, 468a2). His typical sentences with purpose clauses are very simple; if they were more complex, it would certainly be possible to have, for example, "I rule in order that I may kill, punish, and express my hatred with impunity," without the purpose clause being immediately reducible to any of the three real goods Polus accepts. What seems to be excluded, then, is a sentence of the type, "I walk in order to walk," or, "I kill in order to kill." The phrase "for the hell of it" often expresses the whimsicality and conceals the doubling of the same action in both clauses. Whether "for the hell of it" is the same as "for the sake of pleasure" is not easy to say; but the just man who, according to Socrates, wants to do the just things seems to be equally irrational if Socrates wants us to infer that the just man does the just things in order to do the just things. The purity of moral ends looks the same as the arbitrariness of the tyrannical will, and they can only be distinguished if justice is not an art that only serves others.

Polus accepts the difference between rational power and the power to do whatever seems good, but he believes the difference is trivial; and Socrates, he is certain, would choose the latter in the city and would envy anyone whom he saw kill, rob, or arrest anyone he pleased. Polus poses a more interesting question than he knows. What if Socrates were suddenly granted such political power? Would he reject it and obey his *daimonion* that kept him from politics (*Apology of Socrates* 31d2–5)? Or would the *daimonion* cease to hold him back once the threat of losing his life was removed? Polus never says what good the tyrant has; neither he nor Callicles ever speaks of political honor as a possible good (cf. 486c2, 526d5). Polus has been bound too closely to the reality of the goods, wisdom, health, and wealth, to add the seeming of prestige, and Callicles becomes too involved in the dreams of license to stay attached to the reality of political life. Socrates evades Polus' question, whether he would choose the coincidence of philosophy and power, and focuses instead on the second question, whether he envies anyone he sees kill, rob, and arrest in the city. Polus suggests that Socrates cannot but be filled with impotent rage when he sees another wielding the power he himself would use more effectively. Socrates answers that it makes a difference whether the killing is just or not, but in neither case can it be enviable. Because Polus speaks carelessly and does not distinguish between the rhetorician who persuades the city to execute his enemy and the tyrant who might kill off his rivals with his own hands, the issue of the unenviable nature of the city as such never arises. We know that Athens suspended yearly its power to execute criminals it had justly condemned, as if the gods in whose name this suspension was sanctioned wanted the citizens to realize that the power they had was not rightly theirs (*Phaedo* 58a10–b7). Behind the issue of tyrannical power the rationality of the city itself is at stake. What real good does it want and does it know the causes of that good?

Polus believes it makes no difference whether one kills justly or not. He accepts, as Gorgias had, the possibility of just killing. Anyone whose whim coincides with what the city declares to be just is in an enviable position. He has the backing of the city to do what he likes. Had Polus stuck with the rhetoricians and not let the tyrant usurp his place, he could have argued along these lines and shown the rhetorician's power to consist in persuading the city to take his word for it that what he wills is just. Polus would then have united Gorgias with Thrasymachus and made it inevitable that the question What is justice? be raised. Polus takes it for granted that tyranny is unjust without qualification, and even to have the power to act in conformity with one's opinion is unjust (469c5–7). Polus is deeply conventional. Nothing, he believes, could make tyranny the unenviable alternative to chaos. He thus retains his belief in the power of reason in the form of persuasion, however corrupt, while praising the total irrationality of unjust power. All Socrates has to do is split apart his belief in reason from his praise of tyranny in order to win Polus over to his side. Socrates succeeds in making Polus self-consistent without bringing him any closer to the knowledge of justice. Polus becomes the just man who wants to do what is right.

How ungrounded Socrates' argument with Polus is comes to light if one confronts Socrates' assertion before Gorgias that the greatest evil a human being can have is a false opinion about what their discussion is of, and his declaration to Polus that injustice is the greatest of evils. In the original context, Socrates' two assertions would amount to saying that to believe that philosophy can ever be unjust is unjust. That at the core of all injustice is the denial of the justice of philosophy is a hard saying. It is somehow confirmed in Callicles' praise of injustice and assault on philosophy. In the present situation, however, Polus cannot possibly understand Socrates to mean anything else by injustice than what he does; but in that case, regardless of whether the verb *adikein* means to be unjust or to act unjustly, it seems impossible to identify it with a false opinion. That an opinion can be the same as either a state or an action can be true only on the Gorgianic assumption that one is what one knows and is persuaded of, for to be convinced of something must issue in action if there is no impedance, and the soul cannot put up any resistance to its own opinion. Now Socrates cannot possibly maintain this view since he has just had Polus agree that all actions are undertaken for the sake of the good; so not even the tyrant can want to act unjustly, however unjust his action may be. The tyrant or would-be tyrant can have a wholly false opinion about what constitutes his happiness, but he cannot believe simply in the goodness of injustice. Polus, however, must have the tyrant believe in the goodness of tyranny so that he will always will to be and act in conformity with its built-in injustice. Polus asks Socrates whether he would prefer to submit to injustice than to act unjustly; but it is impossible for anyone to will unjustly unless one assumes, as Polus does, that to be a tyrant is to be unjust in every respect. Tyranny is so saturated with injustice in Polus' eyes that the tyrant inevitably gets the contagion of Polus' opinion. The real tyrant is wholly opaque to Polus; he replaces him with an imaginary figure whom he can envy for his happiness and denounce for his injustice. The being of tyranny is the seeming of Polus. His false opinion constitutes injustice.

Polus believes that to submit to injustice is worse than to commit it. To be deprived of some good, then, should be worse than to deprive another of some good; but again everyone wants to acquire some good and not simply take it away. Socrates says he would want neither; but should one or the other be a necessity, he would choose the submission to injustice. It is easy enough to prefer to be robbed than to rob, and even perhaps to be arrested than to arrest, but to be murdered rather than to murder could only be a choice under a tyranny, where the tyrant promises to save your life if you kill someone for him. Why, however, should the tyrant be believed? Under the thirty tyrants, who wanted to protect themselves by spreading their own criminality over as many as possible, Socrates was ordered along with others to arrest someone; and though he walked away he was not executed on the spot for his evasion (*Apology of Socrates* 32c4–d7). As the type of stark alternative Polus proposes cannot be of frequent occurrence, Polus pushes the question to the extreme: Would not Socrates want to be the tyrant? He senses somehow that Socrates cannot mean that injustice is the greatest of evils unless there are either no degrees to injustice or injustice is complete injustice. Polus, however, no longer offers Socrates the choice of being either the agent or the patient of complete injustice. He therefore absolutizes the goodness of injustice without calculating the advantages of nontyranny. That wisdom and health become more available through tyranny would be hard to maintain, and neither Polus nor Callicles ever speaks of wealth as the tyrant's peculiar good.

Polus' response to Socrates' imaginary case of Socrates proposing to kill someone or other in the crowded marketplace as a proof of his tyrannical power is neither to say he must be crazy nor to ask what good he has in mind, but to assert that it is necessary that he suffer a loss, be punished, or fined (*zēmiousthai*). Polus, then, implies that with tyranny comes the power to act unjustly with impunity, and since he is so certain that Socrates cannot get away with his crime, tyranny grants the power to be openly unjust. At this point the rhetorician breaks away from the tyrant, for the former's immunity depends on the unprovability of his injustice. Polus also parts company with Thrasymachus, who had allowed the tyrant to determine what was just. Polus is more concerned, as his example of Archelaus shows, with the way to tyranny than tyrannical rule itself. The unjust way to injustice is happiness. Socrates' example therefore is most telling. Polus is impressed by the isolated man who by daring alone succeeds at a public crime. Callicles is already contained in germ in Polus.

Of the two terms on which the argument so far depends, "good" and "just", "good" is either real or illusory, but "just" is not subject to opinion. Polus cites Archelaus to show that many who are unjust are happy. Socrates has heard of him but does not know him; Polus has heard all about him and knows that he is happy. Happiness is so real a good that hearsay is knowledge (470d5). Justice and happiness, then, turn out to be so rooted in opinion that one does not have to know either to know both. Archelaus is unjust and happy. Socrates says that if Archelaus is unjust he is wretched, but he cannot be happy regardless of how just he is unless his education is of a certain sort. On the basis of Socrates' geometric proportions and sophistry's claim to educate, we can say that Archelaus' happiness depends on the degree to which he is free from sophistry and follows the art of legislation. It is at this point that *Gorgias* and *Protagoras* first intersect and diverge. Socrates now begins to treat justice apart from education. Rationality thus loses out to justice. It had begun to retreat when Socrates offered the simple test of justice to determine whether an action is better or worse. The test is simple because justice is unproblematic for Polus. Justice, according to Polus, makes Archelaus the slave of Alketas, for his mother was his slave; and Archelaus has committed the greatest injustice in murdering his master and not handing back the rule his father Perdikkas had originally taken away from his brother. Not only does Polus assume the justice of slavery and the rule that the offspring of a slave mother and a free father is a slave, but he knows that Archelaus was not out to avenge his mother's enslavement and that his intention to restore the throne to his uncle was a ruse. Just as he knows that Alketas was not caught plotting to kill his slave, so he knows that Archelaus must have lied to Cleopatra when he said that her seven-year-old boy, in running after a goose, fell into a well. Even if Polus' reconstruction of the facts was absolutely correct, how does he know that Archelaus does not now regret his wickedness or at least live in constant fear of assassination? For Polus, hearsay is fact, facts are facts, and there is no experience of facts. Polus does not need to know anything about another's experience; he has the certainty of justice to make up for his ignorance.

Polus indicts Archelaus as if he were bringing him to trial and, as the prosecuting attorney, has to make the case against him as black as possible. He tries to raise moral indignation to the highest pitch and then drive it still higher by stirring up envy of his happiness. He arouses resentment and indignation together in such a way that the audience can enjoy the horror of such great wickedness and picture to themselves the pleasures it must reap. Polus delivers a speech that expresses perfectly the power of rhetoric, but he himself believes it to be true. Just as Gorgias looked like Socrates and provided the first piece of evidence for Socrates' account of rhetoric, so Polus, in falling for the rhetorician's line, proves that rhetoric speaks in the harshest tones of justice as it praises its opposite. It flatters the people on the sternness of their morality and indulges their taste for the happiness of tyranny. What has happened, then, since the beginning of the dialogue can be represented as follows. Socrates came with two fourfold templates (fig. 3). Gorgias confirmed that rhetoric assumes the guise of justice by his version of the identity of knowledge and justice. Polus then took over Gorgianic justice and made it the frame for the content of rhetorical speeches, or the identify of happiness and tyranny. This content takes its character from the corporeal analogue of rhetoric, cookery. The structure of rhetoric is so far of this order (fig.4).

|   |   |
|---|---|
| Gymnastic | Legislative |
| Medicine | Justice |

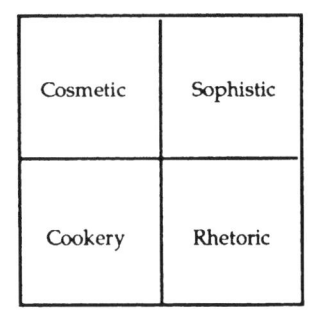

|   |   |
|---|---|
| Cosmetic | Sophistic |
| Cookery | Rhetoric |

Figure 3

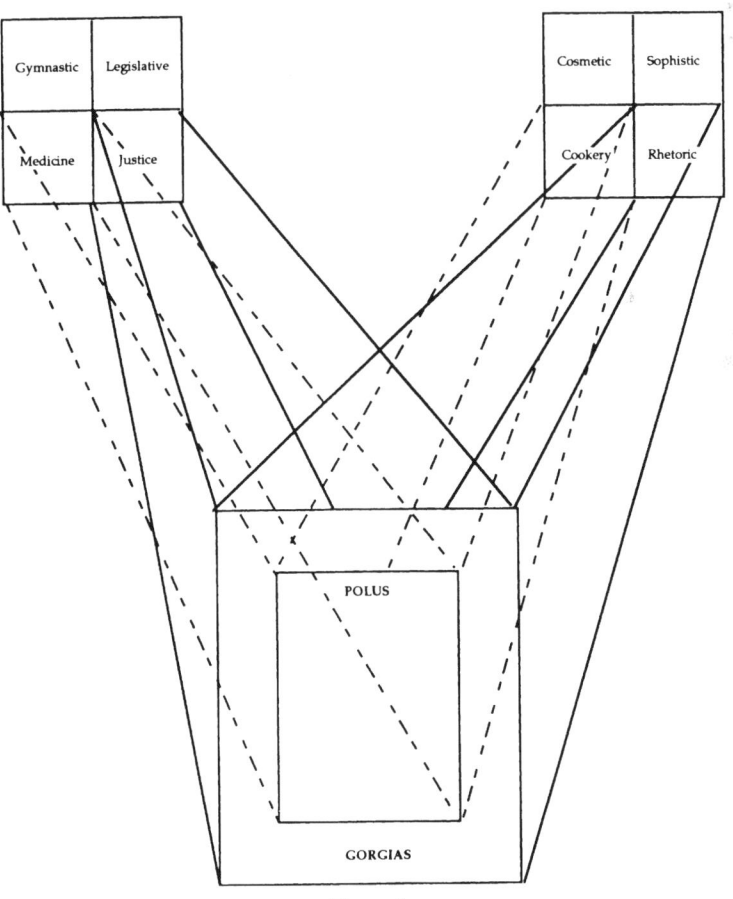

Figure 4

46  Polus

The outer frame is now Gorgias'; the inner picture is Polus'. Polus preserves Gorgias insofar as he too assumes complete knowledge of justice, but now not as part of the teaching of rhetoric but as part of its performance, in which the nonknower, in speaking before nonknowers, utters what they already know. What Socrates intends to do next is to work out with Polus the simulacrum of rhetoric in light of justice's analogue, medicine. The reattachment of rhetoric to a genuine art will be as successful as Socrates' conversion of Gorgias into his representative. Rhetoric will still bear traces of cookery.

Socrates has two theses for which he is going to gain Polus' consent. One is that it is impossible to be unjust and happy, the other that to go unpunished is to be more miserable than to be punished if one is unjust. Polus' counterthesis to Socrates' first is not, as one would expect, that it is possible to be unjust and happy, but rather that he who is unjust is happy if he is not punished (472e1–2). Socrates' schema requires that to be punished, or more literally to obtain justice, must mean either to become just or to become less unjust. Socrates, however, never fully brings this out, so Polus must take punishment in the ordinary sense. If Socrates holds to his understanding of rhetoric, Polus' interpretation of Socrates' notion of punishment must be its phantom image. Socratic punishment when reflected in the ghostly mirror of rhetoric should thus emerge as the exacerbation of injustice rather than its cure. Polus' exaggeration of Archelaus' criminality is likely to spill over into his reformation. Rhetoric will look at the scab over his injustice and give him a clean bill of health. There is, then, going to be a greater separation between Socrates' meaning and Polus' meaning for one and the same speech than there was between Socrates and Gorgias. The facsimile of reason Gorgias retains ultimately vanishes in Polus. Polus thus prepares for Callicles and the sudden emergence of philosophy.

Socrates and Polus each field three theses:

> Socrates (1): To inflict injustice is worse than to submit to injustice.
> Polus (1): To submit to injustice is worse than to inflict it.
> Socrates (2): The unjust are wretched.
> Polus (2): The unjust are happy unless they pay the penalty.
> Socrates (3): The unpunished unjust are most wretched; the unjust in submitting to punishment are less wretched.
> Polus (3): Those submitting to punishment are most wretched.

Polus' refutation of Socrates (2) was Archelaus; Polus' refutation of Socrates (3) is an imaginary case of terrible tortures. These tortures, applied in Polus' example to an unjust man, are indistinguishable from what a just man would undergo at the hands of a tyrant. Glaucon in fact uses a version of Polus' example in his supposition of apparent injustice and real justice (*Republic* 361e3–362a3). Polus, however, never speaks of the tyrant's employment of torture. The capacity to inflict pain is not part of the tyrant's happiness. Torture is solely an instrument of just punishment for Polus. He preserves the literal meaning of *dikē* as justice in the phrase for punishment *didonai dikēn* (cf. 476a7–8), even though in ordinary usage the phrase had long since ceased to be restricted to just punishment.[1] Polus, moreover, does not argue on the basis of the successful tyrant who finally is overthrown and tortured; rather, in order to make it as stark as possible, he picks a man who is caught being unjust because he is plotting tyranny. Since his example does not involve any unjust action on the part of the conspirator, Polus is, it seems, indifferent to the ambiguity of the verb *adikein*, which designates no less an unjust action than a state of injustice. Socrates, in reformulating what Polus says, distinguishes implicitly between the just and the unjust plotting for tyranny (473d5), but this is not a difference for Polus. The tortures Polus imagines include both bodily and psychic pain: the would-be tyrant is put on the rack, castrated, and blinded, and then, after looking on at the outrages his wife and children experience, is crucified or covered with pitch. How he can see though blind Polus does not explain: either the tyrant or Polus has a lively imagination. Just as the tyrant's happiness is decided on independently of the tyrant's own experience, so the tyrant's misery does not involve the tyrant's suffering. Polus, as Socrates says, talks up a bogeyman. It is designed to refute Socrates as if he were planning to take over the government of Athens, but it is not designed to deter the tyrannically ambitious, for if it were, it should certainly mar their prospects for happiness.

Polus first attempts to refute Socrates with the bogeyman; then, when Socrates denies that either the unjust conspirator or the successful tyrant is happier and reasserts that the latter is more wretched, Polus laughs. Socrates wants to know whether laughter is another form of refutation; and Polus says Socrates stands refuted if no human being, including anyone in the audience, will back him up. Ridicule and talk of terror are weapons of refutation; they are not, as they should be, devices for rehabilitation. Polus seems to have at hand the ways of speaking and making noise that would make rhetoric the counterpart to medicine. In the case of the would-be criminal, rhetoric

---

1. Of the six times Herodotus uses the expression, five are in the mouth of others, only one of whom is a Greek (6.11.2) and one in the report of what a Persian is thinking (8.100.1).

48  Polus

would either hold him up to universal contempt or scare him out of his wits. It would make him believe that everyone could not wait to get their hands on him or were about to bury him in scorn. Rhetoric would thus develop a passable version of the conscience, and it might very well be effective. It is truly absurd therefore for Polus to apply these devices against the upholder of justice. Socrates has nothing to be afraid of, and he is immune to comedy. Socrates knows he is funny. Polus, then, illustrates how rhetoric borrows something from corrective justice, mixes it with the cautery and surgery of medicine, and then becomes bewildered and does not know what to do next. The frame of justice, which Polus inherited from Gorgias, and to which Polus' bogeyman and laughter belong, has discharged itself in vain against Socrates. So Polus is ripe for a takeover. He can be redirected against those he is competent to deal with. Polus can be redirected; he cannot be reformed. He becomes the proof of the limit of just punishment.

In turning Polus away from any appeal to the crowd, Socrates promises to prove that Polus believes what Socrates does; but he claims something more: all men believe as they do. Socrates puts forward another paradox. There is a universally held belief about justice and punishment that Socrates himself cannot establish, for he does not even converse with the many, let alone persuade them to confess what they believe. There is some belief that will not come out in any poll. No questionnaire can be devised to elicit it. The alleged reason for the shyness of a perfectly moral stance is the ridicule Socrates would incur were he to try to take the vote of the many. Socrates cites as evidence his ignorance of how to poll the members of the council at the trial of the generals in 406 B.C. Socrates seems to be unnecessarily obscure. What can connect an easily learned procedure with Socrates' incompetence to have any crowd no matter how large roar its approval of morality? At that trial, Socrates resisted the illegal procedure of trying all the generals at once; and since the people later regretted their illegal action, Socrates would have needed a little more persuasiveness or maybe just luck to maintain the law, but not necessarily to save the generals. The issue of procedure conceals a far deeper source of disagreement between Socrates and Athens. The generals were charged with failure to pick up the shipwrecked after their stunning victory; the shipwrecked included the dead, who, on dying, told a survivor to report to the people that the generals had not picked up those who had proved to be best on behalf of their country (Xenophon *Hellenica* 1.7.11; cf. *Menexenus* 243c6). Does Socrates' refusal to converse with the many turn on the issue of burial? Is the belief in Hades the obstacle to Socrates' obtaining a unanimous vote to a universal consensus? The belief in Hades rests on some confusion between body and soul, for without such a confusion no link can be established between burial and the afterlife. Socrates had already hinted that there lurked a similar confusion in sophistry and rhetoric. Polus, then, may be typical of a universal belief that only Polus, as a pretender to the rationality of an art, can express. Polus now has a desire to know what Socrates will say (474c2–4; cf. 467c3–4).

Socrates now adds a third term to "good" and "just." Since Polus proposes that to do wrong is better but uglier or more shameful than to suffer wrong, Socrates must discriminate between "good" and "beautiful." He first mentions, among all possibly beautiful and noble things, bodies, shapes, voices, and practices, but he does not mention souls. His list is solely of corporeal things, and his chief example is bodies. In speaking of beautiful things, Socrates asks Polus whether he looks away from everything else and toward something when he calls them beautiful. Socrates puns on "call" (*kalei*) and "beautiful" (*kala*; cf. *Cratylus* 416b6–d11). At the same time that he uses a verb of seeing (*apoblepein*) in a nonliteral sense he indicates that the beautiful is a linguistic phenomenon. It is through the agency of calling (*kaloun*) that the "called" are *kala*. The ugly and the shameful, then, are the unspeakable things, whatever lies outside the range of speech; but the ugly and shameful also lie outside the range of sight. They are banished from both sight and speech. The law is primarily responsible for this double banishment. The ugly lurks therefore on the fringes of the law and possibly within the law, but on account of the very effectiveness of the law they might escape the notice and the name of law. Callicles believes that Polus made a mistake in refusing to admit that injustice is beautiful and noble, and Socrates manipulated nature and law in such a way as to trip up Polus. Callicles may be either right or wrong about either Polus or Socrates, but Socrates alerts us to the possibility that what Polus calls beautiful might really be ugly, but, in being out of sight and without a name, it might slip past him.

Bodies are beautiful because they afford either some benefit or pleasure to their spectators or possibly both. Socrates needs the disjunction of benefit and pleasure in order to distribute harm to whoever does wrong and pain to whoever suffers wrong; but the disjunction makes the argument deeply flawed as soon as the comparative is introduced. If one thing pleases but does not benefit, and another benefits but does not please, which is more beautiful? And if one thing pains but does no harm, and another harms but does not pain, which is uglier? Furthermore, since the argument is set up in terms of actions and effects but not of subjects, a just man could be more pained in doing an unjust action than the patient of his wrongdoing is. Polus says suffering wrong is worse than doing it, and he must mean that it is more painful; and since doing wrong is less painful, it must be more harmful. But how does Polus know that the wronged is not harmed? Polus preserves the unitary appearance of "beautiful" and "ugly" while he allows what each stands for to be split apart. Polus started with Archelaus, whose injustice and happiness were equally self-evident; and he cannot give up the ugliness of injustice without giving up injustice, since if Archelaus were to represent the union of pleasure and benefit that can also characterize the beautiful, the injustice of Archelaus would have to vanish for Polus. Archelaus is not enviable if he is not unjust. Archelaus, however, is in fact beautiful in both respects despite his injustice, for if Polus' denunciation of Archelaus flatters the audience, Archelaus receives the benefit and Polus delivers the delight. He applies the tyrant's makeup.

What Socrates has done in decoupling the pleasant and the good, of which the beautiful now consists, is to exaggerate a little, to assign to the beautiful either theoretical pleasure or practical good. The tyrant cannot experience any theoretical pleasure because the rhetorician praises the tyrant but the tyrant does not look at himself. Accordingly, in Polus' speech there was an opacity to the tyrant's happiness and a publicity to the tyrant's injustice. If Polus were to work out on this model the greater ugliness of wrongdoing, he would have to say that to suffer wrong is either a benefit or a contemplative pain, that is, to look upon the infliction of injustice is more painful than the submission to injustice. Rather than argue so subtle a point, Polus allows Socrates to shift from the contemplative to the experiential level (475c2). If, however, Socrates had started with harm, after Polus had granted that the ugly was painful, harmful, or both, Polus would certainly have said that the wronged are more harmed, and he would then have been forced to conclude that wrongdoers are more pained, which could hold only on the level of contemplation. Now an argument whose conclusion depends on the order in which the terms are taken up cannot be right. The decoupling of pleasure and benefit is impossible. Rhetoric thus stands exposed as the phantom image of dialectic too. It separates what is together and mixes what is apart.

When Polus hesitates to say whether he would choose the worse and the uglier, Socrates urges him in these words: "You won't be harmed, but nobly submit to the *logos* as if it were a doctor and answer." Socrates offers to cure Polus. The cure consists in Polus no longer *saying* that injustice is happiness. The cure is rational, insofar as Socrates eliminates the inconsistency of Polus blaming injustice and praising tyranny, but it is on the tongue and does not penetrate to the soul, for not a word has been said about the harm injustice does to the soul. Yet Gorgias must still be impressed. Gorgias himself was dependent on physicians and had to persuade his brother's patient to submit to what his brother prescribed; but Socrates has Polus submit to the *logos* which he himself has produced. By doubling himself in the *logos*, as if it were independent of himself, Socrates can speak a speech about a speech about justice and be both rhetorician and physician. Earlier, while Socrates was talking with Gorgias, he wanted Gorgias to disregard the suspicion that Socrates was out to get him and entertain the enlightened belief that they were jointly doing it all "for the sake of the *logos*" (453c3). Now, however, Polus is engaged in another enterprise. The *logos* has ceased to be diagnostic and become therapeutic. It has broken once and for all the unholy alliance between moral indignation and injustice.

The second phase of Socrates' argument with Polus establishes a connection between morality and rhetoric. It is not pretty. Polus first accepts explicitly what he had from the start, that to be punished (*didonai dikēn*) is to be chastised justly if one is unjust, and then, after a complete review, that all just things are beautiful insofar as they are just. In Socrates' original scheme, the political art aimed at the good and its two parts aimed respectively at the beautiful and the just (fig. 5). In the new scheme, the just has mapped itself onto the beautiful and then split once more between the good and the pleasant (fig. 6). The irrational practice of rhetoric comprehends the just and the beautiful under the beautiful and slides in pleasure as the good. Rhetoric is much better looking than justice. It raises the status of justice so that it appears to be the one thing needful. The apparently arbitrary restriction of rhetoric to forensic rhetoric is the truth about rhetoric: the deliberative and epideictic forms of rhetoric are all in the service of justice.

Socrates starts with the general proposition that for every agent there must be a patient; but he is not as precise as he should be. He has the agent do something (*poiein ti*), but he does not add the someone to whom the something is being done. If *poiein* meant "to make," the double accusative would not be needed; but if the action is a beating (*tuptein*), and we imagine the agent to be Achilles, "Achilles beats Hector" describes the will of Achilles, but "Hector is being beaten" holds neither under the circumstances of the *Iliad*, where the gods prevent the action of Achilles from being effective, nor in fact, since Achilles is certainly beating a body, but whether it is Hector's body is moot (*Phaedo* 115c6–d2). If something disgraceful attaches to Achilles' action, there is no contumely undergone by anyone or anything except by his will. The contumely never passes beyond his will. Socrates, then, is proposing to show the operation of

52  Polus

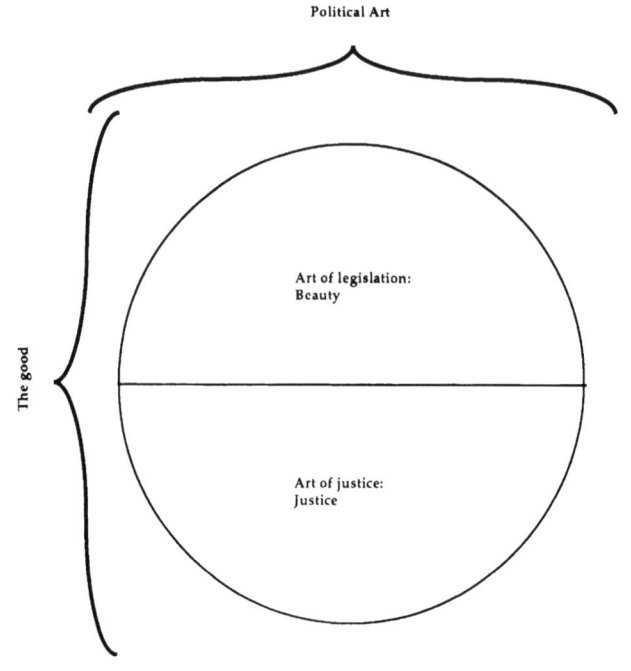

```
                    Political Art
        ⎧⎯⎯⎯⎯⎯⎯⎯⎯⎯⎯⎯⎯⎯⎯⎯⎯⎯⎯⎯⎯⎯⎯⎯⎧
        ⎪      ╱                    ╲
        ⎪    ╱                        ╲
        ⎪   │   Art of legislation:    │
        ⎪   │   Beauty                 │
The good⎨   ├──────────────────────────┤
        ⎪   │                          │
        ⎪   │   Art of justice:        │
        ⎪    ╲  Justice               ╱
        ⎪      ╲                    ╱
        ⎩⎯⎯⎯⎯⎯⎯⎯⎯⎯⎯⎯⎯⎯⎯⎯⎯⎯⎯⎯⎯⎯⎯⎯
```

Figure 5

the will in the guise of the rationality of punishment. Rhetoric, in short, is irrational through its exploitation of the self-ignorance of the will. If the lover says, "I love you very much," no one would conclude, least of all the addressee, that it entails, "You are very much loved." It seems to be true, however, to believe that the sentence in the passive does hold if someone not the lover says, "He loves you very much." The rhetorician, then, enters the picture in order to convince the addressee that his utterance, "I love you very much," and another's, "He loves you very much," are one and the same in their affect, "You are very much loved." Rhetoric thus parades the will under an objective form in which the will vanishes and a spurious sincerity takes on the look of self-evident truth.

Socrates' analysis of adverbs when they limit contact verbs, that the patient experiences the manner in which the agent acts, does seem to hold; but the story of the princess and the pea is enough to warn one to be cautious. From her saying, "I was beaten sorely," it is possible to go back to the active, "They beat her sorely," but not to go forward from agent to patient unless one adds that they intended to beat sorely all the princess-candidates but succeeded only with her. "You hurt me deeply," which can mean bodily harm but usually does not, allows

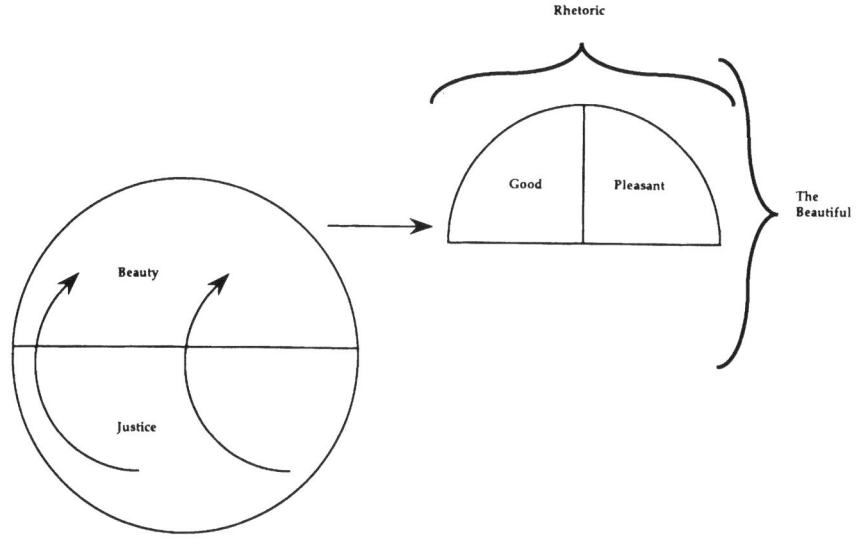

Figure 6

the agent to respond about either his speech or his deed, "I just grazed you." In the case of surgery, the doctor can say, "I cut you healthily," but the patient could agree and still say, "I was cut painfully." A linkage between pain and benefit would have to be established apart from facts if this is going to be the model for just punishment. Rhetoric is irrational because it relies on perception to put together the pain of punishment with the benefit of punishment, but in the absence of a causal analysis the pain of the punishment could induce a fear of further punishment and still leave the disease of injustice intact.

The eight steps in Socrates' proof that to be punished is to be benefited are shadowed by two steps that are truly determining the outcome for Polus.

1. To be punished is to be affected
2. by the chastiser;
3. to chastise rightly is to chastise justly;
4. to chastise justly is to do just things;
5. the chastised in being punished undergoes just things;
6. he undergoes beautiful things;
7. he undergoes good things;
8. he is benefited.

The agent at step 6 must be doing beautiful things, and at step 7 he does either good things or pleasant things. The punisher, then, either

54  Polus

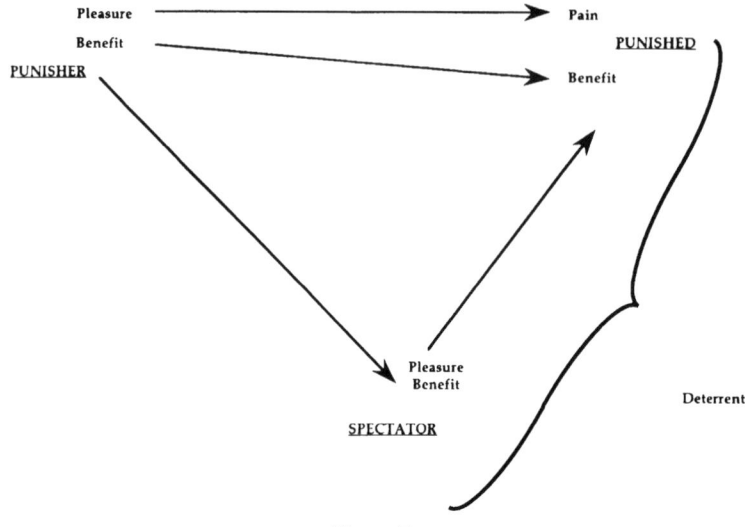

```
Pleasure  ──────────────▶  Pain
Benefit   ──────────────   PUNISHED
PUNISHER                   Benefit

                    Pleasure
                    Benefit
                                       Deterrent
                    SPECTATOR
```

Figure 7

gives pleasure to himself or others or he benefits either himself or others. The sight of punishment is either pleasant or a deterrent, and it is possibly both. The diagram for the situation Socrates has in mind is seen in figure 7. (To what extent it applies to the situation of the *Gorgias* itself can be set aside.)

The rhetorician's role in this scheme is to persuade the punished that he is experiencing exactly what the punisher intends. He is to make the punished into a spectator: Polus already did that in his bogeyman speech. Polus believes that it is noble to punish, but the pleasure he receives in punishing makes punishment noble regardless of how the punished is affected. The punished, then, has to be induced to believe in the transference of the punisher's will.[2] That he could possibly learn to know the punisher's will Socrates has already precluded: pleasure stands in the way of knowledge. Rhetoric, then, must try to make good the proverb *pathei mathos*, "by suffering, understanding." There seems to be something tragic about rhetoric.

In order to convince Polus that the vices of soul cause the greatest harm and not the greatest pain, Socrates asks him whether to be poor and sick is more painful than to be unjust, intemperate, cowardly, and stupid. Polus accepts the view than a criminal who is afraid of getting

---

2. In Latin, *animadvertere* or *animum advertere*, which literally means "to turn one's mind toward" or more generally "to pay attention to," comes to have the specialized meaning "to punish." Here is a case where the will of the punisher is expressly the same as the punishing.

caught, too stupid not to get caught, and who cannot check himself from being a criminal is in less pain that a sick beggar. The evident suffering of Telephus at the tent of Achilles blocks Polus from picturing the suffering of soul; yet he is confident that a thorough basting of the helplessly vicious cannot but do him good. Socrates, on the other hand, implies that the greatest harm and pain would be incorrect punishment or torture; but this is wholly unknown to Polus. Gorgias thus gets a double lesson. He learns the importance of not taking the anticipation of suspicion for the truth of intentions at the same time that he witnesses the display of rhetoric in its commission of this very mistake. The total jumble of medicine and gymnastic with cookery and cosmetics, of law and justice with sophistry and rhetoric, and then the mulling of all these ingredients together must be hard for Gorgias to swallow. Possibly it did him good.

The meaning of the verb *kolazein* covers the range from restraint to punishment; the adjective *akolastos*, "unrestrained" or "licentious," is mostly used as the opposite of *sōphrōn* insofar as it means "sensually moderate." The pain involved in punishment emerges as pleasure if there is no punishment. To punish (*kolazein*) is to knock off, as it were, the alpha-privative of *akolastos*. Pain thus looks like a necessary concomitant of correction, for the possible pain in the life of unrestraint is effectively concealed in its negative relation to what restrains it. Callicles acknowledges that to choose the life of pleasure is to choose a life of pain (494b1–5). Pain, then, has nothing to do in itself with the improvement of soul. Pain no doubt accompanies improvement, but unless the pain of punishment comes in a different flavor from the pain of the vices, it is impossible for the punishment Polus has in mind to get through to soul. The punished would simply have to take his word for it.

Socrates brings Polus back to justice as an art by means of an outrageous pun. He has him agree that just as the chrematistic art gets rid of poverty and the iatric art of illness, so *dikē* gets rid of intemperance and injustice. Socrates pretends that the last three letters in *dikē* are the same suffix as in *khrēmatistikē* and *iatrikē*, so that *D-ikē* looks like the "art of D" or the "Delta-art," for delta is the letter-designation for the number four, and justice is the Pythagorean name for four. The Socrates of the *Cratylus* seems to have intruded for a moment into the severe confines of the *Gorgias*. There is, fortunately, something similar in English to Socrates' pun that at least gives one a handle on what Socrates is up to. We use "medicine" for both the art and a drug; so "to take one's medicine" admits, apart from usage, both meanings. If *dikē*, then, is the art of punishment as well as the punishment, to submit to one is to submit to the other and learning is suffering.

56  Polus

Learning is suffering is the truth of the Gorgianic assumption that knowledge is virtue. It is the penultimate consequence of Gorgias' admission that persuasion comprehends learning and trust.

As a parallel to the doctors, to whom the sick are sent, the unjust and licentious, Polus says, are sent to the *dikastai*, who are either members of the jury or judges; but in neither case do judges administer the punishment they set. How does Polus fail to see the difference? He seems to be thinking of a new kind of judge, whose assessment of the penalty would itself be the penalty. This riddle Socrates solves in a seemingly offhand fashion. He first convinces Polus that he is happiest whoever is rid of vice in his soul, and the second happiest whoever is getting rid of it, "being admonished, rebuked, and paying the penalty." The verb "to admonish" (*nouthetein*) means literally to put mind in someone, and the verb "to rebuke" (*epiplēttein*) means literally to beat upon. Out of twenty-four instances of *epiplēttein* in Plato, this is the only passive use, and nowhere does it have its literal meaning. The confusion between body and soul, upon which the entire argument with Polus rests, reflects the linguistic phenomenon of the extension of corporeal into noncorporeal meanings over time. Rhetoric, then, is not an art but experience, the very experience that almost all languages undergo over time: the verb "to rebuke" also has its origin in a verb "to beat." Socrates can thus speak of the rotten soul (479b8). His exhibition in his speech of what supports the claims of rhetoric suggests that rhetoric, to be truly effective, would have to reproduce experientially the historical drift of language itself. Rhetoric would have to move from the grasp of the hand to the comprehension of the mind, from the beating of the back to the rebuke of effrontery, and from the welts of the lash to the gnawing of conscience. In the argument with Polus, Socrates has shown us how this movement has occurred in the inverse order, since he started from the pseudorationality of Gorgias as an image of his own arts. This movement had the traces of mind in it throughout, for Socrates was always in dialogic control; but the linguistic movement from body to mind is at random, and in stretching itself to include more and more of mind, it is not directed by the mind for any good. It certainly is economical, but it is not rational, for though it acknowledges by its very movement the falseness of the sharp break between body and soul, which Gorgias accepted, it does not come to any understanding of the true relation between body and soul. Any causal account of this movement would invariably start off on the wrong foot. Body would rule soul, and not even the insertion of Anaxagorean mind would help.

The difficulties to which any notion of corrective punishment are exposed come to light no less in what Socrates fails to say than in what he does. Polus agrees that to undergo treatment is not pleasant, and those who are being treated have no joy (478b8); but Socrates' phrasing—*khairousin hoi iatreuomenoi*—allows the insertion of a participle—*khairousin [iatreuomenoi] hoi iatreuomenoi*—that would alter Polus' answer: "Those who are being treated rejoice [at being treated]." The patient, moreover, while he is undergoing the cure would surely have both the evil of the disease and the pain of the cure; hence the unjust, at the start of his punishment at least, is more miserable than the unpunished. In order to deny his greater misery, it would be necessary to introduce the direction or goal of the treatment, either objectively—we decide he is less miserable—or subjectively—he has hope. A successful treatment of the body against the will of the patient is easier to conceive of than such a success for the cure of injustice. Socrates puts together for a comparison the sick and the unjust who equally refuse to undergo treatment. The unjust tries to arrange things so as not to be admonished or chastised, or to submit to *dikē*; he is like someone ill who, caught in the grip of the greatest diseases, arranges not to submit to *dikē* for the errors of his body and be treated, being afraid as if he were a child of cautery and surgery because they are painful (479a5–b1; cf. Aulus Gellius 10.8). The standard is medicine, but Socrates tries to intellectualize the body by speaking of the body's errors and at the same time to give an air of justice to medicine by speaking of the patient's refusal to submit to *dikē*; but his double adjustment, so that mind and right belong to the body and its cure, cannot be carried through. Illnesses are corporeal mistakes, but injustices are not errors of soul, for if they were, punishment would yield to teaching (*Apology of Socrates* 26a1–7). Socrates has no device by which he can hide the primary meaning of cut and burn. He cannot qualify the operation of punishment by calling them scientific, for the unjust patient is like a child and knows nothing of science. The rhetorician, then, who must deal with the reluctant patient, cannot speak scientifically either. He must convince the unjust to take what he says neither literally nor scientifically but morally. Morality exists in the gray area between the literal and the scientific. It has an ally in rhetoric. Both morality and rhetoric handle the "so-called virtues of soul" (*Republic* 518d9).

Socrates illustrates the extent to which the fusion of body and soul is needed in order to justify punishment in the following way. He speaks of those who refuse to be cured of their injustice as *hoi tēn dikēn pheugontes* (479b5). They are those who "flee from justice or punishment"; but *hoi pheugontes* is the standard Attic term for defendants, and *pheugein dikēn* is "to face a charge," with the crime added in the genitive. Socrates has thus reliteralized the verb *pheugein* in order to represent the criminal as the cowardly. To be guilty is to run away. Flight is fear. That there is an allusion to the original meaning of *phobos* as flight and its secondary development as fear is made probable by the verb Socrates uses to draw the parallel between the sick and the unjust. Those who avoid punishment, he says, are probably (*kinduneuousi*) doing the same sort of thing as the sick who avoid treatment. *Kinduneuein* means literally "to run a risk" or "be in danger," but most often it expresses a logical inference with a high degree of plausibility. At the same time, then, that Socrates galvanizes *pheugein* back into life he cannot afford for *kinduneuein* to undergo a similar resurrection, for if it does, the runaways from justice do increase their own risks but at the cost of denying in the argument any validity to the conclusion. The persuasiveness of morality depends entirely on its ability to keep body and soul together in a mix that accords fairly well with experience. It is for this reason that Socrates looks so paradoxical. He can make room for philosophy only if he dissolves the apparent well-being of morality.

Since every action of any sort becomes a patiency of the same sort, the degree and kind of moral indignation determine the degree and kind of unjust action. The actual opacity of wickedness is replaced by the moral certainty of the experience of injustice, which can work backward from its affect to what kind of wickedness initiated its experience. In ignorance of what injustice is, morality speaks of it in terms of what it does, how it is experientially. Since the original proportion was set up—medicine is to justice as health is to justice—two things have happened. Medicine has become the only way to the restoration of health, and injustice has become a disease. Soul accordingly has become a version of body, and proportions have become identities. The likenesses of ratio and science have become the unrecognized metaphors of rhetoric and morality. Punishment as justice is the phantom image of justice. It operates solely within the confines of pleasure and pain.

Socrates is now in a position to reassign rhetoric and disarm its vindictiveness. He proposes that rhetoric denounce the injustice of oneself and one's friends. Archelaus is to be let off the hook. Now that Polus has accepted the split between the tyrant as happy and the tyrant as unjust, Polus can turn around and denounce himself as the would-be tyrant. The pleasure in punishing and the benefit in being punished would finally coincide in the same person, and it would be truly beautiful. In the true counterpart, however, to the proposed relation between rhetoric and punishment, Socrates' pleasure in being refuted and in refuting was equal, but the benefit was greater in his being refuted. In the phantom image, one gives up the pleasure of denouncing and beating another and replaces it with the imaginary picture of his real misery. Self-denunciation is moderate in turning away from others and courageous in turning on oneself; but this courage is grounded in ignorance, for one has to shut one's eyes as one submits to punishment of whatever type and at whoever's hands (480c6). Self-denunciation, then, is the punitive equivalent to the conscious bringing out into the open of one's opinions (480c4, d5; cf. 453c4). Insofar as self-denunciation checks the will from denouncing others and guessing at their wickedness, it retains morally something of Socrates' self-restraint in not guessing at Gorgias' meaning. The will (*boulesthai*) thus emerges as the phantom image of meaning (*boulesthai*). This is the true significance of Polus' failure to answer the question of quiddity before the question of quality. Morality like rhetoric jumps over meaning to will and does not believe that the will is opaque; it knows all about the will of another through itself. But the blindness of the will to the blindness of the will is the beginning of the cure. The failure to know what justice is leads to trust in the effectiveness of punishment. One takes it like a man and is all the better for it.

Socrates was able to bring out the nature of the vindictive will while he made it harmless because punishment as justice could not but seem beneficial if it was directed against one's enemies. Nonpunishment, then, proved to be injurious; nonpunishment punishes and satisfies the desire to punish. Nonpunishment wholly satisfies. Socrates suggests that rhetoric might be useful for denouncing the injustice of one's fatherland. It would prepare the way for the beating, binding, fining, and finally killing of one's fatherland.[3] "Fatherland" (*patris*) is a word that in attenuating its source in "father" (*patēr*) designates a nonbeing (cf. Thucydides 4.95.3, 7.69.2).[4] "Fatherland" is the political equivalent of the moral individual of rhetoric. Its rhetorical power is inseparable from its shadowy nature. It summons something to mind that begins with the graves of one's ancestors and ends in stretching the roots of the city into Hades. The sacredness of its soil gives it a soul. "Fatherland" thus expresses the theme of the Polus section. A nonentity that can do no wrong is to be denounced for its wrongdoing. Only the wicked, Socrates remarks in the *Protagoras*, gladly expose the wickedness of their parents or fatherland and neither seek to hide

3. Cicero speaks of the patricide of the fatherland (*patriae parricidium*), *Philippic* 2.7, 17; cf. 13, 31.

4. Of the twenty-five occurrences of *patris* in Thucydides, only three are his (2.68.3, 4.41.2, 6.4.6), and each refers to a people's former country, while the rest are in speeches (whether quoted or reported). *Patris* occurs most frequently in books 6 and 7 (eleven and four times respectively), and mostly from the mouth of either Nicias or Alcibiades (six and four times respectively).

their faults nor feel compelled to praise them (345e6–346b5). Socrates as a true statesman has nothing to do with the shamelessness of such prosecutions. He abstains from attacking what does not exist. How could he possibly take any pleasure in failing to denounce his country? Nietzsche must have been mistaken in accusing Socrates of killing off Athens (cf. 521b4–c2).

# III
# Callicles 1

(481b6–499b3)

The clearest division in the Callicles section occurs at 499b4–8, where Callicles admits that some pleasures are better and others worse. Coincident with this admission is the total disappearance of prudence and wisdom (last at 499a2) and the virtual disappearance of courage, which recurs twice at the end as a direct consequence of moderation (507b5, c2). Moderation becomes the single virtue into which even justice is absorbed: of the thirty-seven occurrences of "moderation" and "moderate," only six come before 504d3. Prudence and courage, which Callicles himself defines and introduces in order to oppose them to what he understands to be Socrates' justice, do not last the course. Although they are plainly the superior virtues, to which not everyone can lay claim, Callicles does not hold onto them when he becomes sensible enough to discriminate among pleasures. When his case becomes stronger he abandons the weapons to fight it. Does Callicles experience something that forces him to acknowledge his unworthiness to take the high ground? Does Socrates get to him despite his protestations?

That the issue between Callicles and Socrates involves experience is acknowledged not only by Socrates, who makes an elaborate comparison of the two loves each of them has, but by Callicles. He asks Chaerephon whether Socrates is serious or having his fun; Chaerephon says that there is nothing like asking Socrates. Chaerephon alludes to the phrase Callicles had used when Socrates had asked whether Gorgias would be willing to converse or would continue his rhetorical display (447c5). Callicles seems to sense that what he had just heard is not Socrates' opinion but a playful anatomy of rhetoric; but he cannot quite put his finger on the difference between Socrates and Socrates' argument. That the argument followed once Polus granted that injustice was uglier or more shameful he sees, but he is unaware of the extent to which morality is essential to rhetoric or Polus as a rhetorician could not avoid granting what he did. Callicles is even right to say that nature and law have been jumbled by Socrates; but he does not see that that jumble is in the beautiful as rhetoric understands it and not in Socrates' analysis. Callicles gets hold of the

62  Callicles 1

identity of the beautiful and the just, but not of the relation between morality and pleasure. He believes he can restore clarity to the discussion if he can keep apart the beautiful, as it is displayed in wisdom and courage, from the moderation and justice of the just. This split is Callicles' version of Socrates' two arts of politics, through which he attempts to argue for beauty and strength of soul without any footing in the health of soul. It is not obvious why Callicles cannot establish a health of soul that does not involve the justice he finds so repugnant. What is certain, however, is that Callicles does not find in the enlarged arena of the city, into which he invites Socrates, the support he needs for the grandeur he defends. Could it be that Callicles has no more experience of the soul's grandeur than Polus had of Archelaus' happiness, and that Callicles too is nothing but a rhetorician?

Callicles admits that he cannot tell whether Socrates is serious or not, and it is important that he find out. He links the issue of Socrates' earnestness or playfulness with the truth or falseness of what he says. Of the four possibilities his formulation allows for, he mentions one, that Socrates is in earnest and things are as he tells them; but he certainly implies that, though Socrates is in earnest, things are not as he tells them. Callicles takes Socrates for a preacher, who tells us we are doing the contrary of what we ought to be doing, and though he says human life is topsy-turvy, it is right-side up. Of the two other possibilities, one is trivial, that Socrates is playful and what he says is false; but what if Socrates is playful and what he says is true? Human life would be topsy-turvy, but we would not be doing the contrary of what we should. Callicles is too much in earnest to face this possibility. Callicles is too kindly disposed to Socrates to question whether Socrates' feelings match his own. Socrates tells Callicles that he regards him as a touchstone for himself; he lets him draw the inference that he regards him as worthless as a piece of black quartz.

Socrates does not answer Callicles directly; instead, he tries to make himself intelligible to Callicles. They are both lovers. They are in love with something that represents for them the beautiful. The beautiful for both of them shows up in a beautiful body in whose viewing they at least take pleasure; and both of them are in love with an abstraction, as we would say, from which presumably they derive benefit. Socrates tells Callicles that his experience of the whims of his two loves should make him realize that the earnestness of his devotion to them does not depend on the truth of what they say. A corrective rhetoric would either have to break Callicles' devotion or have to stabilize the speeches of Demos the son of Pyrilampes or of the Athenian demos. Now this distinction between unwavering devotion and changeable opinion reflects the ordinary understanding of the difference between morality and knowledge, in whose eyes what one knows and that one knows do not have any consequences for behavior. Socrates tells Callicles, even before Callicles has said a word about where he stands, that the speeches he is going to speak are the speeches of Demos and the Athenian demos, and he ought to know better. He predicts that Callicles' speeches are going to be at times as moral or as infected with morality as are the man in the street's. He is as much of a mouthpiece as Polus: Polus for what everyone believes but cannot be made to say, and Callicles for what the collective nonentity of the city says but no one says. Socrates, on the other hand, just spoke the speeches of philosophy, which never alter. Callicles is called upon to refute philosophy and stop the inconstancy of the demos. The demos cannot be refuted. An exceptional man might just be able to chastise it or shut it up.

Socrates had earlier punned on "beautiful" and "call" (*kalon* and *kalein*). It just so happens that the two parts of Callicles' own name unite in one that pun. "Callicles" contains "the beautiful" (*kallos*) and "the naming of the beautiful."[1] His name is as consistent as the truth of Socrates' pun. Socrates says that his two loves make him constantly inconsistent. His devotion to a manner of speech—"the people"— which seems to be of the same order as "fatherland," falls together with a devotion to Demos. Demos is connected with Plato's own family, for Plato's mother married Demos' father Pyrilampes, his maternal uncle.[2] Demos belongs to the highest stratum of Athenian society. His name is rather unusual and probably reflects an attempt by his father to ingratiate himself with the Athenian demos. Callicles is devoted to Demos and what his name represents. He is devoted to a body and a name that signify the very structure of Athenian politics during the Peloponnesian War. Athenian democracy began with an aristocratic leadership that continued uninterrupted to the death of Pericles. With the rise to power of Cleon, a struggle ensued between men of the people and those who could not lay claim to such origins. In Aristophanes' *Knights*, the overthrow of Cleon is engineered by high-class slaves of Demos who enlist the services of a common man with uncommon talents, and it ends with the restoration of Demos, a figure as real as the sausage seller, to his youthful beauty at the time of Marathon.[3] Callicles, then, in his two passions seems to combine the two components that make up Athens. His praise of courage and wisdom comes from the upper crust; his contempt for moderation and

1. *Klēs* is a suffix from the same root as the word for glory (*kleos*), which became contaminated very early with *kalein*.
2. J. K. Davies, *Athenian Propertied Families 600–300 B.C.* (Oxford 1971), 329–333.
3. Cf. L. Strauss, *Socrates and Aristophanes* (New York 1966), 109–11.

justice repudiates the name of one and the reality of his other love. Callicles, however, cannot quite bring himself to denounce demos. No one except Socrates ever utters the word.

Socrates and Callicles each have two loves; but Socrates complicates his presentation of them by the use of the dual. He makes Callicles and himself into a pair of lovers of two loves (*erōnte . . . duoin,*), but he inserts between the dual participle *erōnte* and the dual object *duoin* another dual participle, *duo onte,* "being two of a pair." The twoness of their loves seems to reflect back on their own twoness, as if Socrates were split in two through his double love of Alcibiades and philosophy, no less than Callicles was through the duplicate demos. Alcibiades belongs to the same stratum as Demos and has the same love of the demos as Callicles (*Symposium* 216b5). Socrates too is tied in with aristocratic Athens, but he has philosophy instead of the Athenian demos to divert him. It is easy enough to say that Callicles and Socrates have each experienced a separation of themselves into body and soul, and whereas Socrates' corporeal love is a love of the lover of the Athenian demos, Callicles' noncorporeal love is of the Athenian demos. Socrates stands two removes from the demos on one side and wholly apart from it on the other; but Callicles is as close to Demos on either side. Socrates is in love with the love of wisdom. What stands in the way of his being a lover of wisdom directly seems to be the equal pleasure he takes in refuting and being refuted; he knows at any rate that because philosophy is the love of wisdom, she cannot love him in return (*Lysis* 212d8). The demos of Athens also cannot love Callicles back. Callicles' love seems more hopeless than Socrates'. It is all the more hopeless if his is a love that dares not speak its name.

Callicles' speech is in two parts (482c4–484c3, 484c4–486d1). They are not quite consistent with one another. The first part declares the right by nature; the second denounces philosophy and the way Socrates exposes himself to base accusers. Callicles too believes that injustice is uglier. In the first part, he defends the great man against the city, which is made up of the contemptible; he then attacks Socrates for not defending himself against the contemptible. First he accuses Socrates of sticking up for the many; then he warns him that one of the many will destroy him. Socrates is guilty of demagoguery or vulgar morality in the first part and of unmanly philosophy in the second. Callicles is thus forced to side with the many in the second part and attack them in the first. He uses philosophy to mount an attack on the city in the first part and in the second attacks philosophy in the name of the city. Philosophy in its noble weakness needs rhetoric—not for its own defense but to further political ambition. Callicles wants to put together education and injustice. Socrates can be said to have done something similar in the *Republic,* insofar as he showed the coincidental necessity of the city and the city's injustice for philosophy. "High culture" and hedonism are not infrequently together. They hardly ever leave room for the political. Indeed, the political usually obtrudes on them with all the suddenness of a pistol shot in the theater.

The inconsistency between the two parts of Callicles' speech recalls Gorgias' difficulty in putting together a praise of the power of rhetoric with a defense of the justice of rhetoric. In place of the unlimited power of rhetoric Callicles puts forward the lion of unlimited appetite and strength; in place of the weakness of rhetoric to defend itself, he blames the weakness of philosophy. In light of the correspondence of the parts of the two speeches, philosophy, we can say, is truly helpless and rhetoric only pretends to be; in turn rhetoric is truly powerless, and Heracles sweeps all before him. But what has Heracles to do with philosophy? More precisely, what has Heracles to do with Callicles? Callicles does not claim to be the naturally superior man himself. He says he is one of the enslavers, and if the other should ever break through the chains and incantations Callicles and everyone else imposed, he along with everyone else would be his slave (483e4–484a6). Callicles is truly just if he can look with such satisfaction upon the loss of his unjustly acquired and exercised power. Callicles' language echoes Aristophanes' *Frogs,* where Aeschylus in Hades offers Athens this advice about Alcibiades: "One ought not rear a lion's cub in the city, but once it is raised, one ought to serve its ways" (1431–32). Callicles, then, praises Alcibiades in the first part of his speech and then, in order to show how really unselfish he is, expresses his indignation at the contumely Socrates is liable to suffer. Callicles is in love with neither Alcibiades nor Socrates, and yet he looks forward to his own debasement at the hands of Alcibiades and cannot bear the equanimity with which Socrates tolerates a slap in the face. Laughter is not, according to Socrates, a proper form of refutation; but we must either admire or be dismayed at the restraint Socrates shows in not laughing in Callicles' face. Does not Socrates take Callicles too seriously to do him any good?

Polus said that wrongdoing was better but more ignoble than suffering wrong; Callicles wants to defend the nobility of wrongdoing, but he begins with the natural disgracefulness of suffering wrong. Wrongdoing is of secondary interest to Callicles. To submit to injustice is simply uglier for real men; it is the experience of a slave for whom it is better to be dead than alive, since on being insulted he can defend neither himself nor anyone else he cares for. The language of insult, it seems, is by nature, but the language of praise is conventional.

Obscenity in speech, one might say, because it calls a spade a spade, is the way in which nature shines out at the edge of convention (cf. 521b2). The real man is someone one does not insult without living to regret it. Whether the real man in turn insults anyone and, if he does, is unjust, Callicles does not say. One would suppose that natural slaves are beneath his notice, and if he had equals it would not be to his advantage to insult them. Of course if Callicles is suggesting that the real man challenges everyone in a contest of abuse, life would be very risky and hardly worth living. If he means, on the other hand, that the real man shows up his inferiors by devising the perfect insult for each, Socrates should be his man; it is difficult to conceive of anyone putting Socrates down. Aristophanes tried to do it, but almost everyone believes he missed the target. Callicles in any case would have to believe that nothing is funny if it is not insulting, and one does not laugh at what one admires. Callicles is rather solemn (cf. 485b2, 4, c1). One cannot imagine him at Agathon's party.

As soon as Callicles turns from suffering to doing wrong, his arguments become less sure. He prefaces his analysis of the equality of the law with "I suspect." The real man alone deserves to live. Since it is not practicable for the undeserving to roll over and die, Callicles proposes that the better should have more than the many. The better should be allowed to flaunt their superiority in a way in which the many can understand, who would be exposed in their incapacity were it not for the law. Callicles can no more set immunity to insults in opposition to profiteering than he can put together equality with the slap in the face. Why should the superior not have less than the many? Perhaps one ought to be compensated for one's inferiority. Socrates' proposal of communism in the *Republic* illustrates this principle. The better one is, the less one has. Callicles' silence about honor is necessary if surprising, for if the many are not willing to admit that they ought to be dead, they are hardly going to be ready to sing the praises of the stronger. The gods of the city exact the requisite humility and admiration from their worshipers; but no man recognized as a man could manage it on its own. Callicles swears by Zeus when he introduces the phrase "in conformity with the law of nature" (483e3), and he cites Zeus' son Heracles as an example of natural right. Callicles admits that he does not know Pindar's poem. He senses that a poet is not the best witness to what is by nature.

The evidence for the natural right of the stronger is the fact that some cities rule others; and though some cities are stronger than others, both are composed of the naturally weak. It must be, then, the rulers of stronger cities who are truly stronger. Callicles mentions Darius and Xerxes, both of whom led unsuccessful expeditions.

Darius and Xerxes must exemplify the truly universal rule that everyone seeks to have more (cf. Herodotus 7.8a) and not the second rule that the right to have more belongs to the stronger. Callicles knows of no one who exemplifies the second rule. The city with its unnatural strength has unmanned the naturally stronger, and under its enchantment they have taken on the shape of equality. If someone born and bred in the city could resist the enchantments of the city, he would bring to light the justice of nature. The city, then, is the indispensable touchstone of natural right. Only cities with the most harshly imposed equality would properly test the naturally superior. The city must be by nature if nature can shine forth only through its laws. Callicles seems to be filled with longing for someone who will prove he is right. If only Socrates were not a philosopher! Heracles and those like Heracles indicate what held by nature prior to the establishment of cities and their laws, but those who once justified violence have surrendered to the power of the law. The original meaning of *kreittōn* ("stronger") has weakened over time and acquired another kind of strength. Callicles needs this extended significance without any loss of its original force. He believed he had found it in Gorgias. Socrates is now his last hope.

The old lyric poet Pindar illustrates prepolitical right; the new tragic poet Euripides illustrates political right. The cattle raid of Heracles yields to a political debate between music and arms. A division of labor has occurred and allowed for the pursuit of excellence. Specialization, however, is stunting. The most stunting of all is philosophy, which, however, has its place in shaping the uncommon ruler of the common. Excessive training in philosophy produces inexperience in the all-too-human things, which include not only pleasures and desires but the laws of the city and the speeches of human associations. The philosopher, then, is free of the law without smashing the law. He alone is equipped to smash the law if he can just be redirected to the city. Callicles' ideal is no longer the lion but the tamed lion, who is strong enough to avoid insults but too weak to resist mockery. Everyone makes fun of what he is no good at, and Callicles does not want to be shown up anywhere. Philosophy, he believes, is needed if one is to be free and partake of the noble and beautiful, but in itself it is naïve and childish. Philosophy keeps one innocent of the ways of the world and, with a side-glance at Alcibiades who was notorious for it, is as deforming as a grownup with a lisp (Aristophanes *Wasps* 44–45). For only one of these two defects does the philosopher deserve a beating (485c2, d2). Callicles can straighten Socrates out about politics, but his lisp demands a straightforward beating. The beating is designed to carry a message, "Grow up!" Socrates has to be snapped out of his baby talk. His ignorance of the hard facts of life is to be brought home to him through the beating itself, which is a representative sample of the hard facts of life. Callicles wants to knock some sense into Socrates. He believes that such a lesson unites body and soul as closely as the expression "to knock sense into one" puts together the literal and the figurative. Callicles picks up the extension of beating into rebuking from Socrates' argument with Polus and reapplies it not to the unjust but to the philosopher. He accepts the notion that punishment conveys the intention of the punisher, but he refines it and believes that in the special case of the philosopher the message is in the cudgeling. Callicles believes the beating will do Socrates good. He certainly supposes that Socrates will be able to discriminate his beating of Socrates and the slap in the face Socrates can expect from a scoundrel. Is he as unaware as Polus was of the pleasure he himself would have?

The Greek word for courage is literally "manliness" (*andreia*), and in recommending the real man to Socrates, Callicles wants to incorporate into *andreia* all that a man should be. It is through the notion of manliness and its natural growth that Callicles' speech does not break into two parts. Callicles himself is from Acharnae, the largest deme of Attica and famous for the number and fierceness of its hoplites (Thucydides 2.19.2, 2.20.4; schol. Aristophanes *Lysistrata* 62). Socrates had apparently anticipated this possibility, for in conversing with Polus he had extended the expression for a gentleman "beautiful and good" (*kalos kai agathos*) to cover a woman as well (470e10).[4] The naturalness of the manly ceases to be all of a piece if nature includes not only form but generation. Callicles needs the city to denature the nature of the manly and perfect it along a single line. Aristophanes' myth of pure males, whose nature persists despite generation, and who on reaching maturity enter politics, would suit Callicles if he could believe it; but Aristophanes, despite the corporeal form of his myth, has to sacrifice the body entirely as it is in itself and make it a symbol of manliness. Only in Hades do lovers truly become one (*Symposium* 192d5–e4). Callicles has not thought as deeply as Aristophanes about his ideal. For a proponent of manliness he is awfully thin-skinned.

Of the three qualities Callicles allegedly has that make him an adequate touchstone for Socrates, Callicles has neither wisdom nor frankness, but he does seem to have good will. He is just but weak. If push comes to shove, he would not help Socrates; but his tolerance,

---

4. Dodds says ad loc that he knows of no other passage where "beautiful and good" is applied to a woman.

insofar as it represents the atmosphere of Athens, suffices to guarantee the survival of Socrates. Callicles would surely not go so far as to kill Socrates in order to teach him a lesson. Socrates distinguishes between Callicles' experience, in light of which he can understand Socrates, and Callicles' qualities, by means of which Socrates can test himself. Socrates can confirm through Callicles' rejection of philosophy in the precise sense his choice of philosophy in the precise sense. Callicles' attempt to frighten Socrates and show the ridiculous figure he cuts is but another version of Polus' bogeyman and laughter, but it is so mild a version that it seems more a promise of Socrates' long life in Athens than an adequate test of his way of life. Callicles must reveal something more than the suitability of a corrupt Athens, upon which both Socrates and Callicles agree, for the life of philosophy in order to justify the length of this part of the *Gorgias*. Perhaps it is Callicles' increasing irritation with Socrates or the rapid exhaustion of his good will that justifies its length. Perhaps it is the absence of any trace of Socrates on Callicles the touchstone that constitutes Callicles' contribution to Socrates' self-knowledge. Perhaps the silence of Callicles is golden.

Socrates casts grave doubts on the possibility of Callicles converting him. First, that Callicles will be franker than either Gorgias or Polus assumes that Callicles was right to ascribe to shame the reason Gorgias and Polus were forced to contradict themselves; but Socrates says that in that case their shame must have been overwhelming if it could bring them to contradict themselves in front of a large audience about the most important matters. Callicles takes it for granted that his premises are Gorgias' and Polus', and though in some sense that may be true, it may not hold for the aspect of rhetoric each defends. By failing to see what Gorgias and Polus are the proponents of—a spurious rhetoric that compels them to speak for it in their own name without the distance knowledge would bring—Callicles misinterprets the morality of rhetoric for a personal reticence on their part. Callicles, then, could be frank only if he really does have knowledge and is not caught up in the experiences rhetoric has induced. The conversation Socrates overheard between Callicles and his friends makes it clear that they guessed at what the right moment was to abandon philosophy. Their very deliberation shows they lacked self-knowledge. As for the possibility that their arbitrary limit on philosophy should set a standard for someone as corrupt as Socrates must be by now is a dream of Callicles. Socrates does take it seriously enough to promise to change his ways if Callicles can move from admonition to demonstration, but he refuses to let Callicles beat him up. If Callicles finds out later that Socrates has reneged on his agreement, he should consider him a worthless dolt. Socrates forestalls a beating. He would be too stupid to get it.

Callicles has to defend three propositions about natural right: (1) the stronger by force or violence drives off the things of the weaker; (2) the better rules the worse; (3) the superior has more than the inferior. The three propositions together represent not only the history of the extension of "stronger" to "better" both socially and morally but also a slide of "weaker" to cover comparable ground. Callicles needs both the identity and nonidentity of the three propositions. If they are distinctly separated from each other, so that they become, respectively, "Might is right," "Virtue makes right," and "Education makes right," he would be hard-pressed to maintain their equivalence either in fact or in principle. Callicles, moreover, speaks of property in the first and third propositions and of rule in the second. The second proposition is a version of Gorgias' claim for rhetoric, and only if all subjects were the ruler's property would it even be talking about the same relation as the first and third. Callicles, then, rejected philosophy for no other reason than its precision. If he is pinned down, he is lost. Callicles' long speeches have a kind of impressive sense that dissolves in argument. He is more thoroughly infected with rhetoric than either of the professionals Gorgias and Polus.

Almost from the first the argument does not go well for Callicles. The issue ought to be the relation between the good and power. It seems impossible either to deny the good power (otherwise the good would be good for nothing) or to identify them (otherwise everything would be in order). Socrates had taken up this issue with Polus, where he had proposed the rational use of power; but Callicles has reduced reason to nothing more than general education, which adheres more to the person than to his power and is unlikely in any case to convince the many that it bestows the right to rule. Socrates easily shows that the many are naturally stronger than the one; but Callicles fails to observe the defect in Socrates' argument, that since the lawful establishments of the stronger are naturally beautiful, the many in establishing the justice of equality prove that it is by nature. Callicles could have answered that whatever the stronger lay down is beautiful by being of the nature of the laying down but not that what they lay down is beautiful. The legislating is in conformity with the principle of Callicles but the legislated is not, and Socrates has not shown that it is. Indeed, Callicles could have argued that either the many have more than they otherwise should, and they call the equal what is more than their share, or else the inferior in laying down the just as the equal are acting in conformity with their nature. The many are blind to what allows them to lay down the law, that is, their collective strength, and the law they do lay down is in conformity with the weakness of their individual natures. Democratic law, then, has the beauty of superior power in its establishment and the ugliness of inferiority in its proclamation. What it says is not what it is. If Callicles had argued in this way, the next question would have been whether any law can embody the principle of its own foundation. Callicles seems to believe that the justice of acquisitiveness could be laid down as a law so that in obeying the law one would be obeying the force behind the law. To obey the law is to listen to a speech and do what it tells you to do (cf. 488c2); but what makes possible the speech of the law is not itself a speech but some force. The law therefore contains in itself the range from body to soul that Callicles needs to bring together Heracles and Gorgias. Callicles in fact uses the word *iskhurizesthai* in its literal sense "to be strong" (489c6) and does not notice its two other meanings, "to persist" and "to insist in speech" (cf. 495b8). Law is the velvet glove over the iron fist. Callicles' case thus seems to express the nature of language and law. Just as for Polus the justness of punishment spilled over into the experience of punishment, so for Callicles the justness of legislative superiority spills over into the justness of whatever is legislated. Pindar is right: law justifies the most violent. The irrational use of power hides behind the enchantment of the law.

In the *Iliad*, Agamemnon proposed to take back the girl he had given Achilles. Achilles was the stronger and the better who had accepted up till then his having less than he deserved. Agamemnon's action is a slap in the face of Achilles. It was a safe way of slapping Achilles, and even so Achilles would have killed him for it had not Athena intervened. Callicles seems to have started from such a situation and proceeded to misinterpret it. He mistakes the girl for the reality of which she is but a sign. Callicles speaks up for Achilles in the language of Thersites, who takes the struggle between natural right and ancestral right as a quarrel over booty (*Iliad* 2.225–242).[5] Callicles' mistaking of Thersites for Achilles began when he spoke of lions. The lion ought to stand for the strength of soul needed to resist the incantations of the law, but Callicles takes it for the ravenous appetite of the voluptuary. Callicles seems to look at the lion from the outside and measure what it needs to live by what he needs. He knows nothing of the nature of the lion; all he sees is how much it gobbles up.

Once Callicles agrees that "stronger" and "better" are not the same, he is no longer arguing fact but principle, and he should appeal to rhetoric as the indispensable means for negotiating between the strength of the many and the goodness of the few. He is very

---

5. Cf. G. E. Lessing, *Laokoon*, chap. 16.

72  Callicles 1

indignant at Socrates' sly way of representing the phantom images of legislation and justice in the form of the doctor consuming great quantities of food and drink, the weaver wearing heaps of beautiful cloaks, and the shoemaker walking around in the largest possible shoes (cf. Seneca the Elder, *Suasoria* 2.17); but his rejection of cookery and cosmetics and celebration of courage and wisdom accompany a praise of the enjoyment of things without their actual consumption or use. Callicles sees no need for a rhetoric of conciliation between wisdom and power, for he proposes to gratify the rulers with the tastes of the ruled. The rhetoric of indulgence has taken the rhetorician from behind. What has happened is this. Prudence and courage, which not unjustly can be identified with the gymnastics of soul, are touted by Callicles over against justice and moderation. The phantom image of the latter is gratification. Callicles accepts gratification no longer as the appeasement of the many but as the reward for the good. Diagrammatically, it looks like figure 8. Callicles, in bringing out into the open the ruler's pleasure, has abandoned Polus' pleasure in punishment and replaced it with the pleasure of the ruled. Hedonism looks more respectable than cruelty. It looks more respectable because the maintenance of law and order within the city, which alone concerned Polus, has yielded to Callicles' experience of Athens' subjugation of other cities, which, as he had said about Persian expansion, has nothing to do with justice. Callicles' fastidiousness, which shows in his contempt for possessions, expresses the individual's experience of the expansion of the imperial city, whose literal greatness does not swell the body but the soul (518e3). The virtues the imperial city needs to maintain itself and grow—prudence and courage—are the agents through their own success of the individual's experience of increasing appetite and pleasure. Callicles' fusion of the perspectives of ruler and ruled is a necessary consequence of his feeling himself to be a part of an imperial people. One outbraves and outsmarts the enemy as Demos and enjoys one's triumph as little man. Callicles expresses perfectly the private Athenian's experience of Pericles' funeral speech in praise of the quasi-tyrannical city (cf. *Menexenus* 234c2–235c5).

Since Plato's aim was different from Thucydides', he could not make Polus into an Athenian Cleon, who would express the pleasure of punishing cities that revolted from Athens as if it were the height of prudence, and then follow him up with Callicles to represent the appetitive apart from the vindictive. Instead, Socrates has set Callicles up as a perfect problem for Polus. Now that Socrates knows that Polus has the will to punish, does he have the art to punish Callicles? Is there any way to convince Callicles to take his medicine without dismantling the city that spawned him? In the following arguments with Callicles,

Figure 8

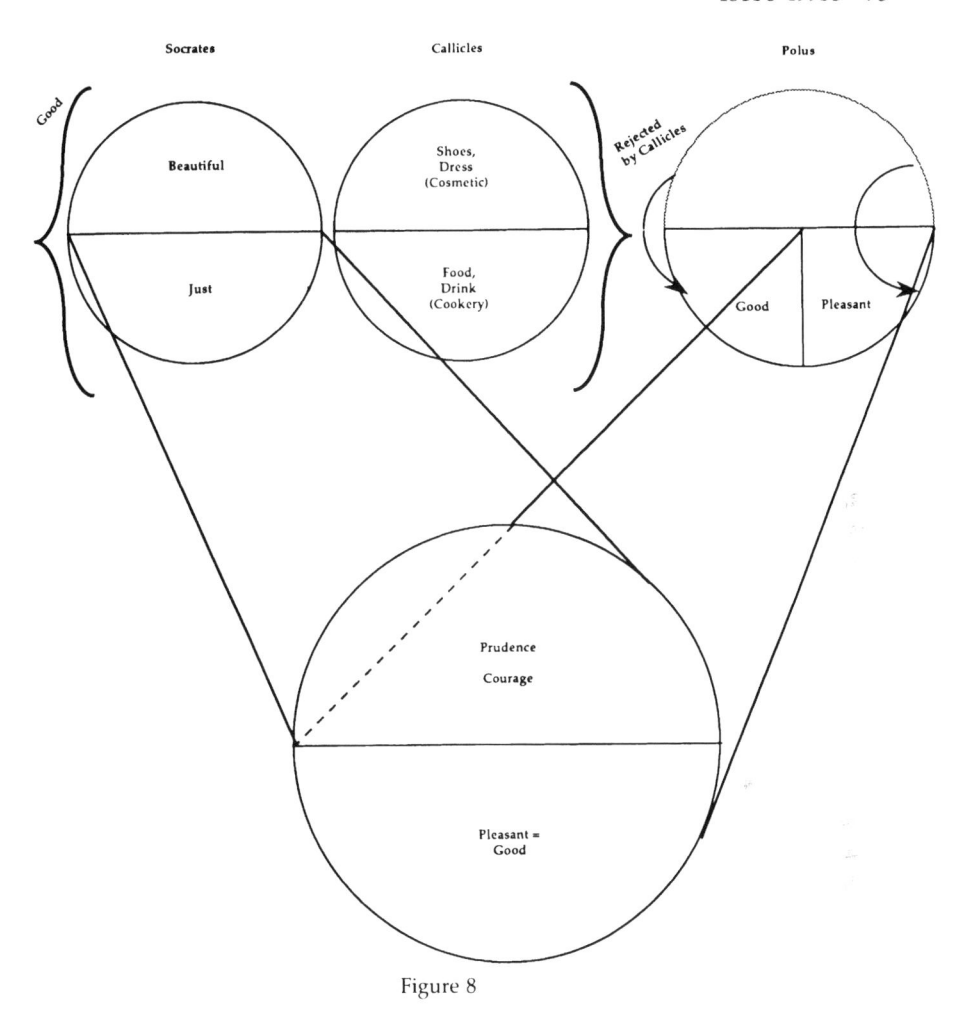

Socrates is discussing with Gorgias and Polus the obstacles to their successful treatment of Callicles. Callicles has, on the one hand, too great support from the city that stands behind him to be wrenched away from it, and, on the other, he is too weak to pry himself loose. He has neither the wit nor the guts to face the music.

Callicles' annoyance at Socrates' literalness is the city's annoyance at its own competence to satisfy perfectly the needs and desires of the body. The imperial city lives on an exaggerated vision of its own enterprise while it acquires the means to offer an eternal source of wages to its citizens (cf. Thucydides 6.24.3). Glaucon had experienced something like Callicles' annoyance when he called Socrates' true and healthy city the city of pigs; but he had been rescued from Callicles' experience of unlimited appetite by the threat of war and the necessity for soldiers to defend the territory his fevered city had taken from its neighbors. Callicles, however, cannot experience this necessity any longer. Within the city the rhetoric of indulgence has prevailed without a word having been spoken about indulgence. That the imperial city does whatever it likes cannot but be experienced in each citizen as the right to do whatever he likes. Democratic equality is on the books, but the strut of the tyrant is in everyone's heart. Socrates has no intention of sobering Callicles; it is enough for him to confirm his diagnosis and hand over to others the therapy.

Socrates' mention of self-rule bursts Callicles wide open. His outburst is the dialogic equivalent of the praise he lavishes on the absence of all restraint. He had been speaking as randomly as the mindlessness he now advocates, but he needed Socrates' speech about self-control to become conscious of his own meaning. Socrates' question is very simple: if the better are the prudent and brave, and the worse the imprudent and cowardly, must not pleasures and desires necessarily be irrational and cowardly and subject to one's prudent and manly control? Callicles then calls Socrates pleasant (*hēdus*), but he means idiomatically "silly," and proves Socrates' point. He then calls the moderate foolish, but "moderate" (*sōphrones*) means literally "sensible," and so he denies that the sanity of moderation (*sōphrosunē*) has anything to do with prudence (*phronēsis*). Throughout his speech Callicles does not once use the word for a real man (*anēr*), but four times "human being" (*anthrōpos*). A human being, he says, cannot be happy if he is a slave to anything whatsoever; if one is to live right one has to let the drives be as great as possible and then be capable of serving them. To be happy is to be free and a slave. Failure seems essential to human happiness, for only if one is impotent in the face of undetermined desires can one be certain that they were the greatest possible desires. The failures of Darius and Xerxes were indispensable for Callicles. If one is going to be what one ought to be, the desires must take off on their own and lead the way irrationally, for otherwise one could plan ahead and adjust them to one's capacity. Callicles cannot designate any pleasure without ruining his case. Infinite longing must not be bound by a nature with finite needs. Callicles rejects self-rule because there must be no self either to rule or to be ruled. The ordinary expression "self-control" implies that the self essentially is desires and pleasures out of control. Callicles accepts that implication and thereby eliminates the self. He replaces "man" with "human being" not because he has come to recognize the partiality of manliness but because he needs a carrier of desires who has no nature.

Callicles' praise of license is so extreme and so vague that its connection with injustice has been attenuated. Socrates had offered Callicles the pleasure of depriving the unworthy of their property; but for all of Callicles' talk of power, those out of control seem to run on no resources. There is nothing vulgar about Callicles' vulgarity. The impress of Athenian imperialism on his soul has been so direct that it has bypassed the money upon which it rests. When he looks at the statue of Athena Parthenos he does not see the gold as the emergency reserve fund it is (Thucydides 2.13.5). Socrates remarks that those without needs are said to be happy; Callicles says that if that were the case, stones and corpses would be happiest. Socrates' answer is complex. He begins by saying that the life Callicles recommends is equally terrifying, "for I would not be surprised, you know, if Euripides tells the truth in saying, 'Who knows whether to live is to die, and to die to live?'; perhaps we are really dead." Behind Socrates' web of puns and allusions is the story of the Danaids, who in Hades were condemned forever to fill up jars of water using sieves. These dead are not miserable because they are dead; they are miserable because they are needy. They are indistinguishable from those Callicles says are the most fully alive. Life, then, is death. Callicles needs Hades, for only in Hades can there be the unconditionality of the selfless self. Man can be truly free only if he is without a body. Hades is not only the place of infinite fulfilling but the place of infinite torture and pain. Callicles' vision unites the pleasure of punishing and the pain of punishment, which Polus had kept apart, into one and the same nonentity. Polus could keep them apart through the difference between the will of the agent and the resistance of the patient; but once the patient no longer has to be won over to accept the agent's intention as his own, the patient has become the agent of his own misery and joy. Callicles believes he is talking about pleasure and desire; he is really talking about crime and punishment. Callicles does not have to be cajoled into submitting to corrective punishment; he has already submitted on his own, and it does not work.

There are four elements that make up Socrates' explanation of Euripides' puzzlement. The first is that our body is a tomb or sign and whatever part of the soul desires are in is subject to constant change and persuasion; the second introduces a likeness of this part of the soul to a jar, and the jar of the senseless leaks; the third says that those in Hades are most miserable if they have to carry water to a leaky jar with a sieve; and the fourth likens the soul of the senseless to a sieve. These extravagant conceits are nothing but what Callicles needs in order for his conception of the best human life to be realized. Only if all of them were literally true would human life meet Callicles'

76   Callicles 1

conditions; whether it would be good or bad is an entirely different matter. Calliclean hedonism is a mystic doctrine. It is so mystical that Callicles has assumed the role of its proponent without ever having been initiated. The dissolution of the literal, which was so essential for the success of morality and rhetoric, has advanced so far that Callicles cannot even be treated unless he is first sobered up. It is Callicles who needs to have some sense knocked into him.

Socrates starts with the disappearance of body (*sōma*) into sign and grave (*sēma*). A tombstone signifies the presence of "some body." It signifies the presence of "no body." Without a body the desires can expand indefinitely within the liberated soul. The soul thus becomes the body and still remains the soul. The soul has something "in" which there are desires, and this something is persuadable and alterable. A change of opinion is a change. What undergoes a change of opinion resembles a jar,—sound if it retains an opinion, leaky if it does not. A leaky jar is not subject to persuasion. No desire can be formulated that can be set as a goal and then satisfied. The insatiate, then, are not those whose desires cannot be satisfied, they are those whose desires themselves drain away and who are constantly redoubling the will to will. This dreamlike state results in the resplitting of the soul into leaky jars and sieve. The leaky jars are now the body for the soul, the sieve is the soul, and the sieve carrier is a phantom which moves endlessly back and forth in an attempt to put body and soul back together. Socrates' final pun is to link distrust (*apistia*) with insatiety (*aplēstia*) and unpersuadability (*apithanon*). The alpha-privative in all three words represents the holes in the leaky jars and sieve. The frustration in incontinence is due to distrust. Animal faith is gone. All that remains is the religion of the incredible for the incredulous.

Callicles' refusal to concede anything to Socrates does not prevent Socrates from trying out another image from the same school. In this image, there is no Hades, no soul, no body, no desires, no persuasion, and no pleasures; all there is are extreme pains (494a1). Callicles accepts it at once and modifies his original objection. He no longer says the moderate are corpses; he grants them a stonelike life, and he identifies the life of pleasure with the life of pleasure and pain. Socrates seems to have done the impossible; the mere mention of pain has brought Callicles up from Hades. Socrates, however, happens to name the liquids in three of the many jars both the moderate and the intemperate man have. Wine, honey, and milk are the ingredients in one kind of libation to the dead (*Odyssey* 10.519–520). The moderate man has already taken care of Hades; he is complete in this respect, at least, even if there is no Hades; but Callicles' man needs Hades. Life on earth can never bring him enough satisfaction. He has to live the life of the insatiable bird *kharadrios* without being a *kharadrios*. He is trapped within a nature to escape from which he needs more than nature. Callicles is deeply into voodoo. Socrates shows to Gorgias and Polus that their rhetoric does not reach the nonknowers to whom it is directed. There is an abyss of fantasy in Callicles at which they have not even guessed. Their rhetoric scratches the surface of the bottomless will of Callicles.

It seems at first quite impossible that courage and prudence could ever be believed to be consistent with a life of pleasure; and without Polus to prepare us for Callicles, we would be inclined to charge it up to a mistake on Callicles' part and not as an essential part of Callicles' mistake. Polus, however, has let us see that if lawful punishment is to be effective, the law must promote the moderation to fear punishment and the courage to face punishment. The law therefore promotes the prudence to evade punishment and the courage to face the pleasures and pains of desires. The moral virtues are in themselves not directly connected with individual happiness; their good is adventitious to the individual and essential to the city; and once the city begins to achieve its good, freedom and empire, the individual picks up that good and makes it his own. The more political the individual is, the more impressionable he will be to the political good; and if he is not frank it will be impossible to discover how his devotion to the nonbeing of the fatherland, reinforced by a devotion to the nonbeing of the demos, has altered him. Callicles' frankness has its limits, but by the time he comes to them it makes no difference to Socrates' argument.

After the funeral speech of Pericles in Thucydides comes his account of the plague (2.47–53). In its last two chapters Thucydides gives the following sequence of the plague's effects. First, the sanctuaries in which some Athenians were living temporarily were filled with corpses; second, all the laws about burial, which they had previously used, were upset, and they buried as they could; third, lawlessness in general spread; fourth, on observing how sudden death made the "happy" and the have-nots so close, men no longer took to hiding their actions in conformity with pleasure; fifth, they made their enjoyments quick, believing equally their bodies and their money as lasting as a day; sixth, no one was eager to work at what was thought noble in the uncertainty whether one would live to achieve it; whatever was pleasant at the moment and profitable for that end became noble and useful; seventh, no fear of gods or laws of men restrained them, judging reverence to be no different from irreverence, since they saw everyone perish alike; and, finally, no one expected to live long enough to pay for his crimes, and, since a far greater condemnation already hung over them, it was only fair, before it swooped down, to have some pleasure in life. The most striking similarity between Thucydides and the *Gorgias* is the emergence of pleasure as the good against the background of divine law and judicial punishment; the greatest difference is the mere juxtaposition of Pericles' funeral speech and the plague in Thucydides and their casual connection in the *Gorgias* (cf. Thucydides 2.37.2 with 2.53.1). Symbolic historiography has become a philosophic psychology. Without Thucydides, perhaps this transformation would not have been possible, but it still is of a different order. What the *Gorgias* contains is a proof that the city and the soul are different in kind, and no mapping of one onto the other is possible. The soul is of necessity incoherent if the city is its model.

Socrates mounts three successive arguments against Callicles before Callicles calls it quits and concedes there are better and worse pleasures. The first purportedly proves that pleasure cannot be good because there can be a co-presence of pleasure and pain but not of faring well and badly; the second that if pleasure were the good, the cessation of pleasure and pain would be the cessation of good and bad; and the third that the presence and absence of pleasure and pain would entail the presence or absence of good. Socrates forces Callicles to be consistent and absurd. Callicles' consistency uncovers his ignorance of the nature of pleasure and pain and his innocence about good and evil. His crude understanding of pleasure accompanies his naïve understanding of good. His hedonism takes its bearings from morality. It is absolute. Callicles wants to say, apparently, that the good life is the life of the greatest variety of experiences regardless of the experiences themselves; and there must be no memory, nature, or circumstances of any experience that could clog the perfect patiency needed for every other experience. The good life, then, is the life devoted to the overcoming of satisfaction and self-satisfaction. It is a life of pain insofar as pain represents the resistance of any nature to be other than itself. Happiness thus consists in having the power to overcome one's resistance to change. Callicles, however, though he plainly refers to such a life (494c2–3), chooses to follow Socrates and identify a life devoted to just one pleasure—scratching an itch—as the happy life. Callicles collapses the sum of all possible experiences into one experience. The democratic principle that every individual has the right to do what he likes takes over from what would result from the operation of that principle over the demos, the greatest variety of every possible experience. Callicles' hedonism is political hedonism if one looks at the sum of all lives in a democracy; but this grandeur and variety disappear if one looks at the trivial and base lives that constitute it. In the whole, the scratch of the itch would hardly be noticed, but Callicles could not explain what guarantee he has that not everyone will choose to scratch and itch together. Callicles is forced either to idealize the demos despite his contempt for it or to put his hopes in philosophy if complete degradation is to be checked. He seems to sense that in an imperial city morality is not strong enough for the job.

Socrates' example of scratching and itching has this striking feature, that one has available within oneself the means to satisfy a desire that one can oneself create, and the relief prolongs the desire. The skin, unfortunately, has a limited capacity to put up with scratching, so one either has to exercise some self-control or discover an eternally elastic skin. Callicles really needs a phantom image of body welded to soul; what he settles for is a physiology of drinking and thirst that does not depend on any account of either body or soul (cf. 496e7–8). Words determine the nature of pleasure and pain: Callicles' hedonism is not just what rhetoric sponsors; it is the invention of rhetoric and bears little relation to experience and no relation to knowledge. Socrates wants to establish as the general formula for the satisfaction of any need or desire *lupoumenon khairein,* "to enjoy while being in pain," but as a general formula it is not true of any particular action and patiency. On each occasion, "being in pain" has to be supplemented with one participle and "to enjoy" with another. In the case of drinking, the complete expression must be this: "Being thirsty/while being in pain to enjoy drinking." What Socrates has done, which Callicles has failed to observe, is to identify the swallowing of a liquid (drinking) with the enjoyment of the swallowing of the liquid, and the pain in the dryness of one's condition with the desire to get rid of the pain. The evil that stands to the left of the slash is the condition for the good to its right. Good and bad, therefore, could well parallel pleasure and pain if every good has attached to it an evil condition without which it could not be. Weightlifters and runners are in different contests. Socrates asks whether strength and weakness can be together or speed and slowness; but he does not ask whether speed and endurance can be together, and whether Ajax is not rather slow. Callicles cannot see the necessary co-presence of good and evil because power is meant to keep them apart. Power grants unconditional freedom. Callicles does not believe the good has any conditions. He saw no difficulty in combining philosophy and politics. He denies implicitly that death is part of living. Once again he needs Hades. His understanding of pleasure therefore is not the opposite of morality but derivative from morality. In its reaction from morality hedonism tries to fulfill the posturing of moral freedom. What it puts in its stead is the scratch and the itch.

Socrates has Callicles agree to the painfulness of "hunger itself"; but he does not ask about "eating itself" whether that is pleasant. Eating has a condition, hunger; but hunger is unconditional. "Hope" never occurs in the *Gorgias*. Socrates transforms Callicles' original assertion, "It is pleasant to eat while being hungry," into an assertion of the co-presence of pleasure and pain. It could be argued that the co-presence of pleasure and pain is experientially true; and Callicles' assertion is a judgment on that experience; and his judgment holds that the assertion "It is painful to eat while being hungry" is not true. Since it is perfectly possible, for hedonist and nonhedonist alike, to replace Callicles' assertion by "It is good to eat while being hungry," and therefore to assign one's welfare to the complex of hunger and eating ("I fare well whenever I eat while being hungry"), it is not obvious why Callicles fuses judgment and experience. Experience is nothing but perception and ignorance of good. What it senses is the same as what it feels. Callicles represents the ultimate consequence of rhetoric, for whom the very speaking of his thesis destroys his thesis. Callicles' failure to see the flaws in Socrates' reasoning is in accord with his thesis. To take any distance from sensation, so as to speak and judge, is to be sensible and lose one's case. The sophistry in Socrates' argument to which Callicles objects is not Socrates' sophistry but Callicles'. He looks into himself and blames another.

Gorgias revealed in his discussion with Socrates that he did not know how rhetoric worked. The echoes of the rhetorician's speeches in the many were as moral as his, but the experiences of his speeches were hidden from view. Gorgias' interest in Callicles' finishing his argument with Socrates is due to his gradually discovering what the effects of rhetoric are. This discovery does not depend on whether Callicles is in earnest or not. His willingness to gratify Gorgias lets the truth emerge regardless of whether he is playing a role or not; indeed, if he were not playing, the truth would never emerge. The city is too serious a place for the reduction of the good, who are prudent and brave, to the bad, who are foolish and cowardly, ever to occur. Were there ever to be perpetual peace, the soldiers and the demos of the city would be the same; but if there were perpetual peace, the ground for Callicles' proposal of the continuous expansion of desires and pleasures would disappear. Freedom and empire, when translated into the individual, become the freedom to do whatever one likes and the power to do whatever one likes; but they cannot be maintained either with the loss of freedom and empire or with the city's stagnation. The individual's breathing is as deep or as shallow as the expansion or contraction of imperialism itself.[6]

6. The collapse of the imperial city into the individual is illustrated by Thucydides having Alcibiades echo Pericles in the following manner. Pericles says, "To excite loathing and distress at the moment belongs from the start to all who claim the right to

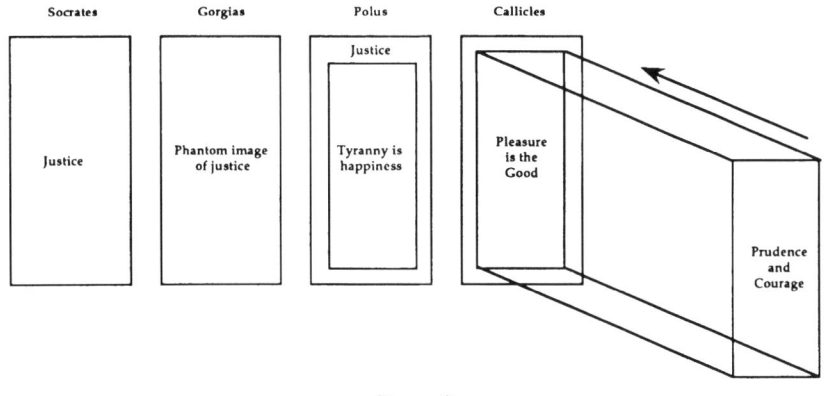

Figure 9

The sequential structure of the *Gorgias* so far is seen in figure 9. Gorgias' spurious version of Socrates' justice became Polus' moral indignation at the injustice of the happiness of the tyrant. Callicles took over the happiness of tyranny as the identity of the pleasant and the good, but he acknowledged the political virtues of prudence and courage to support the expansion of the city. His abandonment of prudence and courage along with the abandonment of indiscriminate pleasures and desires shows what the origin of his hedonism is. Gorgias had not the slightest idea that the freedom and enslavement which rhetoric makes possible are experienced individually as Callicles expresses them. The argument he fell for, that one is what one knows, has its inner truth in the argument Callicles now must accept, that one is what one experiences.

---

rule over others; but whoever incurs resentment for the greatest things deliberates rightly. Loathing does not extend very far, but the immediate brilliance (*lamprotēs*) and the ever-remembered glory are left behind hereafter" (2.64.5); Alcibiades says, "I know that those like myself, and all who stand in brilliance (*lamprotēs*), excite distress in their own lifetime, primarily among their equals, and next in all with whom they associate, but they leave behind the claim on the part of men hereafter to a kinship with them that is not really theirs, and, to whatever fatherland they belong, the possibility for it to boast, not about those who are alien to it and were in error, but about its very own and who did beautiful things" (6.16.5). Although Pericles wants to speak of cities only, his language is equally applicable to individuals.

# IV
# Callicles 2

## (499b4–527e7)

The surgical separation of pleasant from good, which has cut out as well the political virtues of prudence and courage, leaves Callicles squirming before Socrates' threat to cauterize the now-helpless desires (cf. 522e1–4). Socrates expresses pain on discovering Callicles' insincerity. Callicles can no longer be trusted to say what he thinks. He has become as difficult to gauge as the rhetorician's audience usually is. Callicles thus poses a more difficult problem for punitive rhetoric. As he himself will say, Socrates speaks well but he has undergone the experience of the many, for Socrates has scarcely won him over (513c4–6). Part of the difficulty might be thought attributable to Socrates. The radical separation between the pleasant and the good allows them to be put back together in such a way that no degree of pain if good would stand in the way of its being choiceworthy, and likewise no degree of pleasure no matter how little evil it might contain would require its acceptance. The choice of good, moreover, would be up to the expert, and it would be accidental whether anything he chose happened to be pleasant. This severity, however, is not due to Socrates; it is a consequence of Callicles' understanding of the unconditionality of pleasure and the good. In his ignorant rebellion against nature, he allowed pleasure to float free from limitations and at the same time denied the co-presence of good and evil. These two assumptions of Callicles necessarily had the effect, once the wedge was driven between the good and the pleasant, of separating them to the extent that Socrates' original distinction between art and experience required. There is now a retrospective justification of that distinction, which, however, not science but the strict moralism that lurked in rhetoric has grounded. How spurious that distinction is Socrates indicates by remarking on the failure of cookery to have examined the nature of pleasure and its cause (501a5–6), for if there is a science of pleasure it must aim at the good and thus duplicate the sciences of which the parts of flattery are phantom images. If such a duplication is to be avoided, the political sciences of legislation and justice would have to be modified. Socrates hints that the name for this modified practice is philosophy (500c8).

In his summary of the twofold schema of artful and artless treatments of body and soul, Socrates drops all mention of flattery as the phantom image of genuine art. Flattery now aims directly at gratification; it does not pretend any longer that its treatments are good. Rhetoric in its political form is now a way of life in itself; it has turned its back on science. Callicles offers two reasons for conceding to Socrates without casting his vote with Gorgias and Polus: the *logos* is to be brought to a conclusion and Gorgias is to be gratified. The *logos* has a life and shape of its own. Callicles has lost interest in converting Socrates, but Gorgias still has a hold on him. Callicles will indulge Gorgias after he has agreed that everything men do is for the good. The *logos* will be completed even though Callicles does not know whether it is any good for it to be completed. His compliance is blind. He agrees to submit to an unknown end. His submission comes immediately after he has given up a view that committed him to an imitation of the imperial city. The impossibility of there being such an imitation has not led Callicles to sobriety, but it has brought him to the threshold of sobriety. Obedience, in a gracious form, has replaced emulation. The inducement of moderation now seems feasible.

Just as Socrates had tied in the gratification of rhetoric with Polus' gratification of himself, so he now links Callicles' gratification of Gorgias with the issue of collective gratification. Polus gratified his questioner; Callicles gratifies a spectator. He plays to the audience. His insincerity before Socrates makes him an actor whose words are addressed to Socrates but whose intention is to please Gorgias. Callicles joins with Socrates in displaying before Gorgias a variety of crowd-pleasing exhibitions, of which the chief is tragedy. Tragedy performs before a truly comprehensive demos of children, women, and men, slaves and free. Political rhetoric seems to be occupied with a small part of tragedy's range. Callicles grants that tragedy is flattery even after it has been stripped of tune, rhythm, and meter, everything in short that might be thought to make the speeches of tragedy a type of indulgence. Socrates asks whether its whole effort and concern are to gratify the spectators or to fight and strain (*diamakhesthai*) against them, if anything is pleasant but bad, and speak and sing, regardless of whether the spectators like it or not, whatever is unpleasant but useful. Tragedy, however, does speak of the unpleasant and bad—divine punishment, for example—but it does so pleasantly. It is pleasant for the spectators to see and hear unpleasant things. The rhetoric of tragedy has its force through the framing of everything, good and bad, pleasant or not, in the light of pleasure. Tragedy makes good and bad unreal. Tragedy therefore puts in doubt the possibility of a genuine punitive rhetoric. The very fact that the opposite of "gratification" (*kharizesthai*) is a word that has extended its meaning from battle to verbal contention (*diamakhesthai*) is already enough to make one suspect the efficacy of a verbal beating.[1] Tragedy scares one to death, and one enjoys the show.

A rhetoric of pain would have to get its disagreeable message across disagreeably, but still not be as grating as Meles was whose singing to the lyre annoyed the audience. It could be neither unpleasant nor pleasant, but a neutral denunciation of sin is an oxymoron. A possible way out of this dilemma is now before us in the dialogue. Socrates is getting on Callicles' nerves; he submits to the unpleasantness for the sake of the pleasure it gives Gorgias. Callicles therefore must be saying to himself something like this: "It is good for me to be pained and gratify Gorgias." Punitive rhetoric would be possible if the patient believed he was serving someone else's pleasure and not his own. Callicles must understand that Gorgias' pleasure is higher than his own. The demos, then, can be rebuked if it believes it is satisfying some higher being. The tempering of an imperial people through religion is not an unknown practice, but the example of the Athenians' reaction to the mutilation of the Hermae shows how easily it itself gets out of control and contributes nothing to sobriety. Religion, in any case, is not Socrates' way. If, however, the propitiation of the gods is one way to circumvent the self-defeating persuasiveness of punitive rhetoric, Callicles cannot be made subject to it, at least the Callicles in the first part of the argument. Callicles there showed up as someone who needed Hades if he were to fulfill his imperialism of desire. Callicles is curable if there is no Hades; the demos may be curable if there is a Hades, and Hades is not part of tragedy. In the *Republic,* Socrates had proposed a nontragic Hades as a part of his education of the guardians, but he certainly thought it would not work for the demos. The second discussion of poetry in the tenth book of the *Republic* shows that the Hades of tragedy had not been fully disposed of.

On turning to political rhetoric, Socrates asks whether public speakers aim at the improvement of their fellow citizens or, if they, like the tragic poets, aim at gratification only, neglect the common good in favor of their own, and "associate with the peoples (*dēmoi*) as if they were children" (502e7). Since "peoples" is a distributive plural, and it refers to the singular demos in each city, "children" ought to be distributive as well; but if demos is handled as if it were a child, demos is a fiction of rhetorical flattery—"we the people"—and therefore

---

1. In Thucydides, Cleon uses *diamakhesthai* of his own insistence both before and now on the necessity to punish the Mytileneans (3.40.2); Diodotus echoes him (3.44.2). Thucydides uses the verb literally elsewhere.

incompatible with the astringency of punitive rhetoric. Can one improve the souls of citizens while speaking to them as if one soul animated them? It is one thing to satisfy some desires and not others, and in this way to make a human being better (503c7–d2); it is quite another to talk the souls of the many into becoming better without teaching. Socrates tells Callicles flat out that he has never seen a scientific rhetoric. Callicles cites among others Pericles. He seems to believe that the notorious incorruptibility of Pericles proves that he bettered the Athenians. According to Thucydides, Pericles had the power to speak against the Athenians' inclinations: "At any rate, whenever he observed that they were inappropriately confident by insolence he used to strike them dumb with terror" (2.65.9). The induction of temporary fear seems not to be what Socrates has in mind. Thucydides, in any case, though he gives us three speeches of Pericles, does not include among them a sobering speech. He never has Pericles speak of moderation.[2]

Moderation assumes the position of the principal virtue of soul through a discussion of order and arrangement. Socrates' speech on order is even for the *Gorgias* rather disorderly. The aim of the good speaker is the good, but what he looks at in composing his speech is something else. Socrates speaks of the form (*eidos*) each craftsman produces by his nonrandom selection of the things for his work. There is no suggestion that any craftsman is subordinate to an architectonic science that determines the good. Each element is compelled to fit together with every other element in order for there to be an ordered whole, but what one can do with an ordered whole or what an ordered whole can do on its own is left out of the picture. Socrates mentions painters among the craftsmen who make ordered wholes, but the perfect order of a painting seems to be at the price of its unreality and purposelessness. Were the painting to come to life it would have to lose its perfect order (cf. *Timaeus* 19b4–c2). Socrates' account therefore vindicates Callicles' claim that perfect order is the same as death after Callicles has been forced to abandon his praise of the random life. Socrates, however, reinstates randomness in his very speech in praise of order. He distinguishes implicitly between the ordered product made through a nonrandom selection and the random selection in the proof that every craftsman does not operate randomly. Callicles is asked to choose at random any craftsman (503e4, 6), for unless he chooses at random the proof will not be valid. Philosophy therefore must randomize, but it cannot randomize without failing to randomize. Jocasta's injunction to Oedipus cannot be carried out: "It is best

---

2. Cf. L. Strauss, *The City and Man* (Chicago 1964), 152.

86   Callicles 2

to live at random" (*Oedipus Tyrannus* 979). Philosophy needs the unplanned encounter with the random. The haphazard as the condition for all thinking is opposed by Socrates to the arbitrary orderliness of the lawful. Whatever shape the law imposes on human life is better than the shapelessness of the disordered life. Only orderliness can prepare one for the lucky discovery of order. Callicles' demand for maximizing the randomness of life is thus in retrospect an inkling of the condition of philosophy. He superimposed, however, onto the condition for philosophy the individual so that the individual himself became the systematic arranger of his own derangement.

The present restoration of the beautiful to the just so as to reconstitute the good of both in Socrates' original scheme is only apparent. Socrates' science of politics had this structure (fig. 10). Polus reduced it by half through the coincidence of the beautiful and the just, which in turn was made up by the pleasant and the good (fig. 11). After Socrates has forced Callicles to cancel the pleasant, the good has been expanded into the beautiful, and the just has been made to coincide with it (fig. 12). Formally speaking, then, Polus' identification of the just and the beautiful has been incorporated into the present argument with Callicles; but if one looks beyond the form, such an incorporation would involve the incorporation of Polus into Callicles. Callicles can be restrained if it were possible to get Callicles to split himself into himself and Polus, so that the formal identity of the just and the orderly would in practice be the punishing of the self by the self (fig. 13).

Nothing has been suggested so far as to how this self-denunciation can be arranged. The restoration of Socrates' original scheme through

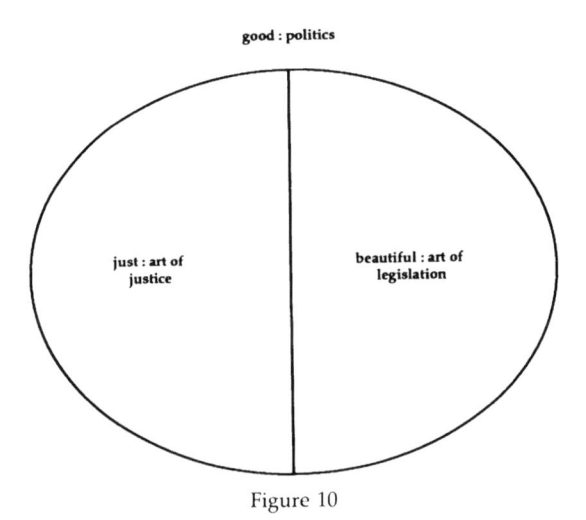

good : politics

just : art of justice | beautiful : art of legislation

Figure 10

Figure 11

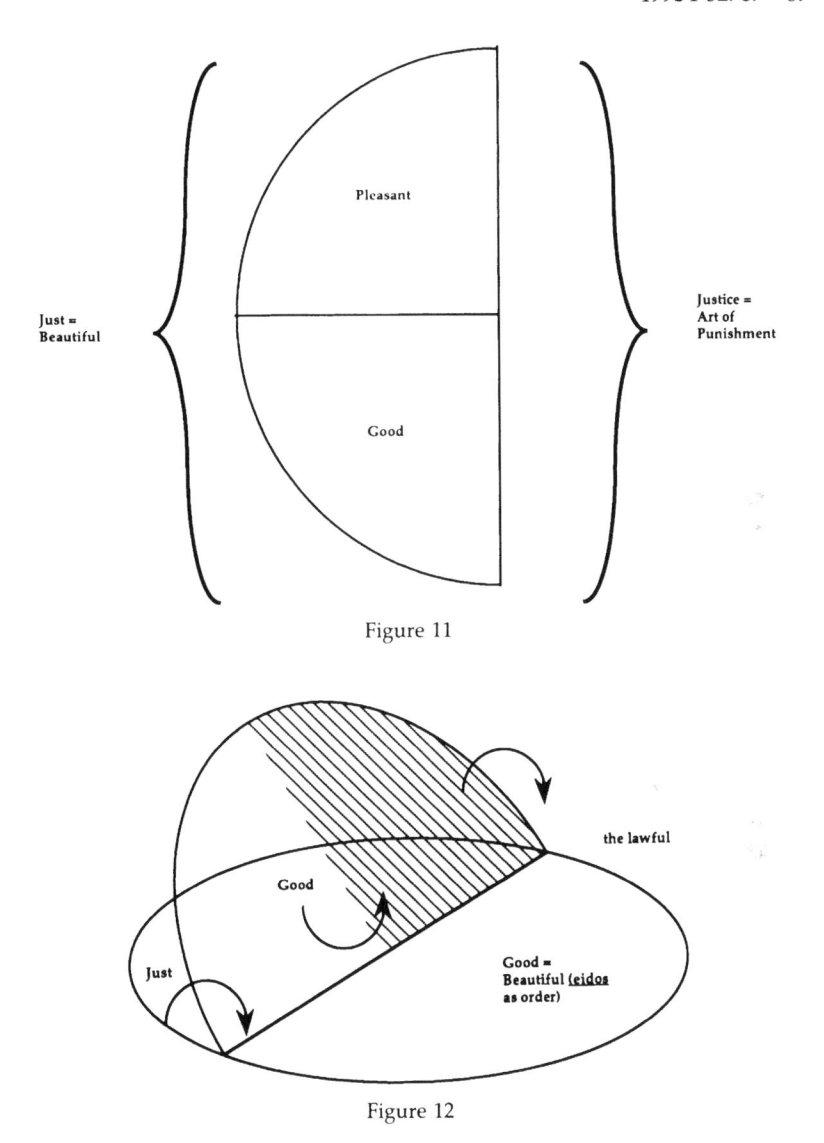

Figure 12

Polus implies that the confusion or assimilation of justice and law is due to the jumble of rhetoric and sophistry which now has infected the arts of which they were the phantom images. Callicles' unwillingness to resist Socrates any longer represents the spurious ease with which Gorgias and Polus believe rhetoric works. His graciousness, in allowing Socrates to complete the argument, is the true measure of the difficulty in inducing the toughness to be the patient of self-correction.

88  Callicles 2

```
        Polus
        Just         Polus
                     Good =
                     Beautiful
                     (order)




                                        ⎫
                                        ⎬  Callicles
                                        ⎭


              Callicles
              Pleasure =
              Good
              (Randomness)
```

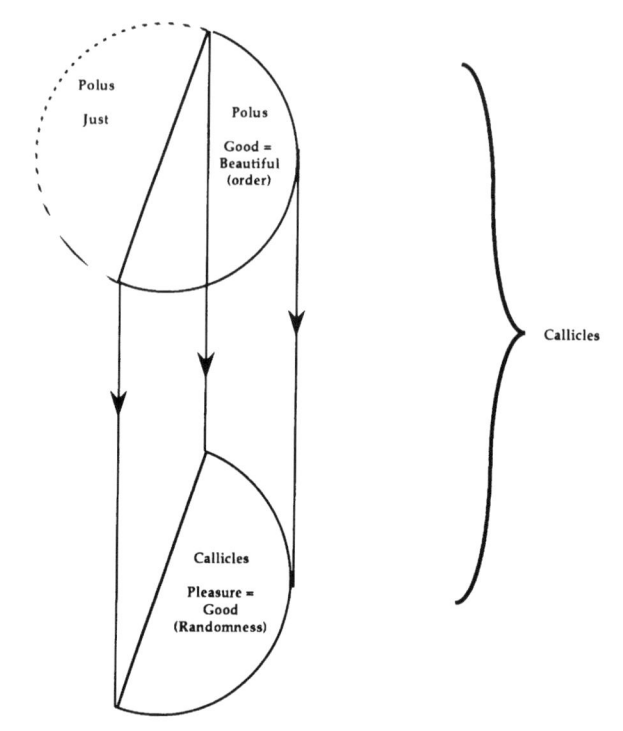

Figure 13

The strict parallelism Socrates' argument requires between body and soul, in order for the lawful ordering of soul to match the ordering of body, is not worked out. It is not worthwhile, Socrates says, and Callicles agrees, to live with a bad condition of body; but Socrates does not say whether it is profitless to live with a bad condition of soul (512b1–2). Polus' assumption that no combination of the soul's vices can be as painful as poverty and sickness still clings to the argument. The doctor, moreover, allows the healthy to satisfy their desires; but the perfectly ordered soul would seem to have no desires to be satisfied. Socrates, at any rate, does not say what they are, anymore than Callicles did; indeed, if the parallel to corporeal appetites is to be maintained, the desires of the healthy soul must be the same as the soul's desires when sick. Finally, Socrates does not say there are any soul doctors to tell us when we are cured. He recommends a course of treatment that does not exist. Its possible nonexistence seems to be connected with his silence about suicide. If treatment is to be found in Hades, he is recommending almost universal suicide; if there is no Hades, and no treatment is to be found on earth, he is being playful and telling the truth. Callicles, at any rate, at exactly this point in the argument, refuses to go on: "I don't know what you mean, Socrates; ask someone else." He refuses, Socrates says, to be punished. Socrates, then, declares he is the soul doctor and is keeping Callicles away from his desires. What are Callicles' desires? Is Socrates keeping him away from the Athenian demos? Callicles is free to leave. Callicles had admitted that all present-day rhetoricians are flatterers; he thereby admitted that the Athenian demos is worse now than it once was. If Callicles were to continue, he would have to admit that the demos must be chastised. He, Callicles, would have to punish his beloved demos. He would have to admit that he desires to punish the demos. Callicles' pleasure has been eliminated from the argument; Polus' pleasure has crept back in under the cover of Callicles' refusal to be punished. The punishment of pleasure has as its recompense the pleasure in punishment.

Callicles had given two reasons for continuing the discussion with Socrates: to complete the *logos* and gratify Gorgias. He now silently drops the first reason and says he only answered for Gorgias' sake. Socrates wants the *logos* to be finished. He wants it to be an ordered whole, for, he says, it is a common good for all those present if it becomes manifest what is true and what false in what he is saying. This is the first and last time the common good is mentioned in the *Gorgias*. A dialogue about political justice has been silent about the common good of political justice. Truth, as the audience's common good, has replaced the common good at the very moment Callicles has balked at being benefited. Callicles has long since known that he could not enlist Socrates into whatever crazy venture he had in mind, and Callicles has now refused to submit to a restraint on his desires. His refusal is not due to the shamefulness of his desires but to terror. Callicles senses that if he checks the desires of the demos he will be killed. He knows from what Gorgias said that the rhetorician is helpless to defend himself if he is thought to be unjust, and he cannot but be thought to be unjust if he attempts to frustrate the desires of the demos. Callicles has already experienced the subsequent argument with Socrates, in which Callicles reveals that his praise of injustice was a cover for his fear of suffering injustice. Callicles' withdrawal from the argument conceals the vanity in his contempt for the many. He is simply afraid of them. His refusal to run any risk for the public good opens up the way for Socrates to return to a common inquiry into truth that had originally been the bond between Gorgias and himself. Socrates' return, however, is not simply a return. Gorgias had agreed to share the inquiry with Socrates; he had tried to say exactly what he meant and not let Socrates anticipate his meaning. Now, however, Socrates delivers a dialogic monologue and presents himself as both Callicles and himself. He splits himself into two and finds he is a whole. He thus shows on the philosophical level what must happen on the level of corrective punishment. Everything is much too easy to do one any good. In the atmosphere created by Callicles' cowardice, philosophy becomes a common good through self-indulgence.

Socrates' questioning and answering of himself summarize fairly accurately his discussion with Callicles, but he adds one item to his list of things whose proper virtue depends on order, correctness, and art. There is now the virtue of not only body and soul but also animal (506d6); but Socrates never discusses what the virtue of animal could be, since his original scheme had not allowed for an architectonic science over political science and the scientific treatment of body. Socrates thus indicates that his pun on *eu prattein*, from which he concludes that whoever does (*prattei*) beautifully and well fares (*prattei*) well and is happy, expresses the omnipotence of the will which, in different ways, Gorgias, Polus, and Callicles had all accepted. Socrates' own version of such omnipotence is in the very dialogue he is conducting with himself. Nothing stands in the way of his intention. His own intention, which Socrates distinguishes from the meaning his interlocutors might attach to his speeches, is the declaration of his ignorance (508e6–509a7; cf. 506a3–5). Between the spurious corporeality of hedonism and the equally spurious morality of soul, philosophy shines through. Its orderliness is grounded in the ordered disorderliness of knowledge of ignorance. Not everything can be in place if philosophy is to be off base. Philosophy always says the same; Socrates does not.

Socrates' deduction of every excellence of soul from moderation has one unfortunate consequence. It is impossible to become moderate without moderation. Courage is impossible without moderation, but courage is necessary to take the punishment needed to induce moderation. Any form of courage the intemperate man might have would allow him to withstand corrective punishment; and if he can bring himself to accept punishment, he does not need it. Either, then, sheer force is necessary or one has to persuade the disorderly that he is not himself. That Callicles could believe he was Socrates seems impossible; but it does not seem as impossible to persuade Callicles that he is Polus and that the shameless desires he has expressed and will continue to express belong to "Demos." Callicles can turn against himself if his true self is Polus and his spurious self is the many. Callicles, then, can be saved if he can be persuaded that everything he said which no one else said but was thinking was not what he himself was thinking. Callicles is curable if the demos is not cured. The demos must be the scapegoat. In this sense, Socrates' pretending to be

Callicles in order to extract a heartfelt agreement from him is the model for Callicles' rising above himself and denying he is he. Callicles' fear of standing up to the demos can lead to his getting the better of himself. He can be frightened into self-control.

Socrates now calls Callicles' attention to the place he has in the argument. Gorgias' concession that the rhetorician must be just and know the just, which Polus said he had conceded out of shame, and Polus' concession that to do wrong was as bad as and more shameful than to suffer wrong, which Callicles in turn said Polus conceded out of shame, are recalled by Socrates in the general context of his identification of moderation with all of virtue and in the local context of his charging Callicles with the neglect of geometrical equality (507e6–508c3). Socrates thus implies that Gorgias is to Polus as Polus is to Callicles. Polus is the bond between them. Polus can be the bond because he shares with Gorgias a belief in rationality and with Callicles a desire for pleasure. Gorgias, Polus, and Callicles therefore represent the soul structure of the *Republic* in light of which the class structure of the city is devised. The rational, the thumoeidetic, and the appetitive have been split apart into three separate persons and then, by the application of a continuous *logos* or ratio, been put back together. They can be joined because the rationality of Gorgias already contained the willfulness of the thumoeidetic, and the vindictiveness of Polus already shared in the pleasures of Callicles. The soul structure of the *Republic* thus turns out to be identical with the structure of "so-called rhetoric." The soul structure is thereby shown to be intelligible if two things are kept in mind: (1) rhetoric's ignorant imitation of political science; (2) the primacy of the city's class structure. Since the classes of the city are more or less permanently separate from one another, the moderation of the lowest class, which Socrates labels indifferently the chrematistic and the appetitive, shows up for the most part in their deference to the soldiers, on the one hand, and their obedience to law, on the other. The self-control of the class does not involve the self-control of any individual in the class; indeed, it could not be the chrematistic and appetitive class if its members individually did what the class must do. As long as they do not meddle in the rule of the city, they can do whatever they want. Each is free in any case to give up his knowledge of his art as long as he behaves himself. The auxiliaries, in turn, can believe as deeply as they want in the unproblematic association of anger with reason as long as they keep the lower class in line and die for their country.

When, however, one sees the soul structure displayed in its exploded form in the *Gorgias*, one realizes that Gorgias, Polus, and Callicles, if they are severally to keep their distinctness, are not combinable into one. Any unification that can be conceived of will move away from the suspended state of systematic ambiguity upon which the analysis of rhetoric in its spuriousness depends. Their unification would force a move toward either the genuine form of political science or the total chaos of Calliclean freedom. With his tincture of philosophy yoked together with a desire for he knows not what, Callicles would just gobble up Gorgias and Polus. Either of these consequences constitutes an extraordinary proof of the necessity for the procedure adopted in the *Republic*. The political would simply vanish into either philosophy or morality if one were not to start from the issue of justice as the common good. Unless Thrasymachus had tied down the Calliclean thesis of the right of the stronger to the political, through his identification of it with the lawful, and had denied to the tyrant anything but political satisfactions, not only would the best city never have been founded, but education would have remained as marginal as it is in the *Gorgias*. Without Polemarchus' threat of force at the beginning of the *Republic*, the proverb Callicles cites at the beginning of the *Gorgias* would have hidden from sight the centrality of war for the understanding of the city. The vacuum in which the *Gorgias* exists reflects the unreality of its topic. If one tries to fill that vacuum, one does nothing but reconstruct the *Republic*.

Socrates is now in a position to bring Callicles face to face with reality. Callicles agrees that will alone does not suffice to avoid doing or suffering wrong; but though power is needed to avoid being wronged, power and knowledge are needed to avoid doing wrong. Socrates casually reveals why no one in the dialogue ever felt the lack of a definition of justice. Justice turns out to be determined backward from the experience of suffering injustice, and everyone is the best judge of that experience. For Callicles, the experience of injustice is the slap in the face.[3] The slap is not an injury to the body but an attack

3. Cf. D. Daube, *The New Testament and Rabbinic Judaism* (London 1956), 260–61: "The XII Tables declared punishable first *membrum ruptum*, secondly *os fractum*, and thirdly *iniuria*. Whereas the two former involved actual damage to a person . . . , *iniuria* signified harmless blows such as a slap in the face. Why was this word, the native meaning of which is 'an unlawful act' or 'illegality,' used to denote a slap in the face? Were not also *membrum ruptum* and *os fractum* instances of *iniuria* in this wider, untechnical sense? They were, and no doubt the Romans knew it. But it was only in cases like a slap in the face that unlawfulness alone, so to speak, constituted the offence; that the rather abstract notion of 'violation' of another person's rights' was in the foreground, not concealed behind any more concrete facts like a broken limb or a torn-out eye; that the plaintiff could show the judge no glaring damage but appealed for redress on the sole ground that a 'wrong,' *iniuria*, had been done to him. Consequently it was cases like a slap in the face, cases of wrong pure and simple, that

upon the soul (cf. Demosthenes *Against Meidias* 72; cited in full in the *Digest* 48.19.16.5, *de poenis*). The slap says, "Callicles, you are nothing!"[4] If Callicles were the lion he praised, no one would ever slap him, and if anyone ever did, the slap would not get through to Callicles; but Callicles is not the lion; he does not know whether in fact he is good for nothing and the slap is fully deserved. Callicles' secret fear is a powerful argument for almost everyone, but his fear had to remain secret if he were not to convict himself of deserving what he fears he deserves; he therefore expressed his fear as his concern and indignation at the possibility of Socrates being slapped. He seems to have picked the wrong man. He wants to beat Socrates in order to take his head out of the clouds, but he could never slap him. Philosophy was Callicles' sole claim to superiority, and in this sense his indignation on behalf of an imaginary slap at Socrates is genuine: if the real thing can be humiliated, what can he expect? Callicles therefore had tried to make himself too big to be slapped by siding with the uneducated and savage tyrant-demos of Athens. Socrates tells him that his imitation of the demos will not secure for him the protection he needs. He must not ape but emulate the demos. He must take pleasure in what he praises and be pained by what he blames. He cannot get away before the demos with what he does before Socrates: Callicles praises Socrates' speech, but his feelings are not behind it (513c4–6). Socrates' warning to Callicles, that nothing but habituation to the way of the demos can guarantee his immunity, is no doubt due in part to the impossibility of knowing nonexperientially the pleasure and pain behind expressions of praise and blame, as Gorgias and Socrates have each in their own way already proved; but Socrates chiefly has in mind this: the demos never punishes one of its own. Only by becoming one of the many can Callicles be sure that he will never be exposed; but by becoming one of the many he will never rule them. Callicles can avoid losing face by losing face; otherwise he is always at risk.

The respectable version of the fear of humiliation is the fear of death; but if life in Athens were as dangerous as Callicles pretends, Gorgianic rhetoric would not be of much use. Callicles, of course, cannot

---

received the technical appellation of *iniuria,* 'unlawfulness proper.' It was they which made early lawyers aware of the existence of a thing like violation of another person's rights as such, independent of real damage. . . . the kind of attack expressed by a slap in the face became the prototype of that spiritual delict, insult."

4. Aulus Gellius (7.14) remarks that Plato in the *Gorgias* fails to mention as a ground for punishment the assault on someone's dignity and authority, "lest the omission of punishment produce contempt and remove honor," but the Callicles section of the *Gorgias* deals with almost nothing else, as Callicles' parenthetical "to be wronged" (483a8) first indicated.

propose the violent seizure of power as the perfect means for self-preservation, for not only is Polus' bogeyman there to deter him, but Gorgias' advertisement offered voluntary enslavement of everyone else to his pupils. Callicles can never repudiate Gorgias or announce his disloyalty to Athens. Socrates poses the issue of disloyalty under the cover of the issue of injustice. He argues that the power to avoid being wronged involves the power to do wrong, since to assimilate to the regime is to assume its understanding of justice. Unless a regime can be perfectly just, to be a ruler or a friend to the ruling power is to be unjust. If, then, politics is a therapeutic science and not just diagnostic, any attempt by its practitioners to make the souls of the citizens as citizens better amounts to a change in the regime. Someone other than the interlocutors of the *Gorgias* could say that the true politicians were really being just while seeming to be unjust (*Statesman* 296c8–d5); but no such distinction has been drawn in the *Gorgias*, and for the interlocutors anything not in conformity with the prevailing law must be unjust. Socrates, however, saves the false politicians who carry the impress of the regime from the charge of injustice since, if to do wrong is always worse than to be wronged, any attempt at improvement on their part would be unjust; and he saves at the same time the true politicians from the charge of injustice by saying that it is impossible to simulate the tastes of the regime while working for its improvement. To succeed as a politician is to lose the power to be rationally good. Every regime has its own pleasures and pains, and there is no art by which they can be known. The tastes of habits are not available to causal knowledge. Nicias and Demosthenes can enlist the sausage seller into their scheme to overthrow Cleon, but they cannot themselves speak as they know he must speak. Science cannot deduce from the structure of a regime the ways of a people. From the fact that an Indian tribe eats their dead parents, it does not follow that they will shout and refuse to listen if they are offered money to burn them, anymore than it is evident to reason that if the Greeks burn their dead they will listen in silence to an offer to eat them and be witnesses to the horror their own practice evokes in others (Herodotus 3.38).

That one cannot gratify insincerely and still come to power receives a remarkable illustration dialogically in Callicles' claim, on the one hand, that he has continued to answer Socrates only to gratify Gorgias, and his actual refusal, on the other, to gratify him. If Callicles were simply Gorgias' tool, there is no reason why he would ever have to balk. He could keep his insincerity to himself and let everyone in on it at the end. Callicles, however, misconceives the purpose of the argument; Socrates had not set out to convince him but show rhetoric to Gorgias. Callicles' inability to keep himself out of the exhibition of rhetoric shows that the rhetorician believes what he says. Gorgias himself has become the spectator of his own rhetoric; he has through his silence freed himself from being its spokesman. Callicles, then, if he is to gratify Gorgias, would have to move to an equally detached level, but he cannot make such a move without discarding his assimilation to the demos of Athens. Gorgias, as a stranger and a teacher of rhetoric, is freer than any of his pupils who come to him with the tastes of the regime in which they have been bred. Gorgias does not affect those tastes. He simply gives them techniques for expressing those tastes with greater frankness. Callicles is his best pupil.

Pericles, according to Callicles, made the Athenians better. They certainly became stronger collectively and prouder individually. Through becoming a great people each became a big man. This is not nothing, but it is hard to defend. Pericles might have used up inherited capital in a vain show. Socrates himself offers a possible defense of Pericles, but Callicles dismisses it as oligarchic propaganda. Socrates says that Pericles made the Athenians idle fellows, cowards, chatterers, and money grubbers. Athens began to babble under Pericles. One might ask whether idle loquaciousness was not the condition for Socrates. Socrates' myth in the *Protagoras,* in which he claims that cauliflower ears and a laconic mode of speech conceal the flourishing of philosophy in Sparta, is as close to a proof as one could wish that Socrates was not possible in Sparta (*Protagoras* 342a7–c3). Callicles, then, could praise Pericles if he cited Socrates as his evidence, and in a way he already has in speaking up on behalf of both Heracles and Socrates. Callicles, however, cannot make such a defense without acknowledging that the city is the condition for, but not the end of, excellence. Callicles, in short, is too loyal to what Athens has become to hear the praise in the blame of her enemies.

After two years of war and one year of a devastating plague, the Athenians condemned Pericles for theft and almost executed him. It is not remarkable that Callicles believes that Socrates' case against Pericles is rather poor, but it is remarkable that Callicles does not mention either the war or the plague in Pericles' defense (cf. Thucydides 2.59). Immediately after Socrates' last mention of the demos (515d6), Callicles accepts the view that Pericles was a caretaker of human beings (510b8; cf. 520a4). The city, therefore, becomes identical with its citizens, and Socrates can go on to ascribe to the city an appetite for ships, walls, and dockyards which Callicles' four heroes were skilled at supplying (517b3). The city thus becomes an entity that can be put on a diet and have its desires checked. We could say that Glaucon and Socrates are shown doing exactly the same in the second book of the *Republic*, where Socrates at Glaucon's urging lets the healthy city become fevered before he applies a remedy; but there are differences. In the first place, the desire is Glaucon's, who has projected its fulfillment onto a city in which he would want to live; in the second place, the expansion and contraction of the city are only in speech. The second defense, however, is not available to the rhetoricians or their spokesman Callicles. For them, everything is already in speech and nothing can resist their words.[5] Indeed, apart from Callicles' quotation from Pindar's song, which he does not know, and Socrates' prose paraphrase of it, force is not mentioned in the *Gorgias* except when Callicles accuses Socrates of being violent in insisting that the argument be finished, and again when Socrates casually pairs force with persuasion as a mode of treatment (484b7, 488b3, 505d4, 517b6). Only in the latter passage does Socrates hint at what limits the power of rhetoric: Gorgias can persuade the sick patient to take his medicine, but it is impossible to persuade the sick soul to submit to its own cure. Deeds are never opposed to speeches in the *Gorgias* (cf. 461c8); and not despite but because Socrates had cut body and soul apart, body and soul have become interchangeable and duplicate one another (cf. 517d1-2). The obvious failure to ask what is justice concealed the failure to ask what is the city. Rhetoric is utopian and at the heart of the city.

All four of Callicles' heroes suffered judicial punishment of one kind or another. In Athens, at least, the speakers who deliberate in the assembly are subject to the courts. Forensic rhetoric should be the protective arm of deliberative rhetoric, but it turns out to have been weak. Its weakness was due to its need to defend the advocates of imperial expansion—of injustice and immoderation—against the charge of injustice and immoderation. The city demands that its leaders be alienated from itself. Suppose someone is a more successful rhetorician than Callicles' four. He is charged with a crime. He pleads his case by gratifying the jury. He indulges them in the pleasure of compassion (cf. *Apology of Socrates* 38d6-e2). The pleasure of compassion is the pleasure the jury takes in the plaintiff's self-abasement. Their power is the power of life and death, and the plaintiff must hold death the ultimate terror and mere life the absolute good. The power of the jury, however, has to be joined with a right to that power. The rhetorician supplies that right in the form of phantom images of the beautiful and the just. His indulgence is morality. As Socrates reminds

---

5. The only time Thucydides speaks of politicians as rhetoricians is at the beginning of the eighth book, when the Athenians have learned of the complete failure of the Sicilian expedition and were harsh against the rhetoricians who had encouraged them in their zeal and were angry at the oracle-mongers and soothsayers who had spoken with the assurance of divine revelation (8.1.1).

this would-be jury, the members call themselves justices (522c2; cf. *Apology of Socrates* 40a2–3; *Statesman* 299c3–4). It was a name Polus had no trouble supplying (478a5).

Socrates' indictment of imperial Athens is framed entirely in terms of the body and things of the body. "Soul" disappears from the argument until it returns in the myth (517d1, 518a5). Accordingly, Socrates elaborates on the foods and drinks, shoes and clothing the services of the body supply; but he omits the corresponding analysis for the soul and never says what rhetoric supplies to the desires of the soul. Callicles began by fully expressing those desires. The distance from his expression of those desires to Socrates' account of their corporeal ground measures the degree to which rhetoric has apparently cut itself free of the body and recognizes only the existence of soul. The distance within the text has its temporal counterpart in the history of Athens, so that Alcibiades and Callicles seem as if they violate the principles embodied in Cimon and Miltiades when in fact those principles have simply sunk deep within them and reemerged with a different look. Athens looks at Alcibiades and recoils in horror at its own tyranny and impiety. Socrates warns Callicles that if he is indicted he will be measured against the great men of the past and found wanting; he will not be able to plead in extenuation that Themistocles, Cimon, and Pericles are really responsible. Socrates tells Callicles as plainly as he can that if he thinks for a moment that he, Socrates, will get up in court and argue this case for him, then he does not know the difference between public speaking and Socrates' facsimile of public speaking (519d5–e2). Socrates admits that he will not be able to tell the truth in court even in his own defense (522b9).

Of the four political practices, sophistry and rhetoric, on the one hand, and their genuine counterparts, on the other, the arts of legislation and justice, Socrates remarks on the public weakness of three of them. The sophists claim to educate and complain that their pupils rob them; the rhetoricians claim to have power and end up in the dock; and Socrates, who claims to be perhaps the only one who is occupied with the true political art in Athens, cannot give the jurors the sweets they crave. His condemnation is assured because he cannot say that he justly bad mouthed the elders—Cimon, Miltiades, Themistocles, and Pericles—and made the young perplexed. Socrates finally tells us what he meant all along by justice. To be just is to make another perplexed—Socrates had done it to Gorgias (cf. 462b4); to be unjust is to flatter another or to fail to instill in him any doubt. It is therefore better to be punished—to be made perplexed—than to punish another, and to denounce oneself—"I don't know"—than to wait around for another to do it for one. To be wronged, then, is to experience a reinforcement of one's dogmatism; but it is far better to be the patient than the agent of dogmatism: the responsibility is less. The city takes to dogmatism as children to candy, and if one makes any pretense to superiority, so as to have the right to rule, it is as senseless as it is degrading to make the city more complacent than it already is.

Socrates concludes his argument with a *logos* which Callicles will believe a myth. The so-called myth is much shorter than Socrates' reasoning about it (523a1–524a7, 524a8–527a4). Socrates' reasoning is in complete agreement with the argument of the *Gorgias*. The *logos* that precedes it should be the premise of that reasoning; but since the reasoning of the *Gorgias* was Socrates' analysis of Gorgianic rhetoric, the premise of its reasoning is the premise Gorgias, Polus, and Callicles all share. None of the interlocutors was clever enough to tell their own *logos*, for had anyone told it, rhetoric would be as deductive an art as geometry, however doubtful its axioms. Callicles especially needs the *logos* if he is to get what he wants, but Callicles will call it an old wives' tale and never come to realize what it is. He will never know why his *logos* is worthless.

There are two peculiarities in the story Socrates tells. He replaces Zeus' violent overthrow of his father Cronus with a peaceful inheritance, and he connects Zeus' improvement in the administration of justice with the deprivation of man's foreknowledge of his own death. The first alteration presents a change of regime for the better without injustice. No force is needed, as in Hesiod, to bring about greater fairness in the application of the unchanging law that the unjust go to prison for punishment and the just to the isles of the blessed to dwell in complete happiness. Zeus' reform does not bring about perfect justice; the first judges are sometimes perplexed, and even Minos the assessor cannot always resolve their puzzlement. In the time of Cronus, and at the beginning of Zeus' rule, living judges judged those who were still living, and the living with foreknowledge of their death were able to bedazzle the judges with witnesses and testimonials. They practiced with complete success Gorgianic rhetoric. Zeus then proposed that the judges and the judged be dead and naked. The judgment that then becomes possible of the soul itself by the soul itself does not involve the presence or lack of education, which, Socrates had said, determines along with justice one's happiness. The change in regime Zeus effected does not go higher than justice. Zeus knows nothing about philosophy.

Zeus arranged for Prometheus to stop men from foreknowledge of their death. In the time of Cronus, everyone made preparations for his trial in the perfect knowledge that the soul was deathless, Hades was, and the divine law was in effect. Zeus denied men knowledge of this kind. He introduced doubt. The issue of piety—whether the gods are—was unknown before Zeus; Zeus made piety an issue—whether he is. Zeus made certain that there was at best trust but no knowledge. At the same time, then, that he tried to make it nearly impossible to get away with wickedness, he deprived men of knowledge of the law. Under Cronus there is knowledge with cheating; under Zeus there is ignorance with little or no cheating. The gods cease to be known, and the soul is wholly separate from the body. The will, then, becomes all powerful. There is no bodily compulsion that can be recognized as a compulsion to commit any crime. Richard III is without his hump. The will becomes all powerful, but the will is not judged. Even under Zeus the order or disorder of the soul remains unknown. Unless the soul does something with the body, it remains scarless. The will therefore is discounted, and actions are judged solely on the basis of the effect they have on the agent's soul. The slap in the face does not show up on the patient's soul; but the patient's interpretation of the slap is accepted: it appears as a scar on the agent's soul. Injustice, then, must be willed as injustice, for if it is willed as justice it leaves no trace. Unless men were deprived of knowledge about the gods, everyone would pass through to paradise; but in the absence of such knowledge, it is now possible to identify injustice with happiness and to will injustice. Polus is right. There must be a coincidence between moral indignation and justice: one sees happiness and concludes injustice. Moral indignation must not ally itself with desire; it must not know that it takes any pleasure in punishment.

Socrates' first deduction from the story is that death is the separation of body and soul. His deduction is equivalent to the union of Gorgias' separation of body and soul and Callicles' need of Hades to carry on his experiment in unconditional freedom. Socrates then concludes that every unjust action leaves a scar on the soul of the agent. His model is the *mastigias,* a slave whose master believes he deserves many whippings and delivered them. The slave is Polus' Archelaus. The master who beat the *mastigias* believed that either he was curing the slave or the slave was incurable; in the first case, he must have believed that his lashes were wiping out the scars the slave by his acts of injustice had wiped onto his soul; if, however, he thought him incurable, he must have believed he was showing to everyone else the incurable scars he alone had detected on his slave's soul. None of this is even plausible unless Polus and Callicles are once more right—Polus with his belief that the will of the punisher goes directly through the experiences of body to the soul, and Callicles with his belief that one can infallibly infer from one's own experience of injustice the will of its agent. Socrates indicates the difficulty in such assumptions by making *en tēi psukhēi* (524d5) exactly parallel to *en tōi sōmati* (524c6). *En tēi psukhēi* must mean "on the soul," as *entōi sōmati* means" on the body." The soul, then, must have an inside, and the scars of the soul must be on the outside, for if they were inside the soul they would be invisible even if the body were removed. The scars would then have to be symptoms of the internal condition of the soul, which do not allow for certain inferences unless the patient of the injustice were the reader of the signs. Since Socrates says punishment works here and in Hades through pains (525b8), it is no less clear that it is the punisher who sees in the beating his own will than that it is the injured who sees in the scar his own interpretation of the other's will.

In Socrates' account of corrective punishment in Hades (525b1–526c1), there is not one mention of the soul. The soul has vanished into a phantom image of body. When Socrates quoted Zeus' proposal, he had him say that the judge must be naked and dead when he examines the naked and dead, and by means of the soul by itself he must observe the soul by itself of each one when he dies (523e1–4). The dead judge has a soul; he is not his soul. He duplicates in the soul the body. Socrates, moreover, in setting up his comparison between the character of the body after death and the soul's character (524b6), inserts an anticipatory particle (*te*)—"both"—without any matching particle (*kai*)—"and." Body (*sōma*) belongs together with soul (*psukhē*) in a living being (*zōion*); corpse (*nekros*) is the body when separated from soul (524c1–3; cf. *Phaedo* 80c3–4). What, then, is the soul when separated from body? Socrates quotes a line from the *Odyssey*: "With his golden scepter, laying down the law for the dead (*nekussin*)." *Nekus* must here be the same as soul, but *nekus* is in fact the same as *nekros*. Soul is simply the soul as rhetoric and morality have conceived it, a metaphorical extension of body with a life of its own.

The judges' main task is to distinguish among the unjust between the curable and the incurable. Since the incurable are to be punished as paradigms for others, the curable are those who can be frightened by such spectacles, and the fear of injustice is nothing but the fear of punishment. Hades, however, thus becomes a tragic show, and it is possible to take pleasure in the suffering of others. The judges' estimation must be extremely refined if they must decide by simply looking at scars whether pleasure in the show will cancel the intention of the showman. Perhaps the gods are not very good poets, but though they may be as bad as Meles they have a captive audience. Socrates says that only big criminals are judged incurable: as a nonentity the Athenian demos will get away with murder. Socrates mentions Thersites. After Agamemnon's plan to test the resolve of the Greeks failed and Odysseus had to restore order to the army, Thersites got up in the assembly and attacked Agamemnon in the words of Achilles. The revolt against Agamemnon's authority had now spread to the ranks, who interpret the issue of honor as a question of spoils. Odysseus then stood up, delivered a sharp rebuke of Thersites, which he coupled with a threat to strip him naked, and then beat him on the back and shoulders with Agamemnon's scepter; Thersites doubled over, a warm tear fell from his eye, and a bloody welt formed on his back; he sat down in fear, and in pain gazed helplessly as he wiped away his tear; but the rest of the assembly was distressed and laughed with pleasure at him. Homer quotes the speech everyone spoke as he looked to his neighbor: "My oh my! Odysseus has done thousands of noble deeds in initiating good plans and marshaling for war, but now this is the best he ever did: he checked the scurrilous slanderer; surely his proud spirit will not stir him again to upbraid the kings with reproaches" (*Iliad* 2.272–277).

The speech of the army is the only effective form of punitive rhetoric. It consists of concealed self-denunciation, in which one wipes off onto another one's own wickedness. There must be a figuration of wickedness as self-evident as Thersites—the ugliest man who came to Troy—who says what everyone is thinking. He must then undergo real punishment and be denounced in such a way that everyone who sees it will say to himself how much he deserved it. The demos must be split between itself and a higher version of itself, so that it can look with satisfaction at its own beating and still be distressed. The poets have in general concentrated too much on the kings, whose punishment has not been salutary precisely because they are kings, and the gloating in their misfortune has overwhelmed any other experience. Socrates, in any case, speaks at length only about the big criminals from Asia; what Aeacus does with those from Europe has not yet been worked out (524d8, 526c6–7). Under the circumstances, Socrates has done as much as he could with Callicles. Callicles came forward as both Achilles and Thersites. Socrates was able to split them apart and urge Callicles to look down upon the Athenian demos, but he was not able to beat demos in a representative figure. Socrates is not in politics (527d2–5), and Thersites is a fiction.[6]

---

6. In the second *Philippic,* Cicero tried to make Antony into a Thersites through words alone. He recalls the scene where Antony, as a half-naked Lupercal, offered Caesar the crown in order to be his first slave: "Oh, that brilliant speech of yours when you addressed the people naked! What is more shameless than this, what more disgusting, what more deserving of every kind of punishment? Are you waiting for us to jab you with goads? This speech slashes *(lacerat)* you, this speech makes you bleed *(cruentat),* if you have a particle of feeling" (34, 86). Cicero delivered the speech in Antony's absence, but it did succeed in prodding the senate to condemn Antony.

At the end of his address to Callicles, Socrates distinguishes between someone who is really beautiful and good, for whom a slap in the face is not a terrible experience, and Callicles, whose lack of moderation consists in his belief that he is a "somebody," and therefore for whom any assault on that belief takes away his very being and turns him into a nobody (527c6–d2). Much to our surprise, however, Socrates associates himself with Callicles, and he says that it is shameful for them to parade as somebodies when they never hold the same opinions about the same things, "and what is more about the greatest things—to so great a point of lack of education have we come" (527d5–e1). We are led to believe that Socrates is being kind and denounces himself in order to conceal his denunciation of Callicles; but Socrates is denouncing himself. He alludes to the experience he shares with Callicles: neither can resist speaking as their loves dictate them to speak, Callicles to the tune of Demos and Socrates to the tune of Alcibiades. Socrates proposes for Callicles and himself castration (cf. 508e1); then they will be pure enough to turn their attention to politics. He suggests more seriously that they have not yet begun the study of nature.

# V
# *Phaedrus*

The initial puzzle for anyone who reads the *Phaedrus* is the ultimate puzzle. The dialogue is in two parts. The first part contains three erotic speeches; the second is concerned with the art of writing. The speeches on Eros seem to be an unprivileged occasion for the conversation on the art of writing, to which any other topic would have given Socrates equal access. In this sense, the *Phaedrus* recalls the *Gorgias,* where the art of rhetoric seems to be eccentric to the issue of justice. One hesitates, however, to accept what seems to be Socrates' own view of the relation between the two parts of the *Phaedrus* (262c10, 265c8–d1). Socrates argues that a perfect writing must be like an animal, with each part fitted exactly with every other part (cf. *Gorgias* 503e1–504a1); and Plato, we believe, would have wanted the *Phaedrus* to be the dialogue that came closest to illustrating Socrates' thesis. We would not want to believe that Plato went out of his way to show himself incompetent, even as he seemed to undermine Socrates' argument for the inferiority of writing to speaking by writing up his argument. The nonevident unity of the dialogue seems to be connected with the nonevident way in which Plato does not contradict in deed Socrates' speech. It is one thing to say that Socrates' twin theses—the inferiority of writing and the wholeness of the perfect writing—amount to the assertion that to be perfect is to fall short, and quite another to say that Plato confirmed Socrates' argument by botching the *Phaedrus.*

The third of the erotic speeches in the first part of the dialogue culminates in the claim that there is an erotic art or science. The erotic art is the last of the four kinds of divine madness to become an art, and it has done so through Socrates. Socrates, who claims that erotic matters are his sole area of expertise (*Symposium* 177d8), claims that erotic madness is completely rational, or that to be outside oneself is the highest form of *sōphrosunē,* or self-control and self-knowledge. That to be out of one's mind is to be rational is not just strange in itself, but the very structure of the *Phaedrus* shows it to be false, since, however dithyrambic Socrates' speech on the erotic art may be, the discussion on the art of writing is as sober as any other argument in

Plato. We could resolve this difficulty perhaps if we took the speech or speeches a lover makes to his beloved, in which he attempts to induce through speech what he himself experienced through the senses, as the model for the transformation of any set of experiences into knowledge. Socrates' erotic art would thus stand for the possibility of science in general; and inasmuch as the erotic art seems to be the same as philosophy, it would represent the aspiration philosophy must have to transcend itself and become wisdom. Socrates' erotic art, then, would be a misnomer, for it would be putting together what are in fact two distinct phases, to each of which correspond the two parts of the *Phaedrus*. The two parts of the *Phaedrus* would represent the truth in the confused claim of Socrates' erotic art, and Plato would have given to a Socratic paradox a rational form.

If we are reluctant to have the pupil dispose so easily of the master, it is not because patricide is an unforgivable crime (*Sophist* 241d1–3), but because Socrates' erotic art is *Socrates'* erotic art and inseparable from him. Its inseparability is due to the inseparability of Socrates' erotic art from Socrates' self-knowledge. Self-knowledge cannot be as universal as knowledge must be without either ceasing to be self-knowledge or becoming knowledge of a thing as general as the ego purports to be. The universality of knowledge and the individuality of self-knowledge seem not to consist with one another. We can be scientific if we forget ourselves and self-aware if we abandon science. Ammon's warning about writing seems to be a warning against the self-forgetting of science, for what cannot be written cannot be a science, and what can be written cannot but subvert self-knowledge.

In order to keep self-knowledge and knowledge together, it would seem to be necessary to keep together the two parts of the *Phaedrus*. The rhetorical nature of the first part and the dialectical nature of the second reflect the difference between soul and mind. Soul and mind are in turn the twin themes of Socrates' second speech, in which soul is self-moving and the hyperuranian beings inform mind. According to Socrates, there are eleven types of erotic soul and nine types of cognitive mind. Wholeness characterizes soul, partiality characterizes mind, for no one gains a complete vision of the beings and everyone follows in the track of an Olympian god. Socrates' erotic art thus seems to be a special case of the union of soul and mind, the Aristotelian expression for which is rational animal. As rational animal, man displays as evidently a disjunction as mysteriously a conjunction, and we seem to be confronted in the *Phaedrus* with the evidence for the disjunction and the mysteriousness of the conjunction in the demand that a perfect writing be like an animal. The *Phaedrus*, however, might not have a human shape and still be rational. It might look like a monster only because we are too much into ourselves and have not yet stepped out of our own skins. Socrates prays at the end of the *Phaedrus* to Pan.

# VI
# Phaedrus and Socrates

(227a1–230e5)

We know three things about Phaedrus. He is good at making people talk; he is a valetudinarian; and eros, whether a god or an experience of the soul, is of more than ordinary interest to him. Speeches are food and drink to him, and if he were not so concerned about his health he would probably waste away like Socrates' cicadas if only there were Muses who could go on enchanting him forever. Phaedrus is all ears. He is literally *philologos*, a lover of speeches, and not *philotheamōn*, a lover of sights. The initiatory experience of eros is to him unknown, but its transformation into speech holds for him a special fascination. Erotic speech is either a speech about Eros or a speech for the promotion of eros. As a speech about Eros, erotic speech expresses the lover's experience of eros; as a speech for the promotion of eros, erotic speech is designed to persuade the beloved to share in the lover's experience. Phaedrus is concerned with both kinds of erotic speech. He wonders why Eros has never been celebrated in prose or verse (*Symposium* 177a5–c5) and why the lover's avowal, "I'm crazy about you," should carry any weight. Phaedrus wants to know why Eros, who is at the heart of the Greek pantheon, has found no one to praise him, and why the lover who is out of his mind should be preferred to the sane. Although Phaedrus' two questions are assigned to different dialogues, Socrates answers both of them in the *Phaedrus*. He accounts for the silence about Eros among the gods of the poets, and he interprets erotic madness as the experience through which everyone transcends the law. The gods of the poets seem to be a way out of the city and its gods that is open to anyone who has ever experienced eros. Socrates, however, has to explain this to Phaedrus, who has a natural immunity to such an experience. He has only what Phaedrus has picked up in his reading and listening to go on. His task is at least as difficult as Theaetetus', who must explain what an image is to a sophist he has never seen and who pretends to be blind (*Sophist* 239e1–240a2).

Phaedrus does everything by the book. When Socrates meets him he is on his way out of the city in accordance with the precepts of his physician, or so he says, but he also wants to learn by heart a speech of Lysias. He wants to refresh his body while he rehearses a speech. On the basis of the few hints Phaedrus lets drop, Socrates has no trouble in reconstructing exactly the series of events that led up to Phaedrus' plan to take a walk in the country. Socrates' knowledge of Phaedrus, however, which he puts on a par with his own self-awareness, cannot detect the fraud beneath the coyness of Phaedrus. Phaedrus wanted to make himself indispensable to Socrates, so that Socrates could not hear Lysias' speech except through Phaedrus' summary of its thought; but as soon as Socrates notices a scroll in Phaedrus' left hand, Phaedrus becomes wholly superfluous to Socrates. Phaedrus can no longer lead him by the nose wherever he wants, for Socrates can now read in town at his own convenience Lysias' speech.

Phaedrus had wanted to incorporate Lysias' speech completely, so that he could pass it off as his own. Baffled from this course by his meeting with Socrates, he chose to be needed by Socrates in some sense at least; and when Socrates saw through him, he took his stand on the distinction between the thought (*dianoia*) of Lysias' speech, which he had pretty much down pat, and its words (*rhēmata*), which he denied he has memorized. Since Phaedrus identifies the thought with the differences between the lover and the nonlover, he implies that the conviction that one ought to gratify the nonlover rather than the lover inheres in the words. Phaedrus begins by making a distinction between dialectic and rhetoric that we then see displayed on the largest possible scale in the two parts of the dialogue.

Thought, Phaedrus implies, is good for noting differences; it is no good for guiding preferences. What we have tentatively identified as soul—the first part of the dialogue—Phaedrus calls words and phrases (*rhēmata*). Words and phrases are all that can be, strictly speaking, in a book. Had Phaedrus succeeded in incorporating Lysias' book, he would have expressed a preference as a type of soul. The nonlover is by definition the beloved. Phaedrus finds in Lysias' speech the speech of the beloved in search of a lover. Socrates would have been that lover as he followed him anywhere in his desire to hear Lysias' speech. Phaedrus would thus have succeeded in dispensing with the need for the lover to transform sight into speech, for the beloved would already be a speech, in which soul and mind would be perfectly together, and the lover in being enchanted by the words would assimilate the thought. If Phaedrus had had his way, love would be as easy as picking up a book and reading it.

Socrates figured out much of what had happened between Lysias and Phaedrus; but once he caught sight of the book and guessed that Phaedrus could be discarded—he did not have to settle for the thought of Lysias with "the speech itself" at hand—all his knowledge of Phaedrus became worthless. At the very moment Phaedrus can no longer stand between Lysias and Socrates, Socrates finds that his own special skill, which he showed even when he met Parmenides and Zeno while he was very young, is at a discount. Socrates' knowledge of Phaedrus, however, is on a par with his self-awareness. Is that too at a discount? That Phaedrus is a tease and that he himself is susceptible are equally worthless pieces of intelligence unless the sharing of an enthusiasm has some advantage over one's direct access to it. Initially, Socrates could not approach Lysias except through Phaedrus, and Lysias could be glimpsed only at Phaedrus' discretion (fig. 14). Once Lysias is fully revealed in the book, Phaedrus becomes a convenience for Socrates (fig. 15). There remains the possibility, however, that Phaedrus and Socrates as fellow Corybants can experience something together that neither would apart from the other (fig.16). This shared experience would have to displace Lysias and present to them a virtual image of Lysias if it were going to be significantly different from a solitary reading (fig. 17). Only in this case could Socrates' knowledge of Phaedrus and himself be indispensable, for in its absence, though they would still experience together the virtual image of Lysias, Socrates would not know it.

Socrates had given a reading, as we might say, of his encounter with Phaedrus. He went so far in distancing the reading from the encounter that he described one Phaedrus to another Phaedrus as if the first Phaedrus were not present but had become so coy that he had vanished into the "third person." All known languages have first- and

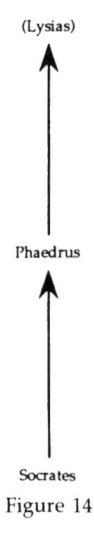

(Lysias)
↑
|
|
Phaedrus
↑
|
|
Socrates

Figure 14

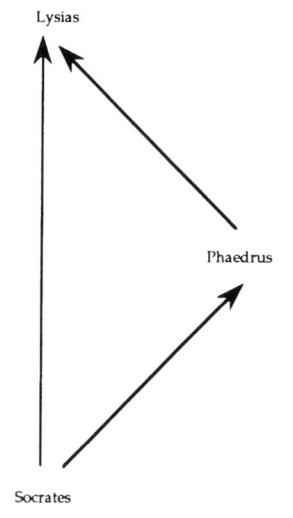

Figure 15

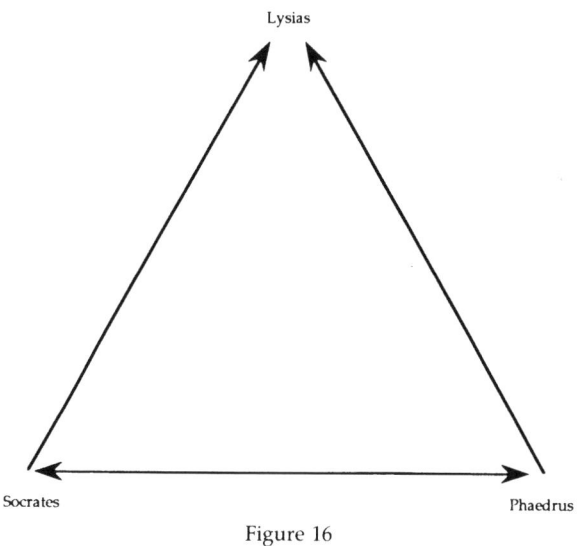

Figure 16

second-person pronouns, "I" and "you," but many, like Greek, have no third-person pronoun, for who neither speaks nor is spoken to does not belong to a conversation.[1] Phaedrus the tease is a present

[1]. E. Benveniste, "La nature des pronoms," chap. 20 of *Problèmes de linguistique generale* (Paris 1966), 251–57.

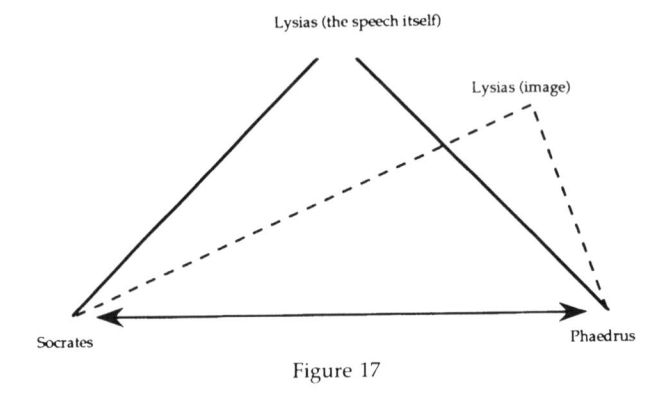

110   Phaedrus and Socrates

```
                    Lysias (the speech itself)
                              ·
                             /|\
                            / | \
                           /  |  \ Lysias (image)
                          /   |  /·
                         /    | / \
                        /     |/   \
                       /      /     \
                      /      /|      \
                     /     /  |       \
                    /    /    |        \
                   /   /      |         \
                  / /         |          \
                 ·<───────────────────────>·
              Socrates                  Phaedrus
                         Figure 17
```

absence; but Lysias, who is his book, is an absent presence. He is there in the book as "I" just as the addressee is there as "you." Phaedrus as the speaker of the book is that "I" as nonlover, and Socrates is automatically its "you." Socrates would listen to a speech that asks him, the nonbeloved, not to gratify the lover and to gratify the nonlover. Phaedrus and Socrates are two nonlovers, one of whom asks the other to gratify him; both of them are lovers of speeches, one of whom, in conformity with Lysias' speech, had refused to gratify the other. As long as Phaedrus does not read the speech to Socrates he is obeying the speech; but as soon as he reads the speech, he urges Socrates not to gratify him as a lover of speeches and to gratify him as a nonlover. One could say that Socrates and Phaedrus are nonlovers because they are lovers of speeches, and that Socrates' extension of "lover" to include himself and Phaedrus complicated Lysias' very simple speech unnecessarily. Lysias' speech may indeed be simple, but the setting of the speech is not. Lysias' speech was, according to Phaedrus, only in a sense an erotic speech. "I do not know in what manner," he had said, "it is an erotic speech"; it is, then, in some sense not an erotic speech, for its speaker neither describes his experience of eros nor promotes the experience of eros in another. Who in fact is the speaker of Lysias' speech is unclear. Phaedrus does not say that Lysias wrote a speech for a nonlover who was attempting to seduce (*peirōmenon*) one of the beauties; instead, he says, "Lysias has written of one of the beauties being seduced (*peirōmenon*), not by a lover, but it is here that he has been ingenious, for he says that a nonlover rather than a lover must be gratified" (227c5–8). Phaedrus certainly does not make it clear who Lysias imagined the speaker of his speech to be. The one addressed cannot be a beloved without the speaker automatically becoming a lover, and the speaker cannot choose which beauty he is to address without asserting by his choice that he is indeed a lover.

Lysias, then, wrote a speech that cannot be spoken, for as soon as it is spoken, relations are established that deny the premise of the speech. Lysias' speech is essentially a written speech addressed to an anonymous reader who is urged to gratify its writer by reading whatever book it prefaces. The speech warns the reader against Socrates, who usurped for himself and philosophy the ordinary word for carrying on a conversation (*dialegesthai*), in which "I" and "you" could be uttered as we ordinarily utter them. Socrates always began from where we are, but now he comes across a writing that first sets aside Phaedrus and then threatens to set himself aside as well. Socrates is put in a writing in which there is a writing that threatens to oust him and philosophy. The *Phaedrus* narrates Socrates' successful thwarting of that threat and hence his failure to do so. He crushes Lysias and is swallowed whole by Plato.

How Socrates discovers that he too may be as dispensable as he found Phaedrus to be takes up just as many exchanges as were needed to expose Phaedrus and then get rid of him. Socrates made use of his self-knowledge on the way to his casting Phaedrus aside. The issue now becomes the status of Socrates' self-knowledge. It arises as the issue through a casual remark of Phaedrus. Phaedrus asks Socrates whether Boreas is said to have seized Oreithyia from somewhere near where they are walking; Socrates says, "So it is said"; but when Phaedrus infers from the charm, purity, and clarity of the waters that the place of the rape was exactly where they are, since it is so suitable for girls to play beside the Ilissus there, Socrates says no. Phaedrus indulges in a mild form of rationalization, and Socrates says the place is two or three stades downstream, for which his evidence seems to be that an altar to Boreas is there. Myths are not those kinds of transpositions of reality, Socrates implies, from which reality can be readily recovered. Myths are not encoded messages the key to which is there before us and at our feet. Socrates places the story in a sacrificial setting that has the backing of what has been publicly decreed. The Athenians established an altar to Boreas on the Ilissus after they had summoned Boreas to help them at the time of Xerxes' invasion of Greece (an oracle had told them to appeal to their son-in-law), and a storm sprang up suddenly off the coast of Magnesia and sank no less than four hundred Persian ships (Herodotus 7.188–192). Socrates implies, then, that the Athenians' choice of the altar's site was based on the official version of the place of Oreithyia's rape. A historical event of the greatest importance, in which a storybook figure gained a political sanction, determines what one is to say about it. There is no reasoning possible about the law. The law has its reasons.

Socrates' denial that they are on the spot of the rape, despite the fact that hearsay and plausibility are in its favor, so astonishes Phaedrus that he asks Socrates whether he is persuaded the story (*muthologēma*) is true. Phaedrus, who has heard that rhetorical persuasion operates on the basis of opinion and not of truth, asks Socrates whether his statement, unqualified as it is by "they say" or "it is said," entails anything about his own convictions. Socrates, however, has not been persuaded (*peithetai*) that the story is true; rather, he obeys (*peithetai*) what is lawfully established ( *to nomizomenon*) about Boreas and every other monster. Socrates implies that obedience to the law and persuasion of the truth of the law are quite separate. He distinguishes implicitly here what he blurs in Plato's *Apology*—*nomizein* and *nomizein einai* (26b3–c8)—of which the former alone is a concern of law, for the law cannot devise a test of belief that goes beyond the practices the law enjoins. The law is necessarily carnal. Its competence cannot include knowledge of soul. Socrates' knowledge of soul, then, is outside the law; but it is not criminal in itself and can become so only if Socrates is forbidden to converse and advance his knowledge. Socrates' identification of conversation with philosophy is the ultimate defense of philosophy against every form of tyranny (Xenophon *Memorabilia* 1.2.33–37).

Socrates offers Phaedrus a way in which one could believe in the story of Boreas and Oreithyia. It would not be a belief in the story as such but in an interpretation of the story that seems to preserve all its essential elements. In the interpretation, Boreas is the North Wind that pushed Oreithyia down nearby rocks while she was playing with Pharmakeia. The rape of Oreithyia glossed her violent death. A tale of desire concealed the truth of randomness. The myth itself was also accidental; it was not a deliberate invention. *Pneuma Boreou* ("blast of Boreas") was shortened to Boreas, and "seized" (*harpasai*) was interpreted as "raped" and not as an imprecise substitute for "pushed" (*ōsai*). Boreas became a conscious being unconsciously. Socrates says he has not fulfilled the Delphic writing to know himself; his lack of knowledge pertains to his ignorance about the simple or complex nature of his soul; but "soul" (*psukhē*) originally meant breath, and its cognate verb to breathe and blow (*psukhō*).[2] The object of Socrates' sole concern, the interpretation of the myth suggests, is no more a being than Boreas is a god. Socrates' attempt to understand

---

2. Cf. *Cratylus* 399d10–e3. The connection between soul and breath was known to Homer; he has Odysseus say that his foolish companion Elpenor went up on the roof of Circe's house to sleep off a drunken stupor, "seeking coolness (*psukhos*)," and when he heard them summon him to the ships, he forgot he was on the roof and broke his neck, "and his soul (*psukhē*) went down to Hades" (*Odyssey* 10.552–560).

soul without tracing it back to the physiology of breathing is as foolish as Socrates says it would be to rationalize away every monster. Socrates argues that he cannot tell whether monsters are possible or not until he knows whether he is a monster; the rationalists argue that they already know the soul is simple, for it is as simple as breathing. Socrates' obedience to the established law about monsters looks as if it prevents him from discovering the truth about soul. He has already been persuaded that what has come to be established about it is true.

A certain kind of rationalism stands in the way of the Socratic enterprise. It questions in particular whether the violence of Boreas is all that different from the possible gentleness of Socrates' soul, and in general whether erotic speech is possible and can overcome the radical difference between lover and beloved. The tale implies that any union between lover and beloved must be violent, for they cannot but be a monster together; and the rationalization implies that there cannot be any exceptions to the uniformity of nature, for every natural kind breeds true. Despite the difference in form of the two accounts, both myth and reason are united against Socrates, who will claim that the soul is essentially a monster but not necessarily a monster that force alone holds together. Socrates, however, is not in principle opposed to some rationalized account of mythical monsters; he simply does not have the time himself to examine anything else but himself. Socrates seems to be thinking of Plato, who did not obey the Delphic writing but devoted himself instead to an explication of a great variety of human souls, among which Socrates' was just one, however preeminent. Plato had the misfortune to turn away from himself to the Gorgiases and Alcibiadeses, Menoses and Callicleses, who could not but be a small number of the infinite variety of human types. Socrates is concerned whether he is a more complex beast than Typhon; but Typhon, who was Earth's last offspring to challenge the Olympian gods, and who after his defeat became the source of all the winds apart from Notos, Boreas, and Zephyros, seems to be the mimetic principle itself, since, according to Hesiod, Typhon could reproduce the sound of every being, whether it be of a god or of a beast (*Theogony* 820–80). The rationalization of monsters is the rationalization of poetry, and Plato has a better claim than any to have rationalized poetry. If the erotic and poetic arts are both rational forms of divine madness, what is the relation between Socrates' self-knowledge and Plato's teratology? Can Silenus survive his representation by Typhon?

Socrates has not yet determined whether he is a beast more complex than Typhon and burning with a smokier flame or a gentler and simpler animal, which naturally partakes in some divine lot without arrogance. Although the "Know thyself" of Delphi evidently warned whoever entered Apollo's shrine that he must realize he was not a god but a man, Socrates made Typhon the sole alternative to god. Man is not between beast and god. The human as such, Socrates implies, does not exist. Socrates' acquiescence in conventions, so that he hesitates to acknowledge that Typhon is nothing but smoke (*tuphos*), prepares the way for a radical departure from convention, in which man himself is put in doubt. Socrates declares this as plainly as possible just before he tells Phaedrus that he does not leave the city because only human beings in town and not places and trees are willing to teach him. There are only human beings available for Socrates to find out whether he is closer to a beast or a god. What he is, is supposed to come to light through what he is not. This Socratic riddle estranges Socrates as much from the country as from the city. He must stay in town in order to discover what he knows in his makeup is from out of town. Now, however, he is willing to leave town provided Phaedrus is willing to read him books. Socrates had first read Phaedrus as easily as he had known himself, only to find out he did not need to know anything about either Phaedrus or himself; Socrates had then declared his lack of interest in the use of reason to demolish mythology in light of his ignorance of himself, only to find out he does not need human beings in the city if there are books. Lysias in a book disposed of Socrates' need for Phaedrus; books in general look as if they dispose of the Socratic riddle. Lysias' rationalization of eros points to the possibility of rationalizing Socrates. His strangeness is of no higher order than the truth about Boreas, soul, and Typhon—wind, breath, and smoke.

Phaedrus comes to realize Socrates' strangeness through Socrates' literary description of the spot where Phaedrus is going to read Lysias' book. The description was literary because it seemed to be addressed to Phaedrus as if he were not experiencing on the spot what Socrates was experiencing. The description is as alien from the immediate as Socrates' interpretation of Phaedrus was, in which Phaedrus became another beside himself. The present absence of the country is due, however, not to Socrates' knowledge of the country but to his ignorance of it. He finds most of the elements that make up the landscape very beautiful and attractive, but they are all dumb and hold no interest for him. Phaedrus was of interest because he had a speech to tell, but the country has nothing to say. However flattering our description of it may be, it cannot be persuaded to join us in an inquiry of its nature. It is in its essence the third person. It is always estranged from itself in our account.

Of the seven items that make up Socrates' description, all but one receive some epithet of praise. The plane, the chaste tree, the spring, the place, the cicadas, and the grass are each given their due; but at the center of Socrates' list, and which can readily be imagined to hold the place together, is a precinct sacred to some Nymphs and Achelous, as Socrates conjectures from the dolls and statues; and of all that Socrates says nothing complimentary. In his ignorance of what he is, he cannot say whether images of human shape are beautiful or not. The gods are as unknown as the monsters. Socrates turns away from everything alien to himself and faces himself as an unknown that holds the clue to many if not all other kinds of beings. The one science needful is a psychology that has Socrates as its one test case, in light of which its own adequacy can be judged. The so-called problem of Socrates began with Socrates.

# VII
# Lysias

(230e6–237a6)

Lysias wrote a speech without any vocatives. The speech is spoken by anyone to anyone. The speech recommends the nonlover to the nonlover, but it does not recommend the speaker and cannot recommend the writer Lysias. Lysias becomes too notorious through the publication of the speech to pass for the nonlover if he is in the train of the nonbeloved (232a8–b2), and the speaker of the speech admits that as one of the infinitely many nonlovers he may not be the best at delivering what he promises (231d6–e2). The speech thus recommends the nonlover to look around for the best friend, who will do the most for him at the price of his sexual favors. The speech cannot prove, however, that one's best friend might not be as good as or better than the speaker at benefiting without demanding any favor in return (233d2–4). Indeed, the speech grants that strong friendships occur within the family without sex, and thus implies that only in the case of incest would the nonlover never be suspected to be a lover. The speech makes sense if the nonbeloved has nothing to offer except his favors (231c1), and it is urging him to make the best deal possible with what he has. The nonlover offers to be his pimp and market him better than he can himself. If the speaker happens to be successful in persuading the nonbeloved to favor him rather than any other nonlover, the nonbeloved will become a lover as he tries to win for himself all that the nonlover promises. The nonbeloved, however, will have entered into an unenforceable contract, since the speaker grants that the nonlover is solely concerned with his own interest and is never grateful.

Lysias' speech is so general that all its arguments are couched in terms of probability. All exlovers may regret their benefactions, but it is only inappropriate and not inevitable for the nonlover to have no regrets; Lysias cannot say the nonlover does not regret the moment after he conferred a benefit. The speech assumes a prior friendship between two nonlovers, from which the speaker withheld all marks of friendship until, as we would say, they became lovers. Since the speaker admits that he is in need, but he cannot state his need without making it sound like a lover's desire (cf.233d5), the speaker, if he is not to confess finally that he is merely the better sort of lover, differs from the lover in only one point: he never says, "I love you." Lysias' argument, then, is that such a declaration, even if one disregards its possible insincerity at the moment and its probable falsehood in the future, should not affect the beloved in any way. The beloved is a patient only in the imagination of the lover, but the person addressed has not altered in himself. The words "I love you" are meant to suggest to the beloved the following: "I have found you to be something special, and before I declared that you were my love, you were nothing; you therefore owe me your favors for my singling you out, for without me, that is, without my constantly reaffirming your superiority through 'I love you', you will fall back into the nullity of everyone else who is unloved." The humiliation the lover experiences in his extreme neediness and sudden awareness that he is radically defective is concealed by a triumphant assertion that the beloved is in his debt for recognizing him to be a somebody. The lover therefore is not a lover but a plaintiff in a suit in which his own shame parades as a right, for the beloved must be made to feel obliged to make up for the lover's loss of self-esteem. Lysias, then, has written a forensic speech against eros; it is an indictment of eros in light of justice. Lysias' speech confirms as well the story of Boreas and Oreithyia, for, once it is granted that the lover's speech is a fraudulent appeal to justice, the lover, if he is to remain a lover and not plead a case he should never win, must resort to violence. The lover must be openly unjust.

Lysias' case against eros is only as strong as a listener finds it to be, and as one charge or another strikes a chord in his own experiences. Socrates, as soon as he had heard from Phaedrus the thesis of the writing, expressed his own wish that Lysias had been more popular and spoken up for the poor rather than the rich and the old rather than the young (227c9–d2); but Lysias had anticipated this objection and had argued that the importunities of lovers ought no more to be gratified than anyone else in the greatest need. Socrates, we know, is in the greatest perplexity about himself and the greatest need of other human beings. His ignorance about himself and his need of others characterize together eros in general. Every other lover is in need of some other, and every other lover is not in his right mind before his beloved; but Socrates does not know himself before himself and needs neither this nor that human being, but human beings as such who live in town. Socrates' distraction is as radical as his attraction to others is general. Insofar as Lysias' speech does not appeal to probabilities but sticks to commonly accepted definitions—the lover is needy and not in his right mind—Socrates alone fits the indictment of eros perfectly. The presence of Socrates, before whom the speech is read, turns a loosely strung series of complaints into something with all the earmarks of "logographic necessity."

118    Lysias

Lysias' speech is meant to arm the would-be beloved against enchantment; Phaedrus is enchanted by a disenchanting and charmless speech, and Socrates is rightly astonished at how Phaedrus gloried in the denunciation of eros. Phaedrus is inspired by an uninspiring speech. A speech with no god within (*entheos*) puts a god within Phaedrus. The god is Justice. He defends Lysias and his speech against Socrates' mild critique and speaks as any lover does when anyone finds fault with his beloved. That he singles out the words (*onomata*) for special praise betrays his conviction, in accordance with his original distinction between thought and phrases (*rhēmata*), that the nonlover is to be preferred to the lover. This conviction means at first no more than that the beloved is always the lover's superior (*Symposium* 180a7–b4), and Lysias is better than any Greek rhetorician and his speech so comprehensive that nothing more can be said. Phaedrus, in other words, refuses to acknowledge that anything in the speech attracts him because Lysias is just his type, and Socrates might not see what he (Phaedrus) sees in him (Lysias). The fact that Lysias said the same thing in different ways only goes to show, according to Phaedrus, that Lysias is universal in his appeal, without any blemishes for which a lover would have to invent a more or less plausible excuse (*Republic* 474d3–475a2). Lysias' plainness of style proves he has nothing to hide. Phaedrus, then, believes that in this special case, rhetoric and dialectic coincide, and the heart has no reasons that reason knows not of. Lysias the nonlover has persuaded Phaedrus the lover to emulate the nonlover. He thus appears as rational as any other nonlover. Socrates, in confessing to the Bacchic frenzy he comes to share with Phaedrus, speaks of Phaedrus as a divine head (234d6).

Socrates himself finds Lysias' speech deficient both dialectically and rhetorically; its language was not as concise and finely turned as it ought to have been, and Lysias did not cover all the ground that the thesis presented to him. Socrates claims to know this not on his own but from a source outside himself, and as he later makes clear the source is Phaedrus (242e1, 244a1). Phaedrus inspires him as any beloved inspires any lover to make a speech which fits the beloved and no one else. The premise will be the same as Lysias'—the speaker will not declare himself to be a lover—but unlike Lysias' speech it will not be directed "To whomever it is of no concern." Socrates will prove in a speech, which supplements Lysias', that Phaedrus is deluded in his belief that nothing of himself colors his choices. Phaedrus is not transparent to reason. This is not surprising; what is surprising is that Phaedrus does not recognize in the love poets Sappho and Anacreon the same intention as Lysias'. Phaedrus does not realize that anyone who ever praised his beloved was praising the nonlover. Stripped of its spurious usurpation of "I" and "you," as if they designated different people, Lysias' speech has the beloved advising himself to look out for his own interests. The core of Lysias' speech is self-interest, but it is equally important that a speech about self-interest is made to look as if it were about the justice of the nonlover and the injustice of the lover. Phaedrus fell for a speech that made his selfishness look moral. His failure to know himself is due to his failure to know his own good without any trappings.

The banter between Socrates and Phaedrus, which precedes Socrates' recitation of Phaedrus' speech, repeats and does not repeat that which preceded Phaedrus' reading of Lysias' speech. In both cases there are two phases. Originally, Socrates' knowledge of Phaedrus forced Phaedrus to concede that he could give the thought but not the words of Lysias' speech; and after Socrates detected the presence of Lysias, Phaedrus proved to be altogether dispensable. In Phaedrus' reading of the parallel to that situation, Phaedrus does not display any knowledge of either Socrates or himself. He cannot reconstruct the process whereby Socrates came to fashion his speech out of his knowledge of Phaedrus. Indeed, Socrates' speech is designed to give Phaedrus the self-knowledge he now vicariously claims. The speech, moreover, requires the presence of Phaedrus and thus restores Phaedrus to the dialogue from which he had been eliminated in principle (244a4). In the second phase of the dialogue's opening, Socrates had declared his own self-ignorance and his need of human beings in town; but later, in admitting that Phaedrus had discovered a cure for his refusal to leave the city, Socrates granted the possibility that he too was dispensable. Now, however, when Socrates balks at speaking extemporaneously, Phaedrus threatens first to use his greater strength and then to withhold from Socrates any report of anyone else's speech. We are somehow back with the issue of violence and monsters. Socrates is first an unlikely Oreithyia who will be forced to speak, and then he is an exile in the country where the plane tree Phaedrus swears by ensures that he will never tell Socrates another speech. Socrates and Phaedrus need each other. Phaedrus assumes that writing is not an alternative to speaking; but Phaedrus cannot strictly be indispensable to Socrates unless he is his Muse, who stands in between Socrates and whatever he wants to understand. Socrates wants to know himself. Socrates' speech, then, in which he offers Phaedrus self-knowledge, would be on the way to his own self-knowledge. We do not yet know what this would mean. Is Phaedrus a version of Socrates, who was allegedly involved in the mutilation of the Hermae and the profanation of the Mysteries, and who now casually makes a plane tree into a god?[1]

---

1. J. K. Davies, *Athenian Propertied Families 600–300 B.C.* (Oxford 1971), 201.

# VIII
# Socrates 1

(237a7–242a2)

Socrates' speech is a deliberative speech cast in the form of a deduction. Its argument is wholly concerned with the good, and it is arranged, after a definition of eros, into five sections: the goods of the soul (238e2–239c2), the goods of the body (239c3–d7), external goods (239d8–240a8), the unpleasantness as opposed to the harmfulness of the lover (240a8–e7), and finally the lover as ex-lover with a summary (240e8–241d1). Socrates' speech is spoken by a lover who had previously convinced his beloved that he does not love him. Socrates thus makes the hypothesis of Lysias' speech able to be spoken and not only written, for there is now a beloved to whom a lover is speaking. The speech, however, is necessarily incomplete, for should the concealed lover once begin to argue for the gratification of the nonlover, he would be arguing against his own gratification. If the beloved is persuaded, on the basis of half the argument, to gratify the one he believes to be the nonlover, he is still gratifying the lover, with all the dire consequences the false nonlover warns against. The issue of how persuasion is related to opinion and truth, which Phaedrus raises in the second half of the dialogue (259e4–260a4), is already present in the setting Socrates has given to his speech; but Socrates might also be suggesting that the lover is always the nonlover when the beloved gratifies him, for the lover by definition does not know himself and therefore might not know what he wants. Sexual pleasure may be nature's way of making sure he never finds out. Lysias, then, would be strangely right that only the true nonlover can properly plead for the nonbeloved to gratify him. The successful lover always has the nonlover by his side.

The deductive mode Socrates chooses for his first speech is good for teaching (265d3–5). It is designed not for discovery but for consistency, so that the conclusion is in agreement with the beginning, and no contradiction in the course of the argument brings one up short and forces a reconsideration of the starting point. Socrates' speech is apparently so much a model of this kind that Socrates' *daimonion* has to intrude and rescue Socrates and Phaedrus from error. Socrates does not take the intervention of the *daimonion* as a reminder that the speaker is a lover who at best, under the inspiration of the Muses, was telling lies like the truth; rather, Socrates interprets the *daimonion* as warning him that Eros is also agreed to be a god. Eros is agreed to be both a predicate and a subject. On the assumption that eros is a predicate—eros is a certain kind of desire—Socrates makes his first speech; and on the assumption that Eros is a subject and a god, Socrates makes his second speech. If we are to believe Socrates' account of Diotima's instruction, in which she proved to him that Eros could not possibly be a god, Socrates' palinode is prompted by a false assumption, and Socrates as the spokesman for Phaedrus begins with the truth. Socrates will later startle us by asserting that his two speeches are in fact one (265e3–4). We are told to make a whole out of two parts that refuse to go together. We seem to be encouraged to use violence to get the lover and the nonlover together, and are thus made to experience the truth in the story of Boreas and Oreithyia. Socrates makes up a monster and tries to pass it off as if it were in conformity with logographic necessity. He seems to include within the *Phaedrus* the riddle of the *Phaedrus*. Plato is merely trying to keep up with him.

Socrates starts off his speech in a very puzzling manner. The many, he says, are unaware that they do not know the being of each thing, but as if they know they do not come to an agreement at the beginning of their deliberation and consequently end with either self-contradiction or mutual disagreement. Socrates admits, however, that it is evident to everyone that eros is a kind of desire; but he denies that eros is a desire for the beautiful things—the dictionary definition (249e3–4)—since, he says, "we know nonlovers too desire the beautiful things" (237d4–5). Socrates thus sets aside the difficulty Lysias did not face—how the nonlover selected someone to address. The nonlover can now desire the beautiful nonbeloved without eros. Socrates then proceeds to work forward to a new definition of eros by surreptitiously working backward from what Phaedrus had conceded, that the lover is without sense (*aphrōn*). To be without sense is to lack *sōphrosunē*, and to lack *sōphrosunē* is to be filled with either madness (*mania*) or insolence (*hubris*). Socrates takes advantage of the fact that *sōphrosunē* can be either sanity or moderation, and consequently it has two contraries. Socrates thus builds into his first speech the grounds for his second, in which he will praise eros as the highest form of madness. Superficially, then, Socrates' two speeches can be combined by uniting the contrary of *sōphrosunē* (madness) with *sōphrosunē* (moderation). The contradiction then disappears and the riddle remains.

Socrates says we have to conceive of a pair of principles or *idea* (the dual) in us, one of which is an inborn desire for pleasure, and the other is acquired opinion (*doxa*) which aims at the best. Nature, we can say, shows up in us as desire for pleasure, and convention or law as some inculcated opinion about the good. There are four possible relations between these two principles: (1) if desire and opinion are in agreement, we believe that pleasure is the good; (2) if desire and opinion are in disagreement, we believe that pleasure is not the good; (3) if opinion gains the upper hand over desire, the name for this mastery is moderation (*sōphrosunē*); and (4) if desire ever rules over opinion, the name for this rule is *hubris*. Desire for pleasure does not have any built-in standard for satiation, since there is no body to which any desire is attached. Gluttony is an excessive desire for pleasure from eating, but it is not said to be excessive in light of a natural desire to satisfy hunger, any more than alcoholism can be understood as excessive thirst, for the desire for pleasure from drinking wine can hardly be said to be a natural craving. The standards over against which gluttony and alcoholism are excessive are determined solely by opinion. There is no natural health.

Socrates wishes to reattach eros to a well-established set of names for excessive desires; but just as he cannot say that gluttony is to hunger as alcoholism is to thirst, so he cannot say what name is given to the desire for pleasure from corporeal beauty when it is not excessive. This desire, he admits, belongs to the nonlover, who by definition is moderate. We would have expected Socrates to distinguish between love and sex or in Greek between *erōs* and *aphrodisia* (cf. 254a7). *Aphrodisia* would then have corresponded to our "lust," but there is no nonhubristic version of it to which a name can be attached. If eros strictly matched gluttony, it would have to be defined in terms of intercourse (*sunousia*), and the pleasure desired be that which comes from friction (*Philebus* 47a3–b9); but had Socrates done so, he could not have introduced the beauty of bodies as the source from which the pleasure of eros comes. By omitting any physiology of eros, Socrates allows the pleasure from corporeal beauty to be either contemplative or sexual; but in either case he denies there is a natural desire for beauty or the beautiful things, since desire is directed only at pleasure. The beautiful, then, must be determined by opinion in its aiming at the best. The beautiful or some part of it is part of the good. Eros, then, desires the pleasure from the beautiful insofar as the beautiful is not good. Socrates' prologue thus takes the form of the argument with Polus in the *Gorgias*, where the beautiful was characterized as either affording pleasure or benefit. Desire and opinion are here the general principles of that argument, and eros is a special case of its exemplification. In the *Gorgias*, however, the beautiful, in which was contained the good or the pleasant, was originally the higher form of the good and health its lower. In the *Gorgias*, the transformation from Socrates' view to Polus' view had been as illustrated in figure 18. In the *Phaedrus*, Socrates gives us a version of Polus' view without its original (fig. 19). We can expect, then, that Socrates in his second speech is going to cancel the right-hand side of the beautiful as hubris and replace it with a madness whose ultimate source will be higher than opinion and which at least in speech will allow it to be recoupled with moderation. In this recoupling, however, it is not clear whether the good would be restored, as in the *Gorgias*, as the comprehensive principle of health and beauty. The good is not among the hyperuranian beings.

The etymological connection Socrates makes so forcibly between eros and strength (*rhōmē*) is certainly in accord with the Boreas story, which likewise presented silent violence as the truth about love; and Socrates' definition itself, since it does not say that corporeal beauty must belong to human beings, also allows for monstrous unions. Socrates' nympholepsy, however, which grants him a more than usual fluency, seems not to square with either the rational deliberation the nonlover calls for or the sober definitions themselves. The inspired Socrates recites a dithyrambic proem to rationality and chastity. Only in the relation between the law and its possible divine source is there a comparable disparity. The manner in which the gods communicate

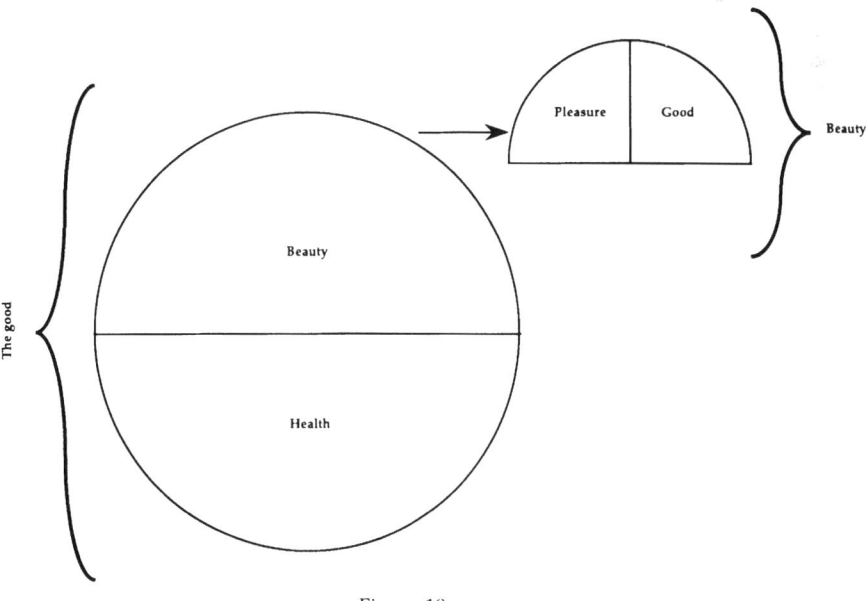

Figure 18

124   Socrates 1

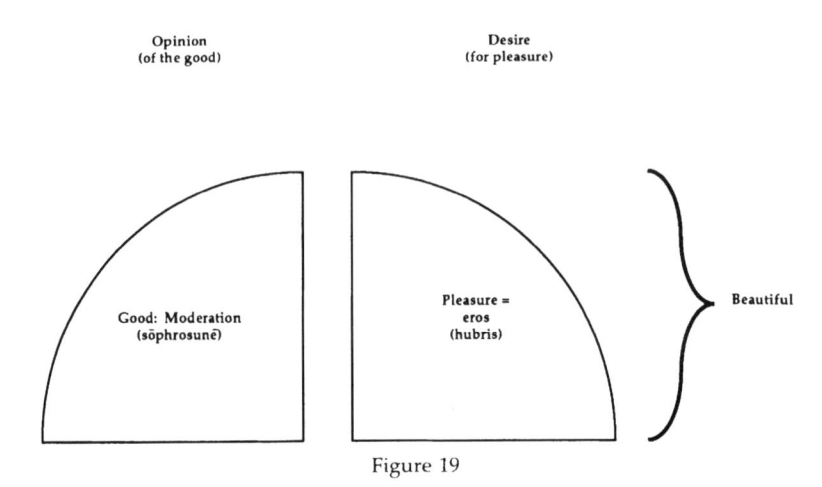

```
       Opinion                    Desire
     (of the good)             (for pleasure)


                                                        ⎫
                                                        ⎬  Beautiful
         Good: Moderation      Pleasure =               ⎭
           (sōphrosunē)           eros
                                 (hubris)


                        Figure 19
```

their commands—even through oak trees Socrates remarks (275b6)—
and the experience their mouthpiece himself undergoes are not
compatible with the behavior and opinions enjoined. By juxtaposing
the "cool" message with the "hot" medium, Socrates seems to imply
that an antinomianism is built into any kind of divine legislation.
According to Aeschylus, divinely ordained matricide was at the root
of trial by jury. The divine law as divine instills the desire to make an
end run around itself and unveil its author. It encourages a mystic
union between man and god while it deliberately sets up a screen
between them. Socrates later reports a conversation two beast-shaped
gods of Egypt had about writing. That story is unintelligible if the
problem of divine law is not kept in mind. The problem is first
adumbrated here, where Socrates renders in vatic speech the glorious
rush Phaedrus felt while he was reading Lysias' speech aloud.

The one thing we know about the lover is that he lacks *sōphrosunē*;
and Socrates now argues that the lover tries to make the beloved as
complaisant as possible, so that he cannot resist the lover from his own
resources and has no one or nothing to summon against him. The
lover enslaves the beloved as completely as possible. He takes away
his manliness and blocks his access to philosophy. Socrates says
nothing about moderation and justice; indeed, the tyrant lover has no
other aim than to instill obedience and lack of hubris in the beloved.
He who is out of control is the perfect agent of control. Socrates does
not explain how the beloved, simply because he gratifies the lover
sexually, loses the rarer virtues of courage and wisdom and acquires
the popular virtues, or, as Callicles would say, the slave virtues of
moderation and justice. The lover has *erōs*; *erōs* gives him strength

(*rhōmē*), and this strength is not corporeal but of the will. The lover has the stronger will. He is hubris incarnate.

This political interpretation of Socrates' first speech puts the virtue of *sōphrosunē* in a peculiar light. It ceases to be praiseworthy if the most effective means for its production depends on the vice it is meant to uproot. Socrates thus prepares the way for the praise of a *sōphrosunē* that cannot be induced by the tyrannical will. Philosophy alone is characterized by such a *sōphrosunē*. Philosophy therefore is the enemy of the tyrant lover who wants to be exclusively admired and obeyed. The lover, however, in rejecting philosophy, promotes the unmanly practices of which philosophy itself is accused. Those who linger in the shade and are inexperienced in sweat and manly toil are precisely those whom the lover too prefers (*Gorgias* 485d3–e2). Phaedrus is simultaneously the representative of the soft, beloved dear to the tyrant and of the philosophically inclined youth whom Socrates is now wooing under a plane tree toward philosophy while he openly praises and silently condemns political or demotic moderation. Socrates sees in Phaedrus those traits which are attractive to him and liable to corruption by tyranny (cf. *Republic* 496b6–c3). Philosophy therefore is also corrupting because it seems to need the natures which make tyranny easier, and so it helps to bring about a situation inimical to itself. Philosophy is thus compelled to be always engaged in a defense of what is potentially hostile to it—old-fashioned virtue that is wholly uninformed by philosophy.

The hidden lover preaches morality. He wants to be unbridled desire who teams up with the beloved on whom he will have imposed the yoke of moderation. The lover plans to split the two principles of Socrates' psychology and keep one for himself and assign the other to the beloved. Socrates' speech therefore is now complete when it is only halfway, for the lover cannot recommend himself as the nonlover without falling into all the difficulties to which Lysias' speech was exposed. If the speech is to continue, it must be of the unconcealed lover, who has to appeal to a principle other than the good if he is to overcome his own speech, a speech that must be almost as sobering to himself as to the beloved. This other principle turns out to be the beautiful. The three erotic speeches of the *Phaedrus* are thus specimens of forensic, deliberative, and epideictic rhetoric, of which the second in the series and the first of Socrates' negotiates in some way between the just and the beautiful. The just and beautiful are the Greek expression for morality, and they had formed the subject matter of Socrates' political science in the *Gorgias;* but in the *Gorgias* they had been taken together as the science of the good, whereas in the *Phaedrus* the good and the beautiful will be coupled in Socrates' two speeches and decoupled as a pair from the just. Justice will not disappear from the Socratic pair, but it will cease to be bound up with the lawful (252a4–6). The tyrant, to whom is allotted the ninth kind of life, can if he is just obtain a better fate the next time around (248e3–5; cf. *Gorgias* 473d8).

From his enthusiastic blame of the lover, Socrates infers that his praise of the nonlover would be beyond all bounds; but if the nonlover is the soul of moderation, it would be difficult to praise him and still not exceed the measure proper to the virtue he esteems (*Statesman* 307a1–3). Socrates avoids this difficulty by saying that all the goods contrary to the faults of the lover belong to the nonlover. The lover, however, is believed to be characterizable as such because eros is thought to dissolve all differences so that, whatever nature anyone had before he became a lover, vanishes when eros stamps him with its own singular die; but if this is the case, the nonlover has not experienced any solvent of his nature and cannot be said to be praiseworthy regardless of what sort he is. The last sections of Socrates' speech, it is true, can be applied negatively to any nonlover as long as he is not favored, for he never forces the unpleasant aspects of his body on the nonbeloved, and he certainly does not renege on anything, for he has promised nothing. If, however, the nonlover is to be chosen for something positive, he must promote the wisdom, the manliness, the eloquence, and the cleverness of the nonbeloved. He must in particular turn the nonbeloved toward philosophy. The nonlover to be preferred, then, must be Socrates, who either steps forward now as the lover of Phaedrus or as the true nonlover who pretends to be his lover. Socrates hints at the possible identity of the lover and the nonlover by speaking in the same sentence of both the lover and the nonlover as "the other" (241e5–6); and he underlines this hint by speaking summarily, as he says, about the goods of the other and the faults of the other. "Summarily" (*heni logōi*) is literally "in a single speech." A single speech of a double other is the formula for Socrates' two speeches.

# IX
# Socrates' *Daimonion*

(242a3–243e8)

Socrates has stirred up in Phaedrus a simultaneous loathing of the lover and the moderation he effects in the beloved; but Phaedrus cannot favor the nonlover, for he has been told he is a lover. Socrates the lover must be the phantom image of the lover, for the true lover tries to induce in the beloved his own state of madness. Socrates must make another speech, but Phaedrus wants to converse now about what has been said (242a5–6). Phaedrus adopts the usual view of Socrates himself, who when offered an oratorical display manages to postpone it until he can discuss the issue the display would hide. The *Phaedrus* is unique in this respect. We are given the whole range of rhetoric before Socrates is willing to discuss it. In the case of the *Gorgias,* where Socrates comes too late for the display, we can say that Gorgianic rhetoric has nothing essential to do with either speech or persuasion, and hence a display by Gorgias could not serve as an illustration of the art of persuasive speech; but the *Phaedrus,* precisely because it is concerned with persuasive speech, cannot dispense with examples of it. The *Phaedrus* must show what conditions have to be satisfied if there is to be no speech at all (Lysias), and what conditions would make it impossible for there to be any persuasion (Socrates' first speech). The ground has now been prepared for the persuasive speech, or more exactly for a persuasive speech that displays the structure of any Socratic persuasive speech. Socrates' second speech harnesses persuasion to philosophy. It is a permanent team.

The opposition between the poetic and the erotic arts, which apparently set Plato against Socrates, emerges in the difference between the Muses, who inspired Socrates' first speech, and Eros, to whom Socrates dedicates his palinode (257a3–6). The Muses do not object to the omission of the gods from their account of eros; they are willing to go along with Lysias and deal with the human by itself. Socrates' *daimonion,* however, though it could not stop the Muses from speaking altogether, is able to check Socrates long enough until he realizes his mistake. The *daimonion,* whose essence according to Diotima is to be an intermediate, had not been part of Socrates' concern with his own self-knowledge; but insofar as Socrates saw

128    Socrates' *Daimonion*

himself as intelligible only in terms of the bestial or the divine, the intervention of the *daimonion* at this point seems to be nothing but the recalling of Socrates to himself. His self-forgetting now seems to be correlated with his knowledge of Phaedrus, and not, as he had first presented it, with his ignorance of Phaedrus. The portrayal of Phaedrus to Phaedrus had involved his own disguise. Impersonation and self-representation do not apparently go together.

Socrates had turned away from the rationalization of mythology until at least he had come to know himself; he had seen himself as possibly either more bestial than Typhon or godlike and had said that human beings in the city could help him to know which he was. The divine, the monstrous, and the human were set up as follows (fig. 20). God and Typhon were paired, and man was separated from both. Socrates had implied that if he were to find himself among the gods, he would be more or less all of a piece, but if he were among the monstrous beasts, he would still be divine, since Typhon too is a god, though without the simplicity that characterizes the Olympian gods; and it was not possible that he could belong to the right of a cut at B, since man in the city was solely a means for deciding between god and beast. Now, however, Socrates had ended his speech in which he impersonated Phaedrus with an epic verse, which likened beloveds to lambs and lovers to wolves who cherish the lambs only to gobble them up (241d1). Socrates' first speech, then, in acknowledging only the human, had linked it with the bestial; and whereas it seemed as if the two principles of soul allowed for the domination of either the bestial or the lawful, it turned out that the alternative concealed a conjunction in which man in the city would be most moderate if the bestial lover were to rule him. This is the brutal truth behind Thrasymachus' view of the relation between ruler and ruled that Thrasymachus himself could not bring himself to say (*Republic* 343b1–c1). Lysias' forensic speech had made the cut at B without reflection; but Socrates' deliberative speech, though it seemed to accept Lysias' premises, had shown that if the cut were superficially made at B, it was deeply made at A. The cut at A necessarily eclipsed Socrates himself, for there is nothing Typhonic about the lover of Socrates' first speech except its speaker Socrates.

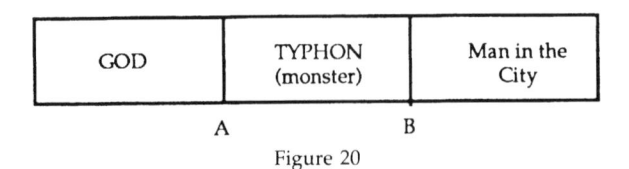

| GOD | TYPHON (monster) | Man in the City |
|---|---|---|
| | A | B |

Figure 20

There are three erotic speeches in the *Phaedrus* (fig. 21). A cut can be made at either A or B. The possibility of either cut is based on Phaedrus' overlapping both rhetoric and philosophy (257b5). Phaedrus *epamphoterizei,* or he extends in both ways and can go either way. The problem Phaedrus sets Socrates is to make the cut at A, so that Phaedrus is united with Socrates and separated from Lysias, despite the fact that the cut has already been made at B and brought Phaedrus and Lysias together through Socrates' first speech. To the extent that Phaedrus has broken with Lysias, it has been due to Socrates showing him that Lysias was not comprehensive, but it could still seem to Phaedrus that Socrates had supplemented Lysias and, if Socrates were to complete his speech in praise of the nonlover, Phaedrus would belong wholly to Lysias and would cease to wander between him and Socrates. An epideictic speech on behalf of the nonlover is impossible in any straightforward way, but it is not clear that Phaedrus realizes this. Socrates, then, must make the cut at A and the join at B. Phaedrus' good, which comes fully into view in Socrates' first speech as that of the manifest nonbeloved and immanifest beloved, must be preserved when Socrates speaks openly to him in praise of the lover. Socrates' first speech began "synthetically"; it brought eros back into the manifold of hubris from which it had drifted away. Socrates' second speech begins "analytically"; it divides what had originally been an undifferentiated divine madness into its four kinds. The dialectical problem we have is whether the joining of Socrates' two speeches at B is related to the synthetic mode of Socrates' first speech, and whether the separating of Socrates' two speeches at A is related to the analytic mode of Socrates' second speech. We have altogether seven terms in the two speeches divided into a triplet of the first and a quaternion of the second (fig. 22). We are asked to put together the third and fourth items despite the gulf that separates them. Socrates' knowledge of others (his first speech) and Socrates' knowledge of himself (his second speech) are to be understood as necessarily together. The constraint we are under to do so reflects the constraint Socrates now experiences in being forced to stay with Phaedrus and not go back to town. It was the *daimonion,* Socrates informs the jury, that always kept him out of politics (*Apology of Socrates* 31c4–32a3).

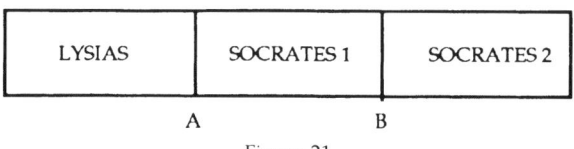

| LYSIAS | SOCRATES 1 | SOCRATES 2 |
|---|---|---|
| | A | B |

Figure 21

130   Socrates' *Daimonion*

Socrates likens his two speeches to Stesichorus' two poems on Helen. Stesichorus' palinode presupposed his ode and did not cancel it. Helen went to Troy in his first ode, the phantom of Helen went to Troy in the palinode, and Helen herself went to Egypt. Since Stesichorus' ode stated that Helen gratified her lover, and the palinode that she did not, Socrates seems to have inverted in his own case the relation between ode and palinode and given his palinode first, since the nonlover lover then urged the beloved not to gratify the lover. The moral Helen, who kept her marriage vows intact, seems to fit the beautiful boy who is not to be seduced; but since Socrates' second speech does not aim at gratification either, it cannot be simply true that an inversion of ode and palinode is intended. It is rather Stesichorus' loss of sight for his blame of Helen that seems to connect him with Socrates. Socrates' first speech had been spoken while his head was covered and he was not looking at Phaedrus; it therefore had bypassed the initial experience of eros in blaming the lover. Socrates' palinode restores sight to the prominence it has for the lover. Stesichorus, moreover, had put into his second ode a reflection on poetry and had thus incorporated into his second ode his first. Stesichorus said that a phantom image of Helen went to Troy. The image of Helen, or Helen as she is imaged in Homer, went to Homer's Troy. The real Helen, the poet is saying, is elusive; and what her lover gets hold of is what the poets supply. The images of poets are the truth of the reality the lover hopes to obtain. The hyperuranian beings of which the beloved is but a reminder seem to be Socrates' version of Stesichorus' insight. The illusion which the lover pursues, and which distracts him from the real, according to Stesichorus, is the reality, according to Socrates, beyond the real that attracts him. The erotic art knows something of which the poetic art has but an inkling.

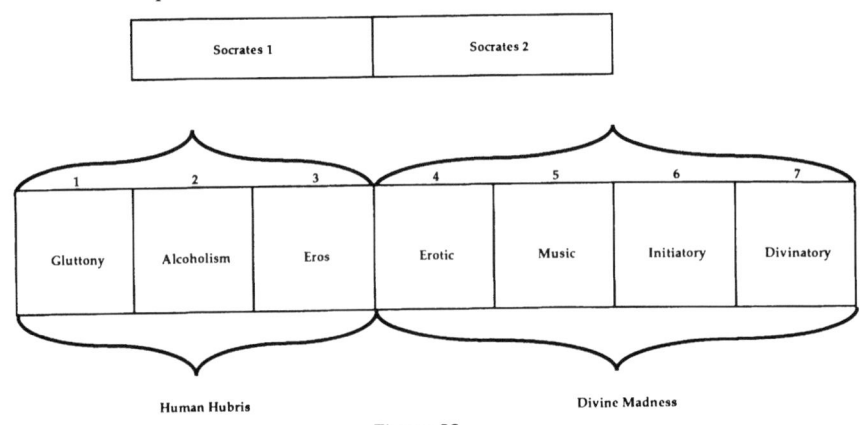

Figure 22

Socrates gives two different reasons for his palinode. In the first place, he must make amends for denying that Eros is a god or something divine; and the ancient mode of purification for an error in mythology is to make a second poem. Socrates alludes not only to Stesichorus but Hesiod, who admits at the beginning of his *Works and Days* that he erred in the *Theogony* about the goddess Eris or Strife: she is not one but two (*Works and Days* 11–26). Socrates, then, should also, it seems, have to declare that Eros is two, for in admitting that the noble lover, who is or has been in love with a noble beloved, would not see himself in the first portrait, Socrates admits that his portrait does fit lovers brought up among sailors and who have never seen any other kind of love. In order to solve a similar difficulty, Pausanias had split Eros into two gods, one to preside over demotic lovers and the other over uranian lovers (*Symposium* 180d3–e3). Pausanias' innovation, however, is not available to Socrates, who has just said that neither Aphrodite nor Eros can be at all bad (242e2–3). Socrates must preserve the unity of Eros despite the disunity of his account, for otherwise he must surrender the unity of his two speeches.

Lysias is now advised to write as soon as possible that one must gratify a lover rather than a nonlover, "everything else being equal" (243d6). It is not immediately obvious what Socrates' qualification means, but at the beginning of his speech he says, "The speech is not true whichever states, when a lover is present, one must gratify a nonlover rather than a lover" (244a3–4). Socrates allows that a lover may not always be present, and in that case the nonlover can be acceptable. Socrates seems to make allowance for his own absence. He seems to make allowance for Plato the writer. The *Phaedrus* is very consciously situated between the past and the future, between a past when divination (*mantikē*) was called the art of madness (*manikē*), without the tasteless insertion of a tau (244b6–c5), and a future to which belongs the destiny of Isocratean rhetoric. In the present there is Socrates and his discovery of the erotic art.[1] It is as unlikely that Socrates will have a successor as that he had a predecessor within the span of human memory (*Republic* 496c3–5). The wise man on the spot is as superior to the law as Socrates is to any writing that represents him (*Statesman* 294a7–8); but we cannot dispense with the law in the hope that a wise man will turn up when we need him, and we cannot in our extreme need for the philosopher to be at our side disregard the absent presence of Socrates. Socrates may well have been the perfect lover, but who are we to say that he would have favored us?

1. Cf. G. R. F. Ferrari, *Listening to the Cicadas* (Cambridge 1987), 117–19.

# X
# Socrates 2

(243e9–257b6)

Socrates' second speech has nine sections, each of which is clearly marked off:

    1. Kinds of madness (243e9–245c4)
    2. Soul as self-motion (245c5–246a2)
    3. Chariot (246a3–d5)
        4. Wing (246d6–247c2)
        5. Hyperuranian beings (247c3–249d3)
        6. Beauty and wing (249d4–252c2)
    7. Soul-types (252c3–253c6)
    8. Chariot (253c7–257a2)
        9. The erotic art (257a3–b6)

    The speech is organized around a central section on the hyperuranian beings, which separates the first four sections—they are about mortal and immortal indifferently—from the last four, which concern the human only. From the point of view of perfect symmetry, the seventh and eighth sections invert the relation between the second and third. Even apart from the puzzle of this inversion, the plan of the speech is not as perspicuous as Socrates' first, in which the order of the parts followed the ranking of the goods. Socrates began there with thought (*dianoia*) and did not mention soul until the end, and there but once (241c5). The absence of a strong connection, or better perhaps the absence of a manifest connection between soul and mind might be reflected in the obscurity of Socrates' palinode, whose sections are as elusively bound together as are the beautiful as it is for sight and the beautiful as it is for mind.
    Whoever wants to blame eros must prove two things—eros is not sent by gods for the benefit of the lover and the beloved; but Socrates has to prove only that erotic madness is bestowed from gods for the greatest good fortune (245b5–c1). Socrates leaves it open whether the good by chance falls equally on lover and beloved, and he emphasizes that eros is an opportunity. It could well be that with rare exceptions eros works out badly and still is bestowed for good. Eros, it seems, would have to be guided by art if its built-in good is to obtain; but how

art can guide it without interfering with it to its detriment is obscure. Socrates cannot cite any ancient example of the beneficence of eros; indeed, it is precisely because he cannot bring any witnesses that he must give a proof instead. Modern proofs replace ancient examples. Socrates is the first to have figured out eros. A universal experience has come to light in the singular science of Socrates' self-knowledge. If the gods have not been exactly ungenerous in the bestowal of this gift, they have certainly been stingy in the granting along with it the knowledge for its use. Socrates is the Prometheus of eros.

## 1. Kinds of Madness

Socrates encroaches on the three other kinds of divine madness. His soul, he said, was somewhat divinatory, though in a poor way, and like those who just write their own names, good only for themselves (242c3–7). Socrates certainly knew how to purify himself from the crime of his first speech; and if Socrates is the first to exhibit eros as it truly is, the crime is ancient enough. Socrates himself had summoned the Muses at the start of his first speech, and he had called attention to its poetic style and rhythm. Erotic madness may thus be the inner truth of divine madness and not just one of its four kinds (cf. 256b6). In the speech itself, divination and ritual purification shape the fifth kind of life, and poetry the sixth (248d7–e2); but neither depends directly on the gods, since each is a fragmented vision of the hyperuranian region. Only eros has a divine source in the strict sense, and of its eleven kinds only one can be said to offer much chance of any good in the strict sense. Socrates of course claims that kind for himself (250b7–c2).

As the ancients used to leave out the tau from the mantic art, so they did not lengthen the omicron into omega in its human counterpart (*oionoistikē*), so as to keep it evident that augury was based on belief (*oiēsis*) and lacked the perfection and dignity of divination. If we think together these two changes, we cannot but note how they recur in the historic change the declension of *erōs* underwent. *Eros* in Homer takes a short ultima in the nominative and accusative (cf. *Cratylus* 420b3–4), and in meaning it covers sexual desire as well as the non-excessive desire for food and drink. It is not yet a god; indeed, it is believed to have been originally a neuter substantive and ceased to be so when it became a god and changed its ultima to omega and was declined with a tau throughout.[1] Eros the god is relatively recent, and eros as a

---

1. Cf. E. Benveniste, *Origines de la formation des noms en indo-européen* (Paris 1935), 124–25. A similar transformation is believed to have happened to Latin *venus*, which was originally a neuter, when an equivalent for Aphrodite was needed; cf. A. Ernout and A. Meillet, *Dictionnaire étymologique de la langue latine* (Paris 1959), s.v.

special kind of hubris is Socrates' own proposal. Phaedrus' surprise that no poet ever praised Eros was perhaps prompted by what he now hears from Socrates, who seems to suggest that without the prior isolation of erotic hubris the divinity of eros could not be praised.

## 2. Soul as Self-Motion

One's first impression of Socrates' argument is this. The soul, whether human or divine, is both an agent and a patient. A reflection on its deeds and its experiences will prove that eros, as an experience of soul, is the same as or as close as possible to the agency of soul. Experientially, eros reproduces with the body what the soul is in itself apart from body. Eros is the experiential "excarnation" of soul. What seems to confirm this first impression is Socrates' pointed use of *ho kekinēmenos* to designate the lover just before he introduces his definition of the soul as that which moves itself (245b4). *Ho kekinēmenos* means literally "he who is in a state of motion" or more broadly "he who is disturbed or agitated." Socrates opposes such a state to the stability of the moderate, who are grave and slow to move. The lover is in motion. He cannot, however, be in any sort of motion, but only in just that motion that recovers the character of the original motion of soul. It is at this point where Socrates' argument becomes obscure. Once he has established the principle of soul as self-motion—that the soul is patient of its own agency—Socrates introduces an image of the structure of soul that contradicts the principle of soul. In the image of the soul's structure, the soul has parts and not one of its parts moves itself. The chariot certainly does not move itself, and the horses and charioteer are composite and move themselves in our ordinary understanding of the expression "a self-moving being." The image of the soul's structure retains the union of body and soul for each of its parts and cannot dispense with that union without ceasing to be intelligible. The manifest contradiction between the principle and the structure of soul makes one wonder why Socrates had to begin with the principle and not restrict his account to the structure. Why must he prove that the soul is deathless in just this way?

Soul as that which moves itself seems to imply the following. Soul is original; it is not derivative from body or being. Like the one it is always; like the other it always becomes. It links body and being in some not yet explicated way. If one had to speak of soul in terms of a standard Platonic speech about a corporeal being—that it is an image of a noetic being or that it participates in that which is just itself—one would have to say that soul carries within itself its own image and partakes of itself only to fall short of itself. Socrates' argument brings none of this out clearly. There are two strands to his argument. The more prominent strand is what he puts first: "Soul in its entirety is deathless."[2] The proof, however, involves the claim that that which moves itself is soul on the grounds that a body with a soul within (*sōma empsukhon*) has motion from itself from within (245e4–6). The model for self-moving soul is self-moving body. Self-moving body and body with an inside go together, for a body is soulless if a body solely submits to motion from without. Soul, then, if it is self-moving, must be characterized by insideness. The essence of soul is interiority; the essence of body is externality. Any body affects another body externally, for whatever of body is within any body can easily be made into another body with its own external surface. Soul, on the other hand, does not have a surface that can be peeled away to expose another surface. If the soul, then, is to be that which moves itself, interiority and self-motion must belong together. "To be within oneself" is a Greek expression meaning to be sane (250a7), just as "to be outside oneself" is to be crazy or to be in a state of motion. To be within itself when it is outside itself would thus be the self-motion of soul. It is of the essence of soul to be ecstatic within itself. Soul as self-motion is intelligible only if sanity and insanity are inseparable in soul. The soul's irrationality and the soul's rationality are not external to one another. Socrates' "I do not yet know myself" would express the essence of soul.

Soul as the single source of both motion and awareness seems to be forced together through the notion that self-knowledge is the ever-elusive goal of soul. The lack of self-identity is the identity of soul. The soul is never itself but always becoming itself. Motion thus seems to emerge as the characteristic of soul through a reflection on the peculiarity of Socrates' "not yet." Socrates himself, however, does not present the self-motion of soul as derivative from self-ignorance but as a cosmological principle. Unless there is something that does not allow that which moves another to separate from that other which is moved, that which is moved will ultimately cease to move. Entropy, we can say, must increase over time if there are only bodies that move bodies. Soul, then, is introduced as a name for an anti-entropic principle. The anti-entropic principle checks the drifting apart of every body from every other body and blocks the collapse of all bodies into one. The necessary eternity of the cosmos seems to demand a source of eternal motion within it. If the universe were a single body in some sense, it

---

2. The other possible translation, "every soul is deathless," would be loosely connected with the present argument and point ahead to Socrates' entire speech; every soul, regardless of whether it is divine, human, or bestial, is deathless.

would be an ensouled animal which could be said to move itself. This would be along the lines of Timaeus' proposal. Socrates, however, seems to allow for soul to be by itself and not be conjoined with body. Consequently, if soul is indeed self-moving, Socrates cannot prove that it necessarily moves another; and if it necessarily moves another, soul is not in the strict sense self-moving. Socrates never shows that that which moves another must itself be in motion. The good or final cause is silently denied. The good is not among the hyperuranian beings.

## 3. Chariot

The cosmological principle of self-motion is so weak cosmologically that it needs to be given a structure that binds it more closely with some possible cosmos; but the structure that makes the cosmological principle cosmological dilutes the cosmological principle, not only because the structure conceals the character of the principle (self-motion) but because the structure must be presented in an image. The true structure of soul belongs to a divine and lengthier exposition; its likeness belongs to a human and a shorter account. The being of soul is to the structure (*idea*) of soul as argument is to image. Socrates implies that the structure of soul cannot be either deduced or inferred from its being; but insofar as the soul is a cosmological principle, it is not hard to infer that, if the being of soul is somewhat indifferent to the shape of soul, the universe, though it could not perhaps be open, could be closed in several ways, and that within a finite time, though the structure of any universe may not be eternal, some universe must emerge. These are strictly cosmological speculations; but in light of the position the Olympian gods occupy later in Socrates' speech, Socrates' restriction of the human account to imagery might refer to the arbitrariness of eleven as the number of possible human soul-types as well as the arbitrariness of the gods as anthropomorphic. Socrates' psychology leaves room for law and convention to give shape to the gods who lead men beyond themselves. The theological dimension of Socrates' psychology is rooted in the gods of the city and the poets, and their conventionality reflects in turn the indeterminacy in the structure of the cosmos. The law fills in what nature sketches. It dots her *i*'s.

Divine and human soul are equally deathless, and the shape of divine and human soul equally consists of a chariot, a team of horses, and a charioteer. Throughout his speech Socrates is silent about the chariot. He is silent about what binds together horses and charioteer, or, more exactly, he does not say in what kind of being horses and charioteer inhere of necessity. Socrates seems to allow the gods to leave their chariot, for when the gods return from their visit to the hyperuranian beings they give ambrosia and nectar to their horses at the manger (247e4–6). Since ambrosia and nectar are the food and drink of the Homeric gods, Socrates implies that the body is the chariot for men, whereas for the gods no body can be assigned them without the gods duplicating men in all respects. "Animal" (*zōion*) is the name for body and soul compounded (cf. *Gorgias* 524b1–c4), but "animal" then applies only to mortal animal and cannot be extended to cover the gods. We fabricate god as some deathless animal, Socrates says, with body and soul naturally together forever. The eternity of that bond would require another principle beside the principle of self-motion. Socrates does not know what it could be. He settles for a weaker principle that every soul cares for everything soulless, and the gods function in his account as caretakers of heaven without necessarily being confined within a body of their own.

If "heaven" (*ouranos*) implies "visible" (*horatos*), as it does in the *Republic* (509d3), the difference between soul caring for body from within or from without would be slight, and the sun, moon, and stars would be the bodies to which divine souls were attached. The gods would then be the gods not of Greece but of Persia or any other country that practices a "natural" religion (cf. Herodotus 1.131.1–2; Aristophanes *Peace* 406–11). Such a religion belongs in the poetic scheme of things to the gods who preceded the Olympian gods and whom the Olympian gods overthrew. If, on the other hand, the gods manage the cosmos, as Socrates says immediately afterward (246c2), the gods rule something that is no longer, like heaven and earth, simply open to sight (245d8–e1), but they control an imperceptible unitary structure of another kind. The unity of such a structure would presumably depend on the unity of soul, which in Socrates' account is explained for the human soul but not for the divine soul. Socrates, in any case, in stating that soul cares for the soulless, implies that nothing cares for soul.

The horses of the divine soul are equally good, but in the human teams one is beautiful and good, the other ugly and bad; this pairing makes for difficult and disagreeable charioteering for us. Socrates fails to say whether the human charioteer is good and of good parentage, and therefore whether the good charioteer of the gods would have an easier time of it if *per impossible* they were in charge of the human team. The experience in any case which men acquire from the sheer cussedness of their team has no counterpart among the gods. Since the gods know nothing about the need for force, they cannot be the model for the human soul, however much we may wish to emulate the

138   Socrates 2

serenity of their rule. For us to look to the gods too much is a dangerous form of self-forgetting. It is not altogether a bad thing if the gravity of the bad horse keeps our feet on the ground. This difference, however, in the composition of the divine and human teams does not make for the difference between mortal and deathless animal. There is nothing in the human soul that is the ground of mortality. To be eternal does not require that one be perfectly good, however much a composite one may be. Socrates asserts that what makes for mortal animal is the loss of wings. Wingedness is characteristic of soul in itself, and the inseparability of its wings characterizes the divine soul. God is wing.

## 4. Wing

For soul to be winged means to be capable of ascent and lofty flight; for soul to have horses in its charge means to be capable of horizontal motion. The self-motion of soul, which is the being of soul, gets resolved in the imaged structure of soul into two different kinds of motion, ascent and locomotion. The soul goes up as it moves along. The soul, then, never goes directly up. If it did, it would bypass the lifeless and proceed vertically to the hyperuranian region. The lifeless becomes a concern of soul on its way up. It is a diversion of soul within soul away from the restoration of soul in itself. The two motions of soul form a parallelogram of forces that are always resolved along a vector at some indeterminate acute angle (fig. 23). Since the wings are powerless unless the horses are already in motion, the operation of

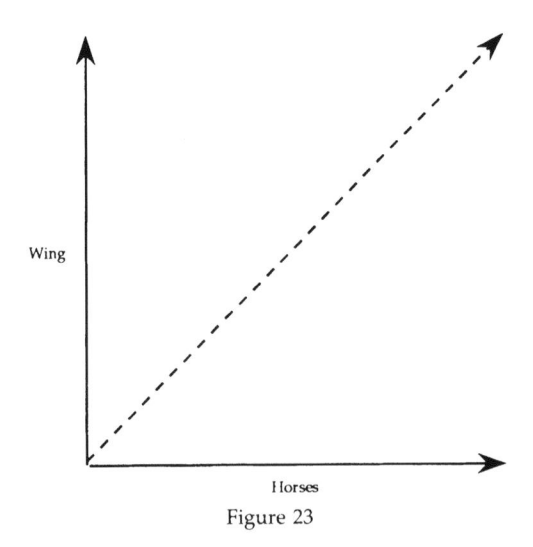

Figure 23

soul is always a compromise between the means available and the end sought. The way for soul is the obstacle. If it should then turn out that this obliquity of soul is good for the animal to which it belongs, but this good is unknown to soul, the self-ignorance of soul and the self-motion of soul would belong together. Indeed, the inner connection between the two characteristics of soul would be all the stronger if the perfection of soul by way of ascent by itself should not be good. The teleology of soul could well be as oblique as its motion[3].

Whether a body or a soul is winged, the meaning of "wing" does not alter. Its power is to lift up the weighty. Loftiness is divine. "The divine," however, has a double meaning. It comprehends both the gods who dwell within the visible, and the beautiful, wise, and good that lie beyond it. What nourishes the wings of soul is not in the region to which the wings convey soul. Hestia is a god even though she has never seen the hyperuranian beings. Whereas it is not possible to be a human being unless one has caught a glimpse of what is beyond heaven, it is possible to be a god and stay at home. To be comfortably at home is a divine principle that does not fully exist on earth. Man's devotion to his own is never complete. There is an idealism in the pursuit of his own that draws man away from his own. Hades, one may say, haunts the hearth of man's home (cf. *Crito* 54b2–c7). The homelessness in man, or his restlessness, records the loss of the soul's wings; but it is not surprising that men interpret that loss as if it meant they have strayed from home. Nostalgia is utopian.

Zeus is at the head of a large army of gods and *daimones*. He orders everything throughout heaven, but he does not order the army. The eleven sections into which the army is arranged are ordered by the eleven gods who severally run their own contingent. Each god does his own thing or minds his own business (*prattōn ta hautou*). No god interferes with the function of any other god, but no god does anything to help anyone. The army of the gods obeys the weak and not the strong principle of justice in the *Republic* (433a1–6). The cosmos is loosely ordered. It has parts, but no part is ordered, and all the parts do not form a whole. Virtue is built in piecemeal into the divine and human souls, but no one has virtue of the soul as a whole, and there is no counterpart to virtue in the cosmos. Everyone is free to follow any god, but whether one follows through on one's

---

3. If we follow Sextus Empiricus (7.112–114) and allegorize Parmenides' proemium, according to which the horses are the irrational impulses, the wheels of the chariot which conveys Parmenides beyond day and night are the ears, and the maidens are the eyes—they are the daughters of the sun— there is the same tension in the aesthetic as the way and the obstacle to the noetic as we find in the conjoined motions of Socrates' image.

following is up to the charioteer. Freedom puts a limit on order; it is due perhaps to the mixture of the two motions in soul. In order to be nourished, the gods have to abandon the cosmos. They cannot care for body and soul at the same time. The gods too descend into the cave, but they can lead others out of the cosmic cave only because they are not perfect rulers. The good shows up in the disorder of the whole.

Any soul is capable of sustained flight aloft, but only the gods find it easy to ascend further. Not even the imbalance in the team bars further ascent, but the guidance of the human charioteer can never be so perfect as to compensate entirely for the viciousness of one of the horses. Once, however, the charioteer has poked his head into the hyperuranian region, his fall is due to his horses, his own poor guidance, or chance (248b1–5). Despite the gods' facility in ascending and descending, they do nothing to prevent accidents in their entourage. The justice and moderation they behold suffices to have them care for lifeless beings; but those virtues either are inadequate for souls or do not involve any care for souls. The gods are not lovers of other souls. There is nothing attractive for them in souls which are fated to be defective forever. They can learn nothing from them. According to Socrates in the *Cratylus*, "hero" has its origin either in "eros," when a god conceived a desire for a mortal woman or a mortal for a goddess, or in "to ask" and "to speak" *erōtan* and *eirein*, and heroes are rhetoricians and sophists (398d1–e3). Although for men there is an intimate bond between these two origins of "hero"—in the best case the bond is nothing else but Socrates' erotic art—nothing comparable to such a heroic enterprise holds for the gods. If there were something comparable, the gods' relation to the lifeless beings they care for would act as an inducement to their visiting the hyperuranian beings, and the science the gods would acquire would be a true cosmology. As it is, Socrates' erotic science is unknown to the gods, and Socrates cannot incorporate what he alone knows into the larger science of heaven and earth.

The gods need their wings for ascent and descent, but the wings are useless once they have gone out onto the back of the world, on which they are carried around without any need to use their horses. The mind of the gods can in principle dispense with the entire apparatus of Socrates' image, but the morality they absorb in their contemplation of justice and moderation keeps them from walking off their jobs. Socrates fails to explain, however, what keeps the world revolving when the gods are away. The Olympian gods are either within the world or outside it, but Ouranos, whom the father of Zeus castrated, is still in motion. The pre-Olympian gods are an indispensable background for the Olympians, but they are unintelligible if there are

Olympian gods. The support the Olympian gods grant to the human has no support in the cosmos for itself.

## 5. Hyperuranian Beings

Human eros consists of two incompatible elements—the desire to be with the beloved and the desire to behold the beloved (*Phaedo* 68a3–7). Apartness precludes pairing, pairing apartness. For the divine mind, however, Socrates seems to see no such difficulty. He says that their mind feasts on the beings they behold (247e2–3). For the human soul, on the other hand, Socrates notes a difference between contemplation and consumption. The great zeal of souls to see the plain of truth is due, he says, as much to the appropriateness of the grazing for the best part of the soul as to the nature of the wing, which the same field nourishes (248b5–c2). Even though consumption and contemplation seem to have collapsed in this account, mind and wing are evidently not the same, and that which makes the soul ascend does not make for comprehension. Light-headedness is not the same as the spirit of levity. Wings lift the whole soul to where the mind alone is at home. Wings belong to the journey and not to the journey's end, but the end of the journey supports the journey. Wing links nature and reason. The way to the understanding of nature is through the understanding of wing. God, however, is wing. The gods, in the contemplation and consumption of the beings, do not come to any understanding of themselves. They guide their easily managed horses and do not have to guide their wings. In the absence of any possibility for error the gods are not forced to ask questions. The union of consumption and contemplation in their case seems to designate their self-forgetfulness. Of the four classical virtues, courage alone is not said to be among the hyperuranian beings. The gods are too soft and have it too easy to know themselves.

In the first account about the hyperuranian region, Socrates mentions only three beings by name: justice, moderation, and knowledge (or science); in his second account, which concerns only the human soul, he adds a fourth, beauty. Beauty is connected experientially with madness through eros. There is no eros for justice, moderation, or knowledge (250d4–6). Man is not outside himself in his longing for sobriety and sanity, but man is outside himself in his longing for the beautiful that is situated in the same region as sobriety and sanity. The simple formula seems to be that as sobriety and sanity are to the charioteer, so beauty is to wing. The human soul at least experiences a division within its structure that reflects its own structure. The gods are innocent of such an experience. The complexity of their own structure shows up in neither their experience nor their mind. The greater simplicity of the gods, in which Socrates did not yet know whether he shared, is not due to a structure any less complex than man's.

The hyperuranian introduces another wrinkle into the tension between the principle and the structure of soul. Not only does it suggest the Aristotelian possibility of an unmoving cause of motion, but the need for the gods to return periodically in order to sustain the wing implies that the gods, who do not need wings to be gods, exhaust over time their capacity to stay aloft, just as their horses need ambrosia and nectar to move. The gods are constantly threatened with the possibility that they will become unmoving images of themselves. In light of Socrates' discovery of the erotic art, that moment may now be at hand. The Olympian gods may not be able to survive Socratic self-knowledge.[4] Socrates prays at the end to a god more monstrous than the Olympians. Pan, according to Socrates, is either *logos* or the brother of *logos* (*Cratylus* 408d2–3).

The gods get to ride on the back of the world; all other souls stay within the world and never lose their need for wings. No nondivine soul sees all the beings (248a6). In the best case, a soul can stay out of trouble if it does not compete in the pack and realizes that the god it follows has no favorites and does not help anyone. That the gods are indifferent to their followers is unknown to their followers. The gods follow the advice of Lysias and Socrates not to gratify the lover. In the prehistory of every human being there was a smashup, and in most cases the cause of the smashup was jealousy. The gods are in charge of an army they never lead to war, but it is not surprising if the troops believe they are in a contest which not everyone can win. "There must be a ranking," each soul says to itself, "in which preference is given to whoever struggles the hardest. Why else are we in a war chariot?" The form of the soul misleads the soul. The soul is two parts eros and one part mind, but when the parts are together it seems to be geared for a fight. Courage is not a hyperuranian being, but its natural ground seems to be built into soul. Socrates' image of soul seems to represent the soul's misunderstanding of itself. It is an image because it is the truth of a falsehood. Self-knowledge must begin with the dismantling of the form of soul.

The fall of soul is due to its failure to know itself; but the degree of self-ignorance does not match up directly with the rank of the life it obtains. That rank does not depend on either the god in whose

---

4. Apuleius' *Metamorphoses* is concerned with the aftermath of the Socratic discovery. It entails the return of the Egyptian gods from whom the Olympian gods had been derived.

contingent it was (otherwise there would be eleven kinds of life) or the damage it sustained in its rivalry with its fellow souls, for the loss of wings is subsequent to the partial vision it had of the beings. The rank of one's life is determined solely by the extent of one's vision. It is determined by the degree to which what one knows is infected by opinion. The lives are these (the "ands" and "ors" are original):

1. philosopher, beauty lover, or *musical* and *erotic* man
2. lawful king or *martial* and *magisterial* man
3. *statesman* (politician), *household manager*, or *moneymaker*
4. toil lover, *gymnast*, or physician
5. *diviner* or *priest involved in initiations*
6. *poet* or imitator
7. *craftsman* or *farmer*
8. *sophist* or *demagogue*
9. *tyrant*

The italicized words are suffixed with *-ikos,* which usually designates a man with a skill. There are sixteen words of this type; of the other six, three have the prefix *philo-* (love). *Eros* shows up in the manifold of cognitive understanding in only two kinds of lives, the first and the fourth. Eros survives in these cases because reason never assumes there the form of an art or science. The philosopher never gains wisdom; the toil lover always sets himself a record to be broken (cf. 229d4). The ranking seems to be heavily politicized, with the best possible regimes set just below the top, and the worst regimes in the last two spots. On the basis of the three hyperuranian beings mentioned so far, one can say that some traces of morality and science are always found together in almost everyone. The city makes it impossible for any science to be as morally neutral as it is (cf. Aristotle *Nicomachean Ethics* 1094a27–b7). In the same way, the prominence war has seems to be due more to the shape the city gives the soul than to any knowledge to be gleaned from the hyperuranian beings. The soul as war chariot anticipates that the fall of man involves him in political life. Only the first kind of life is wholly free of the city and can recover the truth behind the image of the soul's form. In the first generation of every ten thousand–year cycle, if one is a philosopher one cannot be a king. This is the law.

The nine lives a soul has after its first, before it is rewinged and returns to the beings, are no longer subject to the extent of its original vision. It is not clear how one can choose above one's station and not become either unjust or unhappy. Although no human soul knows justice fully, each human soul is judged in accordance with its justice. It is judged apparently in accordance with the prevailing opinion of justice, for neither the sinners who are punished nor those who are rewarded are taught the Adrastean law that forbids any soul to enter a bestial nature the first time around. Men choose to be beasts. They do not understand the connection between the hyperuranian beings and the human shape. At best, there is a weak link between the plain of truth and humanity, even though one cannot even be a human being unless one has glimpsed the truth. To be a human being is to understand what is spoken of by species (*eidos*), in proceeding out of many perceptions and bringing them into one by reasoning (*logismos*). The synthetic power of speech is a recollection of the hyperuranian beings, but only those who choose the human shape understand that the species of perceptible things and speech go together. The fusion of speech lover and sight lover constitutes the union of the human and the human shape. Phaedrus does not represent such a union. He is going to choose to be a cicada. Socrates has the task of converting a lover of speeches into a lover of sights and thus of bringing him to self-knowledge. It is not easy to say whether Socrates succeeds or not. The beautiful that Socrates deploys to strengthen the bond between speech and sight might fall on deaf ears.

## 6. Beauty and Wing

Socrates is about to discuss the fourth kind of madness. He is about to pull moderation away from science and attach reason and speech to eros. He wants to show that to love (*eran*) is to see (*horan*) and ask questions (*erōtan*). There is nothing, he implies, in what we ordinarily say to one another that forcibly makes us look behind the universals of speech. The philosopher alone is devoted to the use of those reminders as reminders. It is his thought (*dianoia*) and not his soul that is winged (249c4). The philosopher therefore heads both the nine types of cognitive mind and the eleven types of erotic soul. In everyone else, eros and mind diverge. Were there not such a divergence, every soul would be fated to love just what it understood, and one would be locked forever into one's original niche. With the divergence, however, one can be attracted to what one does not know and soar beyond one's station. If we leave the philosopher out of account and say that he never stoops—no one is attractive to him except those in his own class—there are eighty-eight other combinations of talents and natures. If we do not discount the philosopher and admit the vagary of eros, the total reaches ninety-nine. Not all of these combinations are equally interesting philosophically, but of those that are, not even Plato perhaps for all his toil represented more than a fraction (cf. *Republic* 618c1–e2).

The philosopher tries to recover those beings that make the gods divine. The many believe the philosopher is going off course (*parakinōn*). Lovers rediscover the gods who care for the universe. They are charged with being crazy, and they are off course. They look up to the Olympian gods and only through them at the being of the beautiful. The beautiful shows up for them in eleven different shapes, which put up the greatest resistance to their being gathered together into a single class. The beautiful that is directly incorporated into speech as a unitary predicate breaks up in the experience of eros as a manifold of eleven distinct subjects. Socrates must argue that this manifold is of a higher order than the discursive one. The discursive one is discursive; it rambles from one thing to another without order or aim. The erotic manifold is distributed experientially over mutually exclusive subjects that direct the lover toward a being. This being is a whole from which nothing is missing. As a whole the god is halfway between the soul and the being to the wholeness of which pair it simultaneously points. The erotic manifold has two surfaces, in one of which the soul discovers what it means for it to be complete and on the other of which the unity of the beautiful itself is reflected. These two surfaces constitute the nature of any discursive paradigm, which in being geared to the learner ceases to make that of which it is a paradigm transparent, and which in maintaining the truth alters the truth of whatever it is a paradigm. The experience of the lover is itself paradigmatic of all philosophic analysis, for in that experience alone does self-knowledge link mind and being.

In Socrates' account of the relation between beauty and wing, the soul has no parts. Horses and charioteer vanish only to return when Socrates turns from the lover to the beloved and has to account for the way in which the beloved undergoes the same experience as the lover. Eros is the experience of the growth of wing, but for neither the lover nor the beloved does this growth occur. *Pteroō* means "to furnish with wings" and is frequent in that sense; it can also mean "to excite," but in this sense it is rare. *Anapteroō,* on the other hand, most frequently means "to excite" and "to put in a state of expectation," but on occasion it has its literal meaning, "to furnish with new wings." When Socrates begins his account of the fourth kind of madness, he says that whoever sees beauty here gets winged (*pterōtai*) and, in being rewinged (*anapteroumenos*), is eager to fly up (*anaptesthai*). *Anaptesthai* is the aorist infinitive of *anapetomai,* which in Sophocles means "to get excited," once in joy and once in fear (*Ajax* 693; *Antigone* 1307). When, however, Socrates describes the stream of the beautiful on its return to the beloved, he says that it excites (*anapterōsan*) the soul (255c7), for he cannot say that it refurnishes the beloved with wings prior to the start of the growth of wings. Wing hovers in a no-man's-land of the literal and the figurative. When wing was first introduced, it belonged to the image of the soul's structure and stood for the power of ascent. Wings were attached to the soul by itself and were lost on the fall of soul into body. Now, however, when Socrates is discussing fallen soul, a physiology of wing is given, and the soul is nothing but an embryonic bird (249d7). Sight, to which Socrates assigns a privileged position among the senses, seems to bring along with it a corporealization of the soul. Socrates' particle-wave theory of sight breaks up the beautiful beloved into parts (*merē*) and thus cancels in the physiology of desire (*himeros*) the whole for which eros longs (251c6–7). In light of this, *anaptesthai*, which presumably means "to fly up" (*ana-ptesthai*), may have to be re-segmented into *an-haptesthai* and mean "to be attached and cling," or "possible to be rekindled" as of a fire (255e3).

What seems to have happened is this. The two incompatible elements that make up eros—to be with and to behold—have been fused together into "wing." The physiology of the growth of wing goes as far as possible in accommodating the sexuality to the transcendentality of eros. It remains true to the experience and yet seems to allow the later split into the black and white horse. "Wing" represents the bewildering character of eros rather than a resolution of the bewilderment. "Wing" is the inarticulate experience of eros. Whom mortals call winged Eros (*erōs potēnos*), the immortals, Socrates says, call *Pterōs*. The immortals fuse noun and epithet into one. Since in that fusion *erōs* survives intact, the immortals' real contribution is to have the word for wing (*pteron*) flow into *erōs* and no longer be detachable from it. *Erōs* makes wing pronounceable. *Pterōs*, then, can be re-segmented into *erōs* and the consonant cluster *pt*, the unpronounceable zero-grade of the verb "to fly" (*petomai*). Eros is wing. God, however, is wing. Eros then is the nonvocalic god, and the eleven Olympian gods are the multiple manifestation of a single human experience. It is no wonder that Socrates calls the nonmetrical verse in which the gods cancel themselves hubristic. He is fairly certain, in any case, that Phaedrus on account of his youth will laugh when he hears it.

The beautiful, like all other hyperuranian beings, has its likenesses here; but it differs from the rest in being in the light. Its being in the light, however, has something mysterious about it. For all its vividness to sight, the beautiful points to something beyond sight. The brightness of the beautiful coincides with its loveliness (250d7–e1). The lovely (*eraston*) is that in which eros and sight meet. What is right in front of us is not right in front of us. What is not right in front of us is what is right in front of us in the being of what appears. This is what is loved. The only form in which the beautiful as the beautiful can be possessed is if the beautiful is a being to be known. To be drawn to the beautiful is to have the beautiful recede unless the beautiful one is drawn to is the image of the beautiful that is. Only in the mode of cognition can the distance of the beautiful, without which the beautiful is not in the light, be reconciled with the attraction of the beautiful, at the moment of contact with which there is nothing beautiful to be seen. Socrates' condemnation of sexual generation as unnatural has less to do with his pederasty than with the denial in the perpetuation of the self and the race that there is anything in the beautiful but a lure to something that does not retain the structure of the beautiful as it first shows itself. At this point of the argument, the structure of the beautiful is retained not by some move to philosophy but by the experience of pleasure and pain. Pleasure and pain of a certain kind point to the hyperuranian being of the beautiful.

The experience of love begins with a shudder of fear. This fear, which changes into the worship of the beloved as if of a god, seems to be the anticipation on the lover's part of his imminent madness and impiety, when he will abandon the lawful and be prepared to sacrifice to the beloved. Every lover is initially on the brink of making a new religion, in which the beloved is both statue and god (251a6). The beloved is himself a god and an image of a god (251a2). On account of this doubleness of the beloved, the lover stays within the law and steps beyond it. He is a heretic and an idolater. The beloved is both a new god with a new name and a representation of an old god with an old name. As a new god he is unapproachable; as a statue he is not present. In the face of this double experience the lover is in a state of disorientation (*atopia*). If he maintains the lawful, the beloved as Apollo or whatever recedes; if he gives himself up to his enthusiasm, he cannot be granted what he believes he wants. Socrates describes this double experience in terms of the growth of wing; but the re-winging can never really occur unless one is no longer alive. The ultimate terror of love is nonbeing. What is experienced in the growth of wing is a false experience, or better perhaps an experience that cannot but be frustrated unless the lover can translate it into a viable equivalent of wing. The presence of the beloved alleviates the pain that accompanies the growth of wing, but it can do no more. Sight alone can never fledge the lover.

## 7. Soul-types

The initial experience of love is no respecter of persons. Its power seems to consist in recovering experientially the complete structure of the soul. As an experiential recovery, however, one is merely excited

148   Socrates 2

(*anapterōtai*) and not re-winged (*anapterōtai*). Socrates, therefore, follows the account of beauty and wing, in which the difference in the natures of lovers made no difference, with an account of soul-types, in which, however, the hyperuranian being of the beautiful disappears. In the central section of Socrates' speech, the relation between the hyperuranian and the Olympian was, for the human soul, as that shown in figure 24. An indirect access to the beings through the Olympian gods was alone possible; but on earth, though the philosophical soul does reason its way to the beings, it must still go through the Olympian gods to realize the connection between human reason and human shape. Now, however, Socrates seems to have split the growth of wing from the Olympian gods, and the Olympian gods from the being of the beautiful. Each soul-type seeks out a soul-type in conformity with its own paradigmatic god. Each soul-type is by nature a lover and finds its beloved before it loves (252e5). Socrates no longer speaks of either sight as the initiatory experience or the growth of wing. Each type deliberately sets out to construct and fashion a kindred nature into a statue and a god: *fingebant simul credebantque* (Tacitus *Annals* 5.10; cf. *Germania* 8.2). The realization of the lover's own nature in the beloved can be done only if there is complete self-knowledge that can divine its own nature in another. Socrates seems to restrict its success to the first generation in the ten thousand–year cycle (252d3). Afterward, the possibility of self-ignorance lurks in every attempt at choosing one's own type and shaping him accordingly. Mismatched lovers and beloveds are very likely to be the rule.

The lover has the beloved emulate his own nature in the guise of a god. He will certainly say and possibly believe that the beloved is the reminder of the god whose ways he urges him to adopt (253a5). His

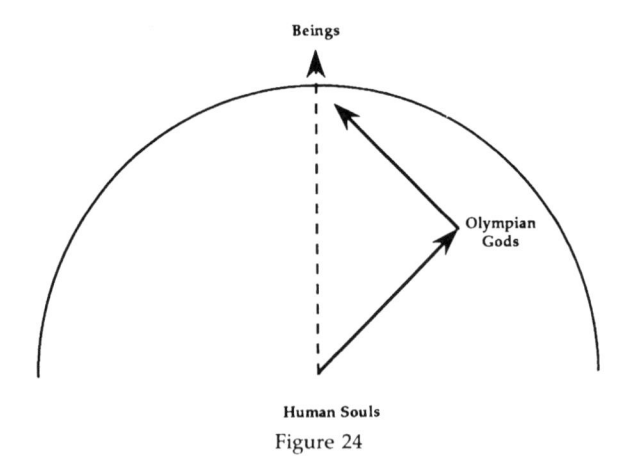

Figure 24

persuasive speech will be guided by either art or nature. If it is by nature, his speeches will conform to the conventions of whatever god his beloved seems to resemble. Indeed, the more misinformed he is about himself and his beloved, the more idealistic the type he proposes for the two of them will be. If his speech is guided by his knowledge, the speaker will be Socrates and the beloved will be Phaedrus. No one else except Socrates has ever had the erotic art. Lysias hit upon by chance a speech adapted to Phaedrus' nature, but he thought it was general and had no restriction on its applicability. Socrates, on the other hand, delivered a speech for which Phaedrus fell completely: he forgot that it was spoken by the lover. Socrates rendered Phaedrus unto Phaedrus, and Phaedrus wanted more. Socrates has now given him more. He has told him what he has done and who he was to do it. Socrates had first told him in an aside that he and Phaedrus were once in the train of Zeus, when they were initiated into and became adepts of complete, simple, unwavering, and blessed apparitions (*phasmata*) set in a pure light (250b7–c6). Socrates antedated his seduction of Phaedrus and represented his art as destiny. We were made for each other, Socrates declares, after he has made him.

In the *Symposium*, Aristophanes the comic poet and Agathon the tragic poet each made a speech in praise of Eros. Aristophanes grounded eros in nothing but the love of one's own, and Agathon in nothing but the love of the beautiful. Socrates has now managed to make a speech in which the love of one's own and the love of the beautiful pair and part in the Olympian gods. Eros is love of one's own better half. Socrates, however, has not yet explained his own art and in what way it shows up in his Jovian nature. His art should be informed by the hyperuranian beings which either were missing in his most recent account of the Olympians or had no cognitive status in the experience of the growth of wing. Socrates therefore must revert back to the chariot and horses in order to show how the charioteer's guidance of eros is related to the understanding of beings and natures. The black and white horses hold the key to Socrates' art.

## 8. Chariot

The ten attributes of the white horse do not quite match up with the thirteen attributes of the black horse. If we supply from each list the contrary item that is missing from the other, the white horse is smallish, weak-necked, and bloodless, and the black horse is a lover of knowledge. It is clear enough that the white horse has the characteristics Socrates assigned to the perfection of opinion as moderation in his first speech, and the black horse exemplifies the hubris of erotic desire. The white and black horses, however, do not represent the split between opinion and desire, but a split within desire itself. The white horse too is a form of eros. For all its outward beauty it is not certain how deep it goes: Meletus, like the white horse, also had a hooked nose (*Euthyphro* 2b11). The black horse is as snubnosed as Socrates. Nearly all of Socrates' account is devoted to the black horse. Without the black horse, the lover would not have approached the beloved, but in shame and awe would have kept his distance and loved in silence. The sexual favors the black horse demands initiates the approach to the beloved. The very possibility that there be a growth of wing depends on the constant concessions the white horse and charioteer have to make to the black horse. Rather surprisingly, the black horse never succeeds in having his way until he has been completely humbled and the beloved shares the love (256b7–c7); but while he is being tamed all the motion belongs to him. The white horse never goes forward on its own; indeed, the white horse drops out of Socrates' account after the black horse compels the white horse and charioteer to live up to their agreement; and whereas in the first encounter the white horse willingly sits on its haunches, in the second and all subsequent encounters, the charioteer seems to deal with a single horse (254e1–5).

In Socrates' first speech, the black horse showed up as hubris with strength and the white horse as the triumph of opinion or moderation; but the speaker of that speech was the black horse, who has disguised himself to look like the white horse. He had disguised himself to look as moderate as any nonlover. The white horse, then, is a complete invention of the black horse, who by splitting himself turned out to seem wholly black in the eyes of the white horse that was no longer part of himself. By contrast to the purified version of himself, the black horse is dyed the deepest black. The black horse conceals himself through a dummy. The white horse, however, is Phaedrus, whose speech it is. It is Phaedrus' noble version of himself presented to him through Socrates. Socrates, then, is the black horse, who can be both himself and another. Phaedrus is on this occasion that other. Socrates is never any other. He does not have in himself any beautiful other, but he never appears as himself but only as the other of some beautiful other. He appears to be in himself pure wing, but he cannot talk with another unless he can join himself with another as other. He must descend. He must descend in order to ascend with another, but he cannot ascend with another unless he diverges from a straight ascent. He therefore never ascends directly, for he cannot ascend without others. Socrates is not pure wing. He differs, however, from the white horse he teams up with by not needing a white horse of one special kind. For everyone else, what Aristophanes says is true: there is a special someone who completes or rather is believed to complete oneself. Socrates' self-knowledge consists in his knowledge that it is contrary to the nature of eros itself that there is or can be someone special. To claim that there is someone special is to claim that the Olympian gods are not gods through their devotion to what is higher than themselves (249c6). It is to deny that man is not man unless he is informed by mind and the things of the mind. Aristophanes drew the consequences of his contrary thesis: mind does not characterize man, and man as he originally was and for which everyone longs was not of human shape.

Phaedrus had wanted to discuss what Lysias and Socrates had said before he had heard Socrates' second speech. He wanted to converse with Socrates before he had teamed up with Socrates. He did not believe there was any need for Socrates to reveal the lover who spoke as the nonlover. "What difference does it make," he would have said with Charmides, "who said it as long as one can ask whether it is true?" (274c1–4; cf. *Charmides* 161c5–6). Socrates, however, had to show that without a prior understanding of the speaker one is apt to take a self-reflection for the truth. This self-reflection would not be so deceptive were it really the self and not the beautiful other the self fails to recognize as itself. Once the black horse has been tamed, the lover associates continuously with the beloved, and the beautiful that streams into the lover flows back to the beloved. "[The beloved] is in love, but with what he is perplexed; and what he has experienced he neither knows nor can he point it out, but as if infected with another's ophthalmia he cannot give the grounds, but just as in a mirror he is unaware that he is seeing himself in the lover" (255d3–6). Socrates does not now say how the lover's presence can occasion the return of eros to its source; but he has already indicated, in the section on soul-types, that the lover constructs a model of the beloved in speech that renders the lover to the beloved in a joint version of their common nature. The beloved moves in pursuit of an illusory other who is in truth himself. He undergoes self-motion through his self-ignorance. This self-ignorance is twofold: the illusory other is neither other nor himself. It is not other because it is himself, and it is not himself because it is the lover who presents himself in the self of the beloved. The lover can make such a self-representation either rationally or irrationally. If he does it irrationally, his self-representation takes on the conventional disguise of an Olympian god; if he does it rationally, he is Socrates, and whatever god he fashions for the beloved is a necessary means for a shared ascent to the hyperuranian beings (cf. 256e1).

## 9. The Erotic Art

Socrates has done several things in his speech. He has inserted his first speech into his second speech, where it is quite different from its appearance when it was apart; he has put Phaedrus and Socrates together so that they can examine the issue of persuasion; and he has shown that his self-knowledge is as inseparable from his knowledge of others as from his knowledge of the double nature of eros. Eros splits into the motion of ascent and the motion of self-motion. These two motions are always split and always paired. The motion of ascent is the motion of Socratic ignorance; the motion of self-motion is the motion of self-ignorance. Just as Socrates cannot know himself whether he is a beast or a god unless human beings in the city teach him, so he cannot work his way back to the beings unless he begins with the opinions of human beings. The opinions of human beings mix their natures with their knowledge or talent. They are informed by what they severally take to be their ideal and a fragment of an "idea." There is in them something that points to what is and away from what is. It is therefore impossible to learn anything from them about what is unless one can draw them to what draws them away from what is. Only in the detection of what is not is there a way of ascent.

Although a version of this relation between conversation and understanding, or in short *dialegesthai*, underlies every Platonic dialogue, only in the *Phaedrus* is it thematic. The issue of persuasion, represented by the impossible case of a nonlover persuading a nonbeloved to favor him, involves simultaneously the triplet of soul, being, and speech. It is characteristic of the *Phaedrus* that it treats the members of the triplet two at a time. Soul and being determine the way of Socrates' second speech; but the use of speech in effecting the union between two souls has been hidden in the speech itself, so that it must be considered later in the confrontation between Lysias' and Socrates' speech. What one learns on the way hides the way. There is a blind spot in every discovery which only self-knowledge can see. Phaedrus' delusion that Socrates' first speech was not his own speech, and which fulfilled him in a way his first lover Lysias could not, distanced him from Lysias. Socrates' second speech brought Phaedrus to himself and made him ripe for a takeover. Phaedrus would certainly have resisted a straightforward appeal to himself in whom there is nothing beautiful for himself. As the nonlover he is beautiful only in the eyes of others. He does not see what they see in him. His love of speeches is not inspired by anything. The white horse inspires Phaedrus. The white horse is the perfect speech.

The spell of the city is broken by eros. Eros presents an individual whole superior in both its individuality and idealism to the whole of the city and its laws. There never was a law lover.[5] The erotic conformation of soul and being issues in a god or an image of a god. Were this conformation of soul not a discovery and invention of the lover, the beloved would be as unpersuadable as Lysias had argued he ought to be; but since this perfect being or image of a perfect being is not self-originating, it carries with it the possibility of being paired with its imperfect and defective inventor. Even though this pairing has already occurred behind the back of the beloved, the conjunction of perfection and defectiveness cannot but seem monstrous. The team of white and black, of Phaedrus or whoever and Socrates, conveys the message that every Socratic dialogue is complete and incomplete. Its completeness reflects the interlocutor back to himself in a form he can follow and aspire to; its incompleteness shows up in Socrates' ignorance. His ignorance is the difference between the satisfaction of the interlocutor and his own dissatisfaction. The difference is determined by the degree of deviation from the straight ascent of Socrates' winged thought, but the degree of deviation is not so easily deductible that the deviation disappears at once. The deviation is not a cosmetic beauty that can be simply peeled away. It has life. Phaedrus' cut between thought and words butchered the patient; the second half of the *Phaedrus* shows how life remains after the surgery.

Socrates' second speech can be summarized as follows. There are three kinds of madness acknowledged to be divine and good; eros has to be shown to be of this kind. The proof requires that the nature of soul be such that it can be ecstatic; and this can be most clearly proved if the soul is of necessity ecstatic, that is, self-moving. Such a proof, however, shows that everyone, man or god, is crazy. One needs therefore an account that allows for the soul to be such in itself, but when bound with body a mover of another. An account, then, has to be given as to how it recovers its true nature while being bound with body. This account concerns ascent and descent; it is introduced through the image of the team, which leads to an insoluble distinction between god and man, for god cannot have a body without being mortal. The account of wing explains this paradox, for Hestia is a god and cannot be winged. Only man as man is essentially winged and follows the eleven gods to the hyperuranian region. The transvisible region is glimpsed by every human soul, and the degree of beholding determines the arts exercised. The glimpse shows up in understanding or collecting (*sunienai*), but it is weakly linked to the human shape.

---

5. *Philonomos* (law lover) occurs on a Jewish inscription from Rome; see L-S-J, s.v.

Erotic madness shows up in being reminded of the nondiscursive beautiful itself by the sight of a phantom image of it. A distinction is thereby made between the syllogistic species (*eidos*) and the contemplative form. The contemplative form shows up in the experience of religious awe. The beloved is experienced as a god and not as a hyperuranian being, and the experience initiates the ever-frustrated growth of wings. This "teething" is relieved by sight of the beloved and the neglect of everything lawful. Wing is said to be eros (*pterōs*). The ascent of soul is erotic and imitates the cognitive ascent of soul in a divergent manner. Eros, then, is soul, and when soul is human it is not eros. The experience of reminding takes different souls differently. The response to the beautiful is shaped by a prior form of soul that depends not on the beings but on the gods. The soul's structure thus duplicates the gods in a variety of soul-types. Accordingly, there is a forced fitting of the beloved into a previously fashioned image (252e4). The lover tries to pair the beloved with himself in his own soul. The white horse is this inserted self as other; it is perfectly obedient. That which does the insertion is the black horse, which thus comes to light as either hubris or madness. The experience of self-motion belongs to the beloved; the lover's is that of ascent. The yoking of ascent and self-motion yields a pseudo-whole under the guidance of the erotic art of Socrates.

# XI
# Writing

(257b7–258d6)

All three erotic speeches argue that one should not gratify the lover; but whereas the third speech is somewhat more permissive and grants that sexual indulgence if it is infrequent is a less serious lapse than the niggard moderation of opinion, only the second speech has as its aim the gratification of the lover. The second speech, however, ceases to have this aim once it is put together with the third speech. There is always the possibility, then, that the second speech get unyoked from the third and lead to the consequence that the lover, disguised in the eyes of the beloved as the nonlover, be sexually indulged. Sexual coupling is a phantom image of dialogic coupling: *dialegesthai* has the nonliteral sense of sexual intercourse (Aristophanes *Ecclesiazousae* 890). Socrates' erotic art consists in his knowledge of how to restore and maintain the original meaning of *dialegesthai*. Socrates, however, is not certain, after the error of his first speech, that is, in light of the possibility of its being misunderstood, that the erotic art will still be his. Socrates is not certain that he can survive the representation of himself as perfect in the partnership of Phaedrus and himself. The white horse Phaedrus is will not move by itself; he will not move unless he is with Socrates. Socrates, however, cannot always be with Phaedrus. He ceases to be present as soon as he too becomes represented. The inscription of Socrates into the orbit of Phaedrus cancels their difference and makes Socrates look as young and beautiful as Phaedrus (cf. *Epistle* 2,313c1–4). The *Phaedrus* in its entirety, which cannot as written avoid assuming the guise of the white horse, parallels the difficulty of preserving in the alphabet the difference between consonant and vowel. The consonant is no less a letter than the vowel is, and its natural silence vanishes in the form it is given. The syllable of consonant and vowel, like the pairing of Socrates and Phaedrus, silences the silence of the consonant in the sounding of itself.

Phaedrus is aware and not aware of this problem. He is as uncertain of the advantage of Lysias' turn to philosophy, so that he (Phaedrus) can be turned as well, as of Lysias' willingness to go on writing, let alone to compete against Socrates' second speech. It is not easy to say how or even whether Phaedrus connects the abandonment of writing with the conversion to philosophy. These issues are in the same speech of Phaedrus, but his speech seems to veer from the issue of Lysias' own conversion to philosophy to the abuse Lysias received recently from a politician for being a speechwriter (*logographos*). Speechwriting is squeezed between philosophy and politics. As a form of sophistry it is neither one nor the other, and Phaedrus seems to doubt whether Lysias could face the humiliation of being worsted by Socrates or endure the reproaches of the politically powerful. Socrates argues that Phaedrus has missed the main point. No one holds writing in more esteem than politicians, and of politicians no one does so more than lawgivers. To lay down for a whole society a written code that will endure for centuries is the highest political ambition. If, however, the law is the antagonist to eros, regardless of whether it is philosophic or not, writing and eros must not go together. The writings of poets and philosophers contradict this conclusion. Writing is just a neutral means to preserve speeches. Whether it is good or not seems to depend on whether one writes well or not. Writing seems to be a nonissue.

The present dismissal of writing in itself as a questionable practice only postpones the problem; it returns after Socrates and Phaedrus have discussed good and bad writing (274b6-7). Their discussion does not distinguish between speaking and writing (258d4-5). Accordingly, if writing in itself, regardless of how beautiful a writing may be, can be at issue, speaking in itself is subject to the same doubts. We know from Socrates' second speech that, even though initially the human soul and the human shape are put together, men are free to choose nine times a nonhuman shape before their souls are allowed to revisit the hyperuranian region and the cycle begins all over again. Many men do not connect the two aspects of their own humanity, and in giving up their shape they sacrifice their capacity to speak. Eros, which leads men to worship other men as gods, does not persuade them that the beauty they behold is strongly linked with their rationality. It would seem, then, that if writing is condemned at the end of the *Phaedrus* but speaking vindicated, writing must be compatible with the rejection of the human shape and the acceptance of the bestiality of man. The Egyptian god who discovered writing had the head of a dog, and the Egyptian god who criticized writing had the head of a ram. Socrates' Egyptian story seems to confirm and not to confirm the connection between writing and bestiality; but it must be kept in mind that the god who criticized writing did not reject it. The Egyptians had writing, and their alphabet was composed of many pictures of beasts. The Greeks called their writings hieroglyphics or sacred writing. The most sacred of writings are religious and legal. Eros, however, is antinomian. The defense of speaking involves an attack on the law. Is Socrates implying that the law is not to be taken altogether seriously?

Writing in itself is never the issue in the *Phaedrus*. Phaedrus makes it clear that the issue is publication, and Socrates that it is the perpetuation of writings in the form of laws and decrees. Socrates speaks of the eros the proudest of politicians have for writing speeches, and, in the best case, of his gaining power to be a deathless speechwriter in the city, so that he believes he is equal to a god (*isotheos*), and those afterward, in beholding his writings, exercise the same belief about him. The lawgiver mimics the erotic nature of soul. His writings are meant to recall their author, just as the beauty of the beloved is meant to inspire the lover to emulate the deity he sees and recall the being of the beautiful. The lover's situation looks like the illustration in figure 25. The law-abiding citizens' looks like the illustration in figure 26. Socrates' objection to the law cannot be the spuriousness of the legislator's claim to divine status, since in his own analysis of eros the gods behind the beloveds are equally doubtful; rather, it must have to do with the incapacity of the law to recall within the law the beings. The law is essentially not rational. It neither argues nor persuades. Socrates made this point as vividly as possible to Crito

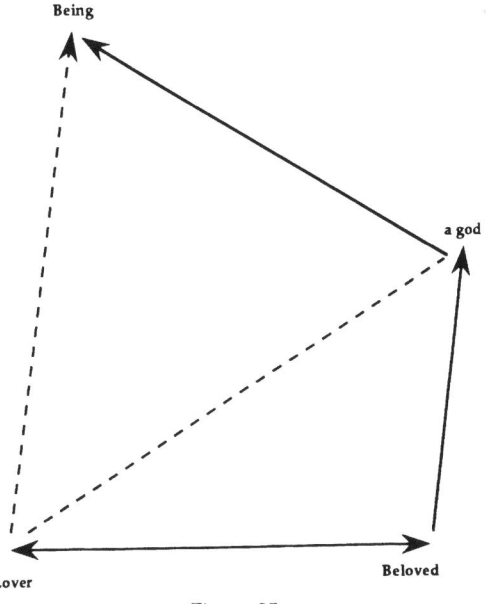

Figure 25

158  Writing

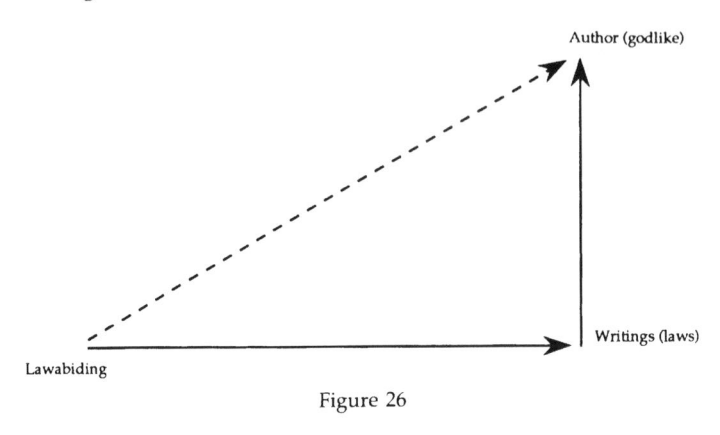

```
                                          Author (godlike)
                                         ↗▲
                                     ╱    │
                                 ╱        │
                             ╱            │
                         ╱                │
                     ╱                    │
                 ╱                        │
             ╱                            │
         ╱                                │
     ╱────────────────────────────────────▶ Writings (laws)
Lawabiding
```

Figure 26

on the occasion of his imminent execution. He imagined the law to be speaking and living beings who tried to meet all of Socrates' objections with arguments and suasions. The animation of the law destroys the law. Even if all its arguments are flawless, how is it to handle those who cannot follow its reasoning? Are they to be acquitted or condemned for disobedience? And if the law is faulty in its arguments, are those who see through it to get off scot-free? The lawgiver, it seems, aspires to be Hestia, the one god who has never seen the hyperuranian beings.

Phaedrus had taken the politician's blame of Lysias straight. He connected the publication of speeches, of which the most powerful in cities were ashamed, with the fear they had of being called sophists. Phaedrus was thinking of persuasive speeches, whose effectiveness on a given occasion and before a given audience must look as sophistical as they are to anyone not caught up in the mood of the moment. Socrates turns Phaedrus completely around on this point by appealing to the decrees and laws that result from the persuasive speech that precedes them. Phaedrus' radical distinction between words and thought finds its realization in the difference between what politicians say on behalf of a law and what the law says. The law manages to hide the sophistry of its enactment in the formulation of its commands. The sophists the city finds fault with screen the city from its own sophists (*Republic* 492a5–b3; *Statesman* 303b8–c5). Phaedrus, however, takes it for granted that whatever politician is hostile to Lysias cannot be finding fault with his own desire. Phaedrus denies that it is possible to take out on another what one finds reprehensible in oneself. There are no scapegoats for Phaedrus. It does not occur to him that in the eyes of the best politicians written legislation might be an unavoidable evil (*Statesman* 294a10–301e5). Phaedrus concedes the neutrality of writing in itself because he takes the writings of the city as authoritative.

A politician, Socrates says, who succeeds in passing a proposal of his own puts first the name of those who praised it, whether the council or the people. The politician incorporates into his writing the audience he persuaded. Every nonpolitical writing goes into the world looking for an audience. It has to persuade noncircumstantially; but the politician, in contrast, has already persuaded and does not leave in his writing any traces of the means he used to get it adopted. The politician then puts his name after his partisans: "So-and-so said." Socrates implies that the name of the politician too is part of his writing. The name identifies the wisdom as his. In a nonpolitical writing, it is hard to ensure, as Zeno learned to his cost, that the writer remain attached to his writing (*Parmenides* 128d6–e1). Nonpolitical writings are essentially subject to plagiarism unless the name of their author is woven into them. Nonpolitical writings aspire, it seems, to a legislative status, for unless they become authoritative neither the author nor his text can be guaranteed. The transmission of wisdom as one's own wisdom seems impossible outside the political domain, and the transmission within it cannot be of wisdom if it is to be rational. It is not immediately obvious why the wise, if they are not spuriously wise (i.e., sophists), should want to sign their wisdom. If they put all they know into a single writing, it should make no difference whether it is anonymous or pseudonymous. Only if their wisdom is parceled out over several writings, and necessarily so, would their signature be indispensable. Two or more writings require a single name, but the risk of nonrecognition is thereby increased. The necessary manifold of the beings to be known disperses the singularity of the knower. They are bound in the knower through self-knowledge; they are bound in the reader through a name.

If we suppose, then, that the beings are essentially different, and therefore that they do not admit any presentation of them together before they are presented apart, the single author of their representation must have recourse to stamping them with a unity of another order. We call this order "style"; Phaedrus called it "words" (*rhēmata*). Rhetoric is the necessary means for the display of dialectic, so that the unity of style can keep together in appearance the real unity of self-knowledge.[1] Uniformity of style, however, might be neither attainable nor desirable; Lysias seemed to one ancient critic more

---

1. There is no better example of the problem style poses than Lysias' speech in the *Phaedrus*, for what seems to mark it as Plato's own work is his extravagance in the use of a Lysian trait (cf. P. Shorey, *Classical Philology* [1933], 2: 131–32).

successful than Plato in fusing style and thought (Aulus Gellius 2.5); and the author might have to institutionalize his writings in order to keep them together. He might have to rely on some men who look up to him, so that he can find others who look to him on their way to look at what is past him. It would be close to miraculous if what drew his guardians to him did not repel his rivals. The more deeply, it seems, an author reflects on his self-perpetuation, the more playful to him his writings must become.

# XII
# Horses and Asses

(258d7–260d2)

Socrates asks Phaedrus whether they are to examine about good and bad writing anyone who has written or will ever write a political or private (*idiōtikon*) writing, in meter as a poet or without meter as a nonprofessional or layman (*idiōtēs*). Socrates' contrast between public and private, on the one hand, and poetry and prose, on the other, shows that there have been shifts of meaning over time with which the language has not kept pace. As a poet Plato certainly wrote private political writings without meter; but inasmuch as they were published they were not private, and though they were political they were not political, for he did not offer even the *Laws* for adoption as laws; and despite Plato being a poet he wrote as a nonprofessional. The language does not accommodate Plato. He is as much an innovator within writing as Socrates was a discoverer with his erotic art. Socrates seems to be suggesting how his discovery prepares the way for Plato.

Socrates asks Phaedrus whether they need (*deometha*) to inquire into good and bad writing. The word he uses for "need" Lysias had put at the beginning of his speech, when he had the nonlover say that he did not deserve to miss out on what he needed (*deomai*) because he was not the lover (231a1). Phaedrus falls at once for the apparent sanity and painlessness of need: "Are you asking (*erōtas*) whether we need? For what would anyone live virtually except for pleasures of this kind? Surely not for those things in which there must be a preceding pain or else there is not any pleasure at all; and that is pretty nearly true of all corporeal pleasures, and therefore justly they are called slavish" (258e1–5). Socrates has not won Phaedrus over to philosophy through his second speech, for that speech merely coupled Phaedrus with him for the ascent and argued for the deep attraction Phaedrus felt for his chaster self and the greater weakness of desire in the beloved. Phaedrus would not want to live unless the mind could be pure and free of pain. Phaedrus denies the inseparability of body, soul, and mind through eros. His valetudinarianism is a way of tinkering with the body so as to ensure its noninterference with the mind. Phaedrus must be convinced that he does not make up the illnesses he does his best to forestall. A *malade imaginaire,* Phaedrus is wholly unimaginative. His belief in the purity of mind goes along with his acceptance of the essential sickness of eros. Socrates has tried to show the essential impurity of mind and the naturalness of pain. Phaedrus would rather die if Socrates were right.

Socrates does not respond directly to Phaedrus' reason for living; instead, he tells a story that introduces the question of truth and opinion as ambiguously as the story of Boreas had introduced the question of Socrates' self-knowledge. Socrates had given meaning to monsters like Pegasus through his analysis of the soul and eros; but he had not settled the issue whether monsters are possible, since the hybrids he had argued for were not the offspring of natural generation. Now Socrates tells a story about cicadas, which, like all insects with their segmented bodies and compound eyes, would certainly be called monsters if they were on the supposed scale of Pegasus and Chimaera. Phaedrus does not know the story and has no interest in its truth. The story has no official backing, but it carries a moral. The exhortation it contains more than makes up for its being a fiction. It is enough that it persuades.

The story goes that before the birth of the Muses the cicadas were once men. At their birth and the appearance of song, these men were so overwhelmed by pleasure that while singing they failed to eat and drink; on their death they became cicadas, with the reward that they could sing as soon as they were born and did not have to eat or drink until their death, when they were to report back to the Muses and tell them which men honored which Muse, and in doing so make each man dearer to whichever Muse he emulates. In the case of Phaedrus and Socrates there are two Muses involved, Urania and Calliope, for the former concerns heaven (*ouranos*) and the latter divine and human speeches. Every detail in Socrates' story signals a change in the direction of the dialogue. The Muses had been invoked for Socrates' first speech in favor of the nonlover; but they had been subordinated as a lesser kind of divine madness in his second speech. There Eros had been separated from the Muses and assigned as the link between the Olympian gods and the hyperuranian beings; but now Erato is the Muse concerned with erotic things, and she is separate from Calliope and Urania, or philosophy. To discard eros is to keep philosophy within the visible cosmos; but such a restriction is not all bad. The Muses, whose number cannot but remind us of the number of lives the partial vision of the hyperuranian beings determined, replace the Olympian gods. Socrates lets us know that all we know of the Olympian gods is through the Muses (*Ion* 534c7), whose mouthpiece Hesiod has them say: "We tell lies like the truth, and we know whenever we wish how to tell the truth" (*Theogony* 27–28). The only gods besides Zeus whom Hesiod calls Olympian are the Muses. There were men before there was song; there were men before there was song that mixed in a conscious way truth and falsehood. The Olympian gods were one consequence of this kind of song. Being themselves the illusions of self-ignorance, the Olympian gods made a weak link between human reason and human shape. Human beings became human over time through the Olympian gods of the Muses; but the Muses themselves made those who were enchanted by them directly into cicadas. Song in itself does not suffice to keep one human. It makes one drowsy and enslaved. Only if one resists the enchantment of the cicadas do the Muses reward one. Only if Phaedrus and Socrates continue conversing will they remain disenchanted. The Muses will favor Socrates and Phaedrus only if Phaedrus' nature is overcome.

The *Phaedrus* had almost begun with the disenchantment of a certain kind of rationalism. Another kind of rationalism had then been praised that seemed to require erotic enchantment if the beings were to be comprehended. Now the common source of enchantment, whether erotic or not, is attributed to the Muses, who test through enchantment those who sail past it. If we put together the Olympian gods of Socrates' second speech with the Olympian Muses of the present story, we could say that to succumb to enchantment and to resist enchantment belong together. No disenchantment without enchantment. No discovery of the truth of speeches without the illusion of being. The beauty of speeches cannot be discussed prior to the beauty of being. In putting together in this way the sequence of the *Phaedrus* we are not fully attending to the sequence, in which Phaedrus, whom eros cannot tempt, is an easy victim of the Muses. The cicadas represent what Phaedrus wants to be. He wants to give up the human condition for the sake of speeches. Speeches have no necessity in them; nothing stands in their way. The enchantment of eros, however, is experienced as a compulsion; it forces one to face what is as it draws one to what is not. There is no such compulsion in speech. Speech does not force the issue of self-knowledge. In Socrates' story, the Muses know nothing of men directly.

The *Phaedrus* is concerned with three things—soul, being, and speech. Soul and being were put together in Socrates' second speech but at the expense of speech. Now soul and speech are about to be put together but at the expense of being. Phaedrus' question whether the rhetorician ought to know the really just, good, and beautiful simply denies, in presupposing that the beings can be fully known, the thesis of Socrates' second speech. Phaedrus would have to reformulate his question quite differently if the rhetorician as persuader could not be opposed to the dialectician as knower, but only to a Socrates who knows his own ignorance. Olympian Muses and Olympian gods cannot be in the same myth; or, in nonmythical terms, speeches and beings cannot be together. Their incompatibility can be summed up in the word "likeness" or "image." A lie like the truth seems not to be of the same order as an image of what is. Timaeus seemed to think they were when he proposed to give a likely story (*eikōs muthos*) of the visible cosmos as an image (*eikōn*) of what is (*Timaeus* 29b1–d3); but we do not know whether the likely story is a likeness of the image of the cosmos or of that which the cosmos images. If the speech matched the visible cosmos, we would be able to read off from it the true account; if its mixture of false and true differs from their mixture in the cosmos, Socrates was right to keep being and speech apart. The Eleatic stranger, who sets out to catch the sophist Socrates, does not do any better than Timaeus. He cannot or at any rate does not bring into line his account of speech as the interweaving of species, by means of which the problem of nonbeing is solved, with his definition of speech as the interweaving of noun and verb, by means of which the problem of false speech is solved (*Sophist* 259e5–6, 262b9–c7).

Socrates puts to Phaedrus a difficult question; Phaedrus simplifies it so that it conforms with what he has heard. Socrates' question is: "In order for things to be spoken beautifully and well, must not the speaker's thought, with knowledge of the truth about whatever he is going to say, be there at the start?" Socrates too makes a distinction between thought and words, but it is unclear whether it involves as radical a cut as Phaedrus had made between the discrimination of thought and the persuasiveness of words. Socrates seems to allow for the thought of the speaker not to appear in what is said but merely to guide it, and he certainly allows for the truth to be that full knowledge is unavailable (cf. *Gorgias* 459e6–8). Phaedrus, however, opposes the really just, beautiful, and good things to the opinions the many hold about them, and asks whether the rhetorician has to learn the former as well, since in the case of justice it is the many who decide on the guilt or innocence of a man, and they do so on the basis of their opinions. Phaedrus accepts without question the differences among the kinds of oratory and assigns to each of them its own being. What is said in the courtroom concerns justice, in an assembly the common good, and at a funeral or other gathering the beautiful (cf. *Symposium* 198d3–7). In its classification of speeches, rhetoric insists on the total separability of these three "ideas." A region like the hyperuranian, where it is possible to behold the beautiful apart from the just, seems to be presupposed by rhetoric. As a science, rhetoric must appeal to what really holds and is not just an opinion, even if it only uses in the speeches it writes the opinions of the many. The difference, then, between Socrates' position and rhetoric's is hard to make out. Socrates' "thought of the speaker," which knows the truth, could well be the same as the art of rhetoric, which knows that the just, the beautiful, and the good as they really are ground the species of its own art. One may wonder, however, whether the issue between Socrates and rhetoric does not just turn on the knowability or unknowability of the beings, but at a deeper level on the relations that obtain among the beings themselves. Socrates' omission of the good as a being allowed it to be beyond being, as either the orderer or the order of the beings. The order of the beings would deny that the various species of rhetoric are a proper match to it. Not only would the spoken speeches have to overlap, but they would have to be ordered hierarchically, that is, they would have to be ordered by the good. As the split between Socrates' two speeches, which concerned respectively the good and the beautiful, might be due to a concession made to rhetoric, so the separation between the being of the beautiful and the being of justice, which was indispensable for the vindication of eros in Socrates' second speech, might likewise be dependent on rhetoric's false understanding of itself. Socrates' immediate challenge to rhetoric's claim that it needs to know only the opinions of the many involves the question of the good.

Socrates proposes an examination of what the wise say about rhetoric. Whatever may hold for the opinions of the many, the opinions of the wise lack the authority to enforce our speaking in conformity with them. However successful in its practice, its teaching is subject to review. Socrates quotes three or four words from Homer: "The speech is not to be tossed aside." They are from a speech addressed by Nestor to Agamemnon before the full assembly of the troops at Troy, which Odysseus has just managed to bring under control after Agamemnon disordered them and Thersites incited them to disobey. Nestor spoke as follows: "But, my Lord, you yourself take good counsel and be persuaded by another; the speech is not to be tossed aside, whatever I say: discriminate the men according to tribes, according to clans, Agamemnon, in order that clan help clan, and tribes tribes. If you act in this way and the Achaeans are persuaded by you, then you will get to know who of the chieftains and who of the people are bad and who good; for they will fight on their own for themselves. And you'll come to know whether in fact you will not sack the city by divine commandment or by the baseness of men and their failure to understand war" (*Iliad* 2.360–368). Nestor urges that a classification be made in order to discover the good and the bad, and to settle the question whether the human or the divine is responsible for their failure. Nestor connects the marshaling into kinds with the discovery of the good. The kinds must be known before the good can be known, and the good must be known in order to know the power of the good and what limits its power. Socrates is persuaded by the eloquent Nestor to practice dialectics.

Nestor's proposal is in the midst of a war. Socrates takes up Nestor's proposal by turning back to his image of the soul and asking what difference it makes that his image described a war chariot and not a cart drawn by two asses. He puts to us the question why the soul, which in all its parts was erotic, should assume as a whole the form of spiritedness (*to thumoeides*). His funny question alerts us to the peculiarity in his account of the taming of the black horse, that though the black horse is filled with the strongest possible desire for the beloved, in whom it sees or imagines a god, the ultimate consequence of its desire is fear. Fear of the beautiful gods arises from the forced constraint on the desire for the beautiful gods. This fear of punishment vanishes as soon as the soul resumes its wings. It then fights to get ahead of its rivals and closest to the god it follows in the army of Zeus. Zeus, however, has no Nestor to instruct him. The disarray in the heavenly host seems to be due not only to the absence of the good as an ordering principle either on earth or beyond heaven, but to a failure on Socrates' part to consider the political in its relation to soul. Socrates' departure from the city led him to celebrate the erotic repudiation of the lawful, but it did not free him from the city if war still clung to the soul in an inexplicable manner. What it would have meant to strip the city entirely from the soul is now before us in the absurd image of an ass with wings (cf. Apuleius *Metamorphoses* 11.8). The opinions of the many about the beautiful at least do infect the beautiful.

Socrates asks Phaedrus the following: "Should I persuade you to ward off enemies of war by the acquisition of a horse, and we both should not know horse, but I should happen to know about you that Phaedrus believes the tame animal with the longest ears is a horse; and when I should persuade you in earnest, composing a speech in praise of an ass, calling it a horse and saying the creature is worth everything to have at home and on campaign, useful as it is to fight from and capable besides of carrying baggage and useful in many other respects," then Phaedrus admits it would be altogether ridiculous (260b1–c2).[1] In applying this example to the case of the rhetorician persuading a city, Socrates asks Phaedrus to replace "horse" with

---

1. Antisthenes advised the Athenians to decree asses horses, and when they thought this irrational, he said, "And yet you have generals who know nothing and are only elected" (Diognes Laertius 6.8); cf. D. Daube, "Greek and Roman Reflections on Impossible Laws", *Natural Law Forum* 12 (1967), 5–6.

"good" and "ass" with "bad." It is obvious that a city which acted on this advice would lose the war. In Socrates' example, the horse is as a whole unknown, and the one characteristic believed to be equine is asinine; but the praise is the praise of a horse and not of an ass. In the political application, this would mean that the good is unknown but that which is believed to be a property of the good is a property of the bad, but the praise is of the good. What is praiseworthy, then, is known in the sense that the language of praise is known, but the referent is unknown to such an extent that everything said of the good is true of the bad (and it is equally good for both) except for one attribute, and that attribute pertains to war. Socrates does not say what property of the bad is believed to belong to the good; but if we take his use of the proverb "a shadow of an ass" as a sign of worthlessness, the bad, he would imply, shows up as something worthless in the presumed good for the sake of which there is fierce competition on the part of the ignorant.

It is important to keep in mind, in reflecting on Socrates' example, that there is no known connection between the long ears of the ass and its incapacity to be the animal of choice in warfare. Whatever bad, then, stands in for the good has an irrelevant characteristic that just so happens to be linked necessarily in an unknown way to something useless for the purpose at hand. A conspicuous but neutral property that cannot fail to designate just one thing out of all things recalls the snub nose of the black horse and Socrates. Socrates asks us to consider two things simultaneously. On the one hand, there is the problem of properties and essence in natural beings, in which the accidental must be distinguished from the invariant, and the invariant traced back to its cause; and there is, on the other hand, the problem of logographic necessity, in which nothing is accidental but not everything has the same weight or coheres in a straightforward manner. The ugliness of Socrates could not be more necessary logographically and less inevitable by nature. The meaning of things is not the being of things, for the world is not a book.

Socrates' example shows the need for the most careful discrimination of kinds; but it also suggests that precise discrimination might not be possible in all cases. A he-ass and a mare generate a mule (as a she-ass and a stallion a hinny), and the mule borrows traits from both its parents and combines them into its own sterile form. The mule already answers Socrates' question about the possibility of natural monsters. It is a sterile hybrid that cannot be deduced from the separate kinds that are its makeup. Just as heroes are not necessary if there are gods and men (*Apology of Socrates* 27d5–28c1; Herodotus 2.143.4), so the mule is a fact that defies the speciation of things. The mule can stand no less for the cosmological problem Socrates avoided—how the self-motion of soul is related to becoming—than for the hybrid the soul itself seems to be. Insofar as Socrates' ignorance of himself turns on the nature of the composition of soul, the ass would be, in his example, the bad element in soul that has been mistaken for the good. It would be a false god. The ass indeed is the symbol of the evil Egyptian god Set, who was identified with Typhon (Plutarch *On Isis and Osiris* 49–50 [371] ). The mule, however, undercuts the opposition of black and white, and allows for whatever is Typhonic in Socrates to be at one with whatever is divine. Socrates' white horse now looks once more as if it were a poetic separation from the original black. Socrates' ghost of a suggestion throws a curious light at any rate on Herodotus' claim that Homer and Hesiod made most of the Greek pantheon out of Egyptian gods (2.53.1–2).[2]

2. Ovid captures the transformation perfectly when he tells the story of the contest between the Pierides and the Muses, in which the former sing the Egyptian story of Typhon and the Muses the Greek (*Metamorphoses* 5.318–358). The Pierides are sometimes the same as the Muses.

# XIII
# The Art of Speeches

(260d3–262c4)

Socrates' argument gives a privileged position to the good, for an error about it shows up on the battlefield or elsewhere, whereas a consistent departure from the truth in the case of the just and the beautiful (or morality) does not apparently have any consequences for which a city must pay; otherwise, systems of law and convention would shatter at once in face of the real (cf. *Theaetetus* 172a1–b6). Surprisingly, Socrates is not satisfied with his own argument; he wonders whether the art of speeches does not have a defense. The issue now is whether the art of rhetoric can be an art if it is not the same as knowledge of the truth. Rhetoric advises that one learn the truth first, but she cannot compel one to learn it, for rhetoric is an art by itself without which it is impossible to persuade even if one knows the beings. Rhetoric denies that knowledge of the beings includes knowledge of the nonbeings of opinion. Knowledge of truth does not comprehend knowledge of error.

The power of rhetoric does not consist in her bare claim that the knower of the beings will fail to persuade without her, but in the very personification of rhetoric Socrates now employs, and in light of which Phaedrus asks: "Won't she, if she says this, be speaking justly?" One has the sense that, had Socrates phrased the question neutrally, Phaedrus would have asked, "Isn't it true?" or "Isn't there a point in this?" The indignation in Socrates' animation seems to prompt Phaedrus' response in terms of justice. However this may be, rhetoric is asking how the effectiveness of her defense draws any support from the knowledge of the beings. Socrates counters rhetoric with an animation of her critics; these critics are speeches who deny rhetoric is an art, and whom Socrates addresses as noble creatures with beautiful children (261a3).[1] These speeches ask Phaedrus whether the rhetorical art must not be a leading of the soul through speeches, regardless of whether they are spoken in court and other public assemblies or in private, and about big or small matters, with the art itself indifferent whether the matters are serious or trivial. Phaedrus

---

1. If one punctuates after *kallipaida te* and not before.

believes that the scope of rhetoric as an art does not extend beyond forensic and deliberative speeches, at least to the extent that there are writings about pleadings in court and some talk as well about public addresses. Phaedrus prefaces his speech with an oath, "No, by Zeus" (261b3). He backs up his belief with an oath, but he is unaware of the psychagogic element in his oath. He believes in the rhetorically neutral character of ordinary conversation and is unaware that the relation between the gods and the beings, which Socrates outlined in his second speech, holds the key to the art of rhetoric.

Socrates had made an elaborate speech, filled with gods and divine things, and designed to turn Lysias to philosophy; but now Socrates addresses speeches, which he himself has ensouled, to persuade Phaedrus that unless he is competent in philosophy he will not be a competent speaker about anything (261a3–5). Rhetoric is no longer to be abandoned in favor of philosophy; it is merely to be subordinated to philosophy; and this lesser goal, which consequently requires a knowledge of the beings superior to what the simple conversion to philosophy required, is to be achieved by speeches endowed with all the life the gods had earlier shared with the souls of men. The gods could not be bothered with men on their upward flight; but now speeches condescend to instruct Phaedrus. Their first question involves the literalization of a noun (*psukhagōgia*), whose verbal equivalent had long been used to characterize the magical practices by means of which the dead are raised (*psukhagōgein*). Persuasion is presented in terms of necromancy. Ascent is no longer from earth to the uranian and hyperuranian but from Hades to earth. The body in such an ascent is a phantom image, and the soul is appealed to directly without encumbrances. Will Socrates' psychagogy too meet with no obstacles, and its speeches be as unlimited in their power? One wonders at any rate how far from necromancy Socrates' psychagogy can be when the assumption of necromancy, that there can be living beings without body, still adheres to Socrates' psychagogy, insofar as he employs the rhetorical device of personification. Rhetoric seems to be just as much an attenuated version of superstitions as the Olympian gods are refined and beautified fictions of more primitive deities. Rhetoric still resists its incorporation into philosophy.

In order to comprehend forensic and deliberative rhetoric within a single science of speech, Socrates hides Gorgias and Thrasymachus behind the masks of Nestor and Odysseus, so that Palamedes can stand in for Zeno, who could by art make appear the same things as alike and unlike, one and many, at rest and in motion (261d6–8). Phaedrus easily sees through the likenesses of Gorgias and Thrasymachus, but Palamedes baffles him. Perhaps what distracts him is the story that Odysseus' unjust accusation of Palamedes led to his death. If the comprehensive art is Palamedean, it is not capable of defending itself against its own forensic arm, and rhetoric is vindicated in the very image that was meant to put her in her place. Callicles' argument against Socrates is lurking in the fate of Palamedes. Perhaps the weakness in Zeno's art was due to the Parmenidean One which it wanted to defend, and the manifold of beings limits the possibility of a universal art. Socrates seems to hint at this weakness when he says that the art of assimilating anything to anything must stay within the feasible.

The art of persuasion is the art of incremental deformation; it knows how to deviate from what is, little by little, so that what finally appears looks like what is but is its opposite; and it likewise knows how to protect one against another trying to deceive in the same way. Socrates says of the art that it brings into the light (*eis phōs agein*) the hiding of things through likenesses; but he also says that the art makes the same things come to light (*phainesthai*) as either like or unlike. The light in which things come to light is different from the light in which things come to light hiddenly. Socrates does not explain this difference; but the difference is important because he tells Phaedrus, when he asks how the art of contradiction works, "I imagine it will come to light (*phaneisthai*) if we examine it in the following way" (261e6). By 262c4, Phaedrus has been convinced that "knowledge" of opinions by itself will make rhetoric artless. In fifty exchanges, which begin at 259e7, Phaedrus has been incrementally turned around to believe the contrary of what he has heard, that the rhetorician does not have to know the truth. Phaedrus has submitted to the very art of speaking Socrates is talking about; but his conversion has not been accompanied by any understanding of his conversion. Indeed, it is difficult to conceive how anyone could understand anything if understanding of the way of the understanding had to coincide with the understanding. It seems to follow, then, that motion in thought is incompatible with self-knowledge, and therefore philosophy, which cannot be philosophy unless it can combine self-knowledge and knowledge, is impossible. We might now want to say that the division in the *Phaedrus* itself, which looked at first simply as that between rhetoric and dialectic, is that between self-knowledge and knowledge, which are thereby shown not to coalesce. The argument, however, which now turns Phaedrus around, assumes the truth is known, and Socrates' second speech argues for philosophy precisely because the truth is unknown. Self-knowledge, then, seems to be possible if one does not presuppose knowledge; but it then becomes unclear how an art of speaking is possible if it cannot start from what is and gradually deform it. Were

Socrates' argument now straightforward, it would have an unfortunate consequence. Since it is self-evident that knowledge of the truth is necessary if one is to proceed from what is not to what is, Socrates' proposal to find how in his two speeches the conversion from one position to its opposite was made by art would amount to asserting that his second speech was false and the first true. The absorption of the art of Odysseus and Nestor into the art of Palamedes cannot be as simple as Socrates makes it out to be. Rhetoric has not yet lost its independence.

Rhetoric would seem to be able to claim that the art of incremental deformation can be practiced simply on the basis of the manifold of opinions, and the skill of the rhetorician consists in arranging a series of opinions in a proper order (fig. 27). Socrates' counterargument seems to be that this series of opinions cannot be ordered properly without a knowledge of the sequence of likenesses among the beings (fig. 28). Likeness$_c$ shades off into likeness$_p$, whereas likeness$_a$, though it has a match in likeness$_r$, is too gross to deceive anyone into taking Being$_1$ for Being$_2$. Likeness$_a$, however, looks as if it corresponds in figure 27 to the dodecagon Opinion$_2$, and likeness$_c$ to the hexagon Opinion$_4$. The opinion series and the likeness series, therefore, seem equally effective if one is to deceive; but if one is not to be deceived, knowledge of the beings in their essential differences and phenomenal resemblances is necessary. The art of speaking Socrates proposes would be essentially a defensive art. As a defensive art, it is bound up with self-knowledge, for the slippery slope of deviant likenesses is greased by self-ignorance. Once, however, self-ignorance is factored in as the perspective in light of which an opinion is accepted, then neither the knowledge of opinion nor knowledge of truth suffices; but now there is a third element that links the two sequences (fig. 29). Rhetoric, then, cannot arrange the sequence of opinions correctly because of its ignorance of soul-types. The new situation, however, parallels that which Socrates presented in his second speech, where the being-likeness series was the species of things as they are given to

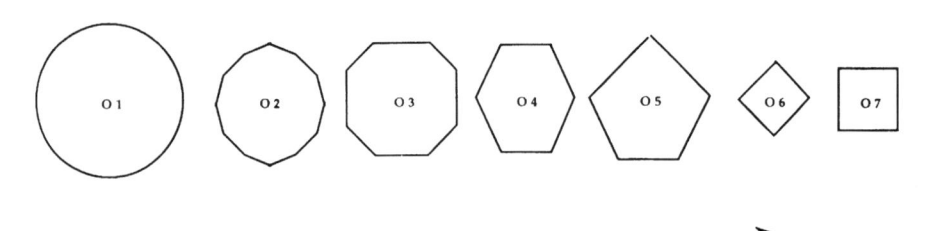

Figure 27

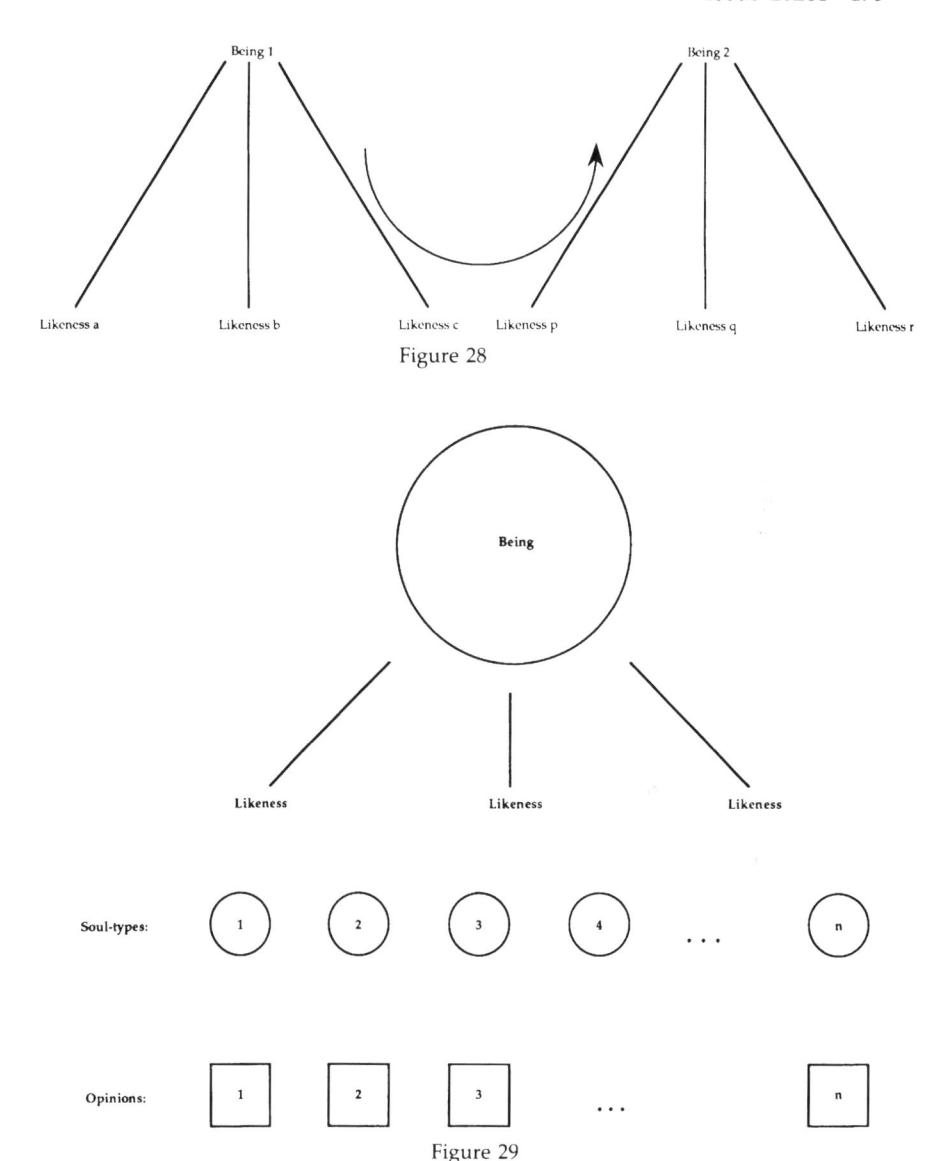

![Figure 28: Two peaks labeled Being 1 and Being 2, each with likenesses beneath them (Likeness a, b, c, p for Being 1; Likeness q, r for Being 2), with a curved arrow from between Likeness c and p pointing up toward Being 2.]

Figure 28

![Figure 29: A circle labeled Being with three lines descending to three items labeled Likeness. Below are soul-types numbered 1, 2, 3, 4, ..., n as circles, and opinions numbered 1, 2, 3, ..., n as squares.]

Figure 29

us in speech, and without the understanding of which one could not be a human being. It is clear that the opinion series is not the same as the likeness series, for the gods are among the opinions and are not images of beings (246c6–d3).

That the truth needs to be known in order for the proper sequence of likenesses to be set up now admits of the following proof. It was misleading to give in figure 27 such a sequence of opinions; rather, the connections among opinions are not determined by opinions; opinions appear apart from one another and cannot be ordered doxastically. Only through a casual science can the inner connection of disjoint opinions be confirmed so that it becomes possible to glide from one opinion to another on the basis of an understanding of their unitary origin. The resemblance exists only through knowledge of the being and not through opinion by itself. The soul-types interfere with and disarrange the ontological-likeness series in so fundamental a manner that any speech that tries to stick to the opinion series will become as incoherent and fragmentary as the opinion series itself. Lysias' speech is the paradigm of such incoherence and disunity.

# XIV
# Lysias and Socrates Examined

(262c5–266c1)

By a kind of chance, Socrates says, a pair of speeches (*logō*) was spoken that exemplify how the knower of truth would lead astray his listeners. The dual of "speech" (*logō*) seems at first to refer to Lysias' speech and Socrates' own two speeches counted as one; but Socrates' very next sentence, in which he charges the gods of the place and the cicadas for the artfulness of the speeches, implies that the pair of speeches are his first and second speeches which moved from the blame to the praise of eros (265c5–6). The dual, however, is then somewhat unsuitable, for his two speeches must be one if they are to illustrate the gradual transition from one thesis to its opposite. The instability in the counting of the speeches seems to make Socrates' distinction between the noncontroversial and the controversial more doubtful than it ought to be. Socrates distinguishes between iron and silver, on the one hand, and the just and good, on the other. What men disagree about is subject to greater manipulation and deceit than anything whose name brings the same thing to mind in everyone. If this distinction between justice and silver is applied to the notion that deception most easily occurs when one deviates gradually from one thing to its opposite, then the highest rhetorical skill would lie in moving either something noncontroversial into the controversial or something controversial into the noncontroversial by means of a series of likenesses. The latter kind of movement often happens in poetry, where, for example, the just ceases to be controversial at the very moment the poet speaks of the golden age (cf. *Cratylus* 398a4–6). In general, names that are noncontroversial—"Rose is a rose is a rose"—tend to supply images for what is controversial: "My love is like a red, red rose." As for the contrary movement, when one casts doubt on the noncontroversial, we have an example in Socrates' first speech, in which justice and moderation were shown to be the products of the greatest injustice and wantonness. Since Lysias had started with the indisputable goodness of moderation and sanity, Socrates' first speech, which apparently took the same premise, was essential for laying the groundwork for the praise of divine madness. It would therefore follow that the dual Socrates uses for the pair of speeches spoken by chance does refer after all to Lysias' speech as one of the two. Socrates' first speech, which focuses on the good, functions retrospectively as the deviant image of the just, with which Lysias was exclusively concerned, and prospectively as the deviant image of the beautiful, which underlies the praise of madness. By showing the ugliness of moderation, Socrates' first speech vindicates the beautiful in itself.

Socrates seems to argue that the controversial, of which eros is one, can be handled by stating outright what it is and deducing everything from the definition, as he did at the start of his first speech. Even if one grants that everything Socrates says is consistent with his definition, it is hard to see how eros ceases to be controversial. His criticism of the opening of Lysias' speech, that it lacked a definition of eros, is connected with the rambling character of Lysias' whole speech which Socrates also criticizes; but it is really because Lysias does define eros implicitly that he ruins his speech. Socrates first stops Phaedrus at the words "That they regret" (262e4); but in the second recital he lets him add, "whatever benefits they bestowed when they have ceased from their desire" (264a2–3). Love, then, according to Lysias, is sexual desire for some human being accompanied by beneficence. The definition is widely accepted and noncontroversial. So Lysias' mistake was not in failing to define eros but in letting his principle be identical with what the nonlover must admit holds for himself. Lysias defeated himself in two ways. First, the nonlover was simply the lover in disguise, as Socrates had supposed at the beginning of his first speech; second, if eros is to be blamed it is necessary for it to be presented as controversial if one is going to argue so paradoxical a position as Lysias had. One cannot rely entirely on opinion if one is out to subvert opinion. There has to be argument and not a collection of observations.

What Socrates calls logographic necessity, in conformity with which each item in a speech follows close upon its predecessor, is connected with his likening a speech to an animal, with its own body, so as not to be either headless or footless, but its middle and extremities to have been written to fit one another and the whole (264c2–5). The introduction of the likeness produces a slide from a temporal structure to a formal structure of whole and parts. That a speech is a living whole can emerge only after one has read it through; that a speech is "logical" can be judged while one is reading it. It would be surprising if these two different perspectives coincided at all times and throughout all the parts of a speech. What does not fit in the temporal reading might well belong to the whole, and what does fit in the temporal reading might not fit in the same way in light of the whole. Socrates phrases his description in such a way that he makes it evident that the whole is not written; what is written are the parts. These parts form a speech that is not spoken. If the animal Socrates has in mind is a dialogue, the unspoken speech is a monster. The unspoken speech has a head; the head, if the likeness holds, should signify the beginning of the speech; but to put a head on a speech means proverbially to complete it and thus corresponds to what Socrates calls the foot (*Gorgias* 505d1). If, then, one tries to put together the temporal order of speaking and reading with the synoptic order, the temporal order becomes the life of the animal. As a living being the speech changes, and changes as the reader goes through it. The reader must be the animator of the speech.

Socrates contrasts the perfect writing with the epigram on Midas' tomb:

A bronze maiden am I; I have been set up on the tomb of Midas.
As long as water flows and tall trees flourish,
Remaining at this very spot on the much-lamented tomb,
I shall report to passersby that Midas has been buried here.

A nonliving being speaks, shaped in the likeness of a living being; it utters a speech about a nonliving being as if he were not nonliving. The speech itself is without any temporal order; any line can be put before or after any other. Its indifference to temporal order seems to be at one with its speaking of eternity. Like Lysias' speech, it can be written but not spoken by anyone. The speech of the girl is random; the image of the girl is lifeless. The juxtaposition of the two points to the difficulty of putting them together. No tinkering with the syntax, though it may impose a necessity on the sequence, would make the utterance a whole. It cannot be a whole unless it can be the utterance of the girl, and it cannot be her utterance unless she is alive. Socrates' insistence that the truth must be known for persuasion now looks quite different. To know the truth is to know what is impossible for human life. It is to have self-knowledge.

Socrates claims for his own two speeches a certain plausibility in proceeding from an argument in favor of the nonlover to one in favor of the lover. His attempt, however, at making his two speeches consistent seems to break down. The definition of eros in his first speech is combinable, he claims, with his second speech if a distinction is made between human and divine madness, the former of which is a disease and the latter a release from the lawful and customary (265a9–11).[1] Socrates seems to have in mind a scheme like the one in

---

1. Socrates first hints at the instability of classification by citing a line from Pindar's *Isthmian* I (227b9–10), for in that poem Pindar yokes together two poems, one in celebration of a Theban charioteer and one in celebration of Apollo at Ceos (6). The forced pairing of man and god occasions a succession of unstable pairings and separations throughout the poem.

178   Lysias and Socrates Examined

figure 30. At first glance, it seems impossible to map erotic hubris onto the black horse, for one is human and the other divine; but the black horse splits between a tamed and an untamed version, and the tamed is controlled by terror before the beautiful gods. Socrates' second speech acknowledges the need for force as well as opinion, but the first speech is much more idealistic and believes that opinion by itself can prevail. If this is correct, it is necessary to incorporate Socrates' first speech into his second speech and observe the difference between a part apart from and a part as a part of a whole.

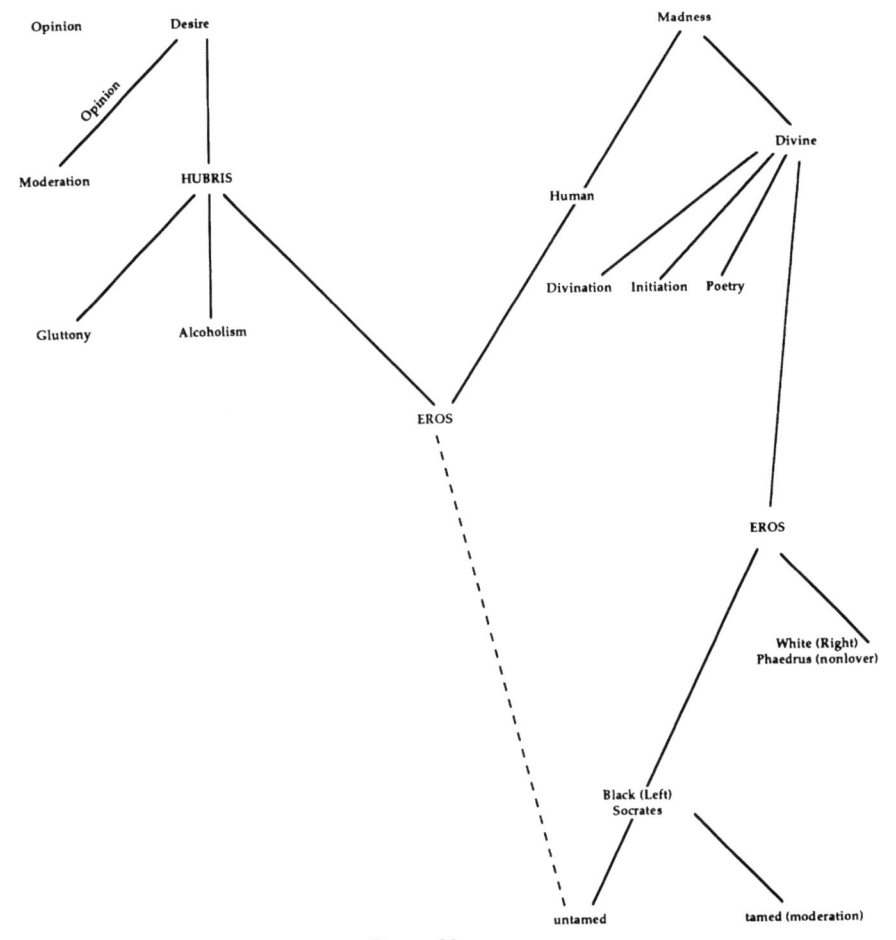

Figure 30

The two speeches exemplify two species of procedure. One is to take a synoptic view and gather into one kind (*idea*) widely scattered things, so that by defining each thing one may make evident whatever one wants to teach. This is the way of Socrates' first speech. The other species is to be able to cut according to species at their natural joints and not break off any part in the manner of a bad butcher; "but just as lately the two speeches (dual) took in common the folly of thought (*dianoia*) as some one species, but just as in the case of the body, there are double and homonymous parts by nature, [one] the left (*skaia*),[2] the other called the right (*dexia*), so too the two speeches (dual), in the belief that the natural species of aberrant mind is one, one speech, constantly cutting the part to the left, did not let up its cutting until it found in them an eros called left (*skaios*) and reproached it rightly, and the other speech brought us to the right of madness, and found there in turn an eros homonymous with the former but divine, and having held it out praised it as the cause of the greatest possible good for us" (265e1–266b1).

Socrates' speech exemplifies the analytic way. It includes Socrates' first speech by letting the whole of it be the right side of a single speech with bilateral symmetry. Its right side is the pseudo-moderation of the first speech as a whole. It is the projection of the left or black side. It therefore only appears as "right" to Phaedrus, who in facing Socrates must reverse his right and left if he is unaware that he is looking into a mirror. The two speeches side by side look like the illustration in figure 31.

Socrates gives a double presentation of his first speech and a single presentation of his second speech, since the second speech shows the first speech in its transformation from a speech of logographic necessity (i.e., of a temporal order) into a speech as part of a living whole. The first speech was given by the black/left horse and heard by Phaedrus as the white/right horse, and, as we know from the story of the cicadas, Phaedrus himself has or believes that he has no black/left horse. A second speech was then given by the black/left horse, which presented itself as both itself and the white/right horse, but in this presentation it still shows up for Phaedrus as the white horse. There is no other Platonic dialogue, I suspect, in which what must occur of necessity in every dialogue is shown to us in its logico-temporal and periagogic modes. The logico-temporal mode is didactic and synoptic;

---

2. Socrates omits the particle *men* as well as the article with "left"; the full expression would have been *ta men skaia, ta de dexia*. He thus calls attention to the possibility that "left" may also be "right" by nature if not by name. Every cut on the left branch makes a right, and every cut on the right a left. There is a similar ambiguity about right and left at Aeschylus *PV* 489–90.

180   Lysias and Socrates Examined

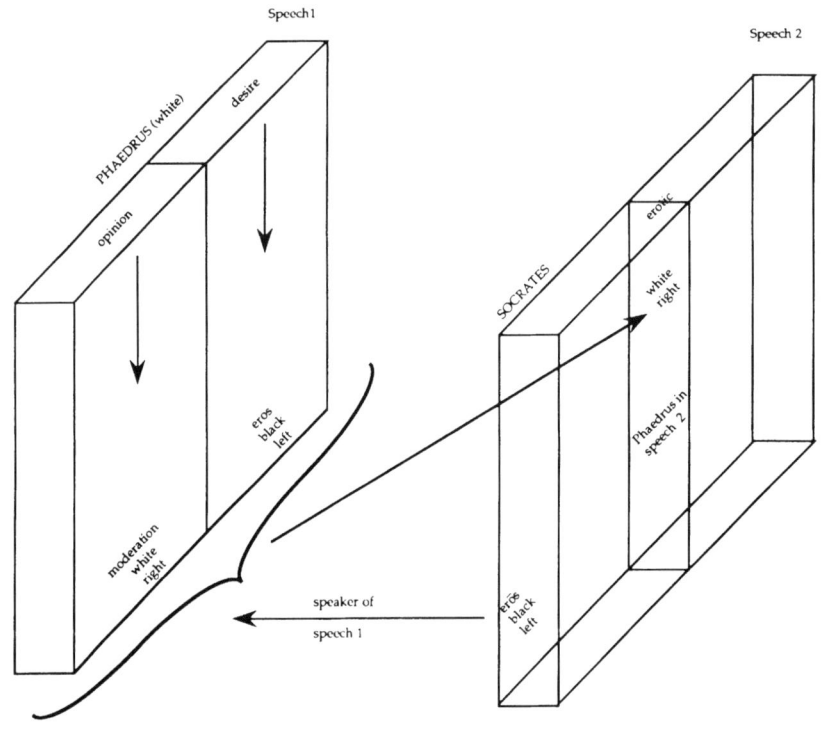

Figure 31

the periagogic mode is zetetic and analytic. The synoptic mode, however, is in fact a fragmentation of a whole into a pseudo-whole, and the analytic mode is the unification of parts into a whole.

Socrates says he is a lover of divisions and collections, in order that he may speak and think; and if he believes anyone else is capable of seeing the unity and the manifold of things as they are by nature, he pursues him "behind in his footsteps as if of a god." We have just seen Socrates practicing his love as he pursued Lysias' book into the country. The book was the carrot Phaedrus held in front of him (230d6–e1). The book affirmed the indisputable right of indifference of the beloved. It set the problem which Socrates side by side with Phaedrus tried to solve. The solution involved the displacement of the problem into a pseudo-solution that drew Phaedrus the beloved to Phaedrus the ideal. This displacement let the problem come to light as a problem. The true outline of the problem is whatever is not contained in the pseudo-solution. The pseudo-solution is the Platonic dialogue in itself, that is, Phaedrus as the white horse; the true problem is what lies outside the *Phaedrus,* or the hyperuranian. The pseudo-solution is fed by the hyperuranian; it is not an answer to a totally spurious question. The discovery of the true question requires the determination of the refractive index of the pseudo-solution. The refractive index is determined by Socrates' relation to his interlocutor. It is a relation Socrates establishes on the basis of his knowledge of himself and the other. Every dialogue displays the greatest self-restraint on Socrates' part in order that the zetetic may be paired with the didactic. There cannot be any discrimination of things unless there is communication, and there cannot be perfect discrimination if there is communication. Socrates calls those who can juggle discrimination with communication dialecticians. They are those who converse in the middle voice (*dialegesthai*) as they discriminate in the active (*dialegein*).[3]

---

3. Cf. Xenophon *Memorabilia* 4.5.12: "[Socrates] said that *dialegesthai* is named from the fact that people come together and deliberate in common by dividing (*dialegontas*) the matters of interest (*ta pragmata*) by kinds (*kata genē*)." Xenophon, by following this remark almost immediately with the assertion that Socrates never ceased to examine what each of the beings (*ta onta*) is with his companions (4.6.1), indicates his awareness of the difficulty of keeping together the good as one's own interest with the beings as they are in themselves.

# XV
# Rhetoric

(266c1–274b4)

Socrates' highly condensed account of his two speeches convinces Phaedrus that they exemplified dialectic; but without self-knowledge Phaedrus cannot see that dialectic is rhetoric as well, and nothing that is susceptible to science has been omitted. Phaedrus' failure to know himself leads to Socrates sketching an art of rhetoric that is formally independent of his practice. A sign of this difference is the mention of Anaxagoras, who attempted to solve the problem of causation through mind (270a4); and we know that Socrates turned away from any teleological physics because he thought Anaxagoras had failed to establish it, and there were insuperable difficulties besides (*Phaedo* 96a6–100b3). On the basis of the *Phaedrus* we could say that Socrates reflected on a new kind of causation, persuasion, which was unlike any known efficient causation and was not rational; and he certainly was not as speculative as Timaeus, who claimed he discerned on a cosmic scale the persuasion of necessity. The weak cosmological links Socrates' account of soul had allowed are enough to show that he did not know how to proceed from a human psychology, in which the effect of speech on soul was studied, to a comprehensive physics. There was, however, a compensation for the abandonment of cosmology. It was the opening up of the hyperuranian in the lowly collection and division of species.[1] This opening up is about to be closed off. It cannot survive the allowance for a science apart from philosophy, for philosophy is not a science.

There seem to be three topics of rhetoric: likeness-making, passion-making, and parts of speech. The first, Socrates had already argued, depends on knowledge of the truth; the second must be grounded in a psychology; but the third, which alone seems to have been touched upon by the rhetoricians themselves, seems to be a puzzling addition. The rhetoricians show a confused awareness of the difference and inner connection between logographic necessity and a speech as a

---

1. Apuleius has Psyche (Soul), after she has been abandoned by Amor (Eros), discover in her wanderings the scattered tools of peasants before the temple of Ceres, and he has her proceed to separate and collect them by kinds (*Metamorphoses* 6.1). When Psyche is apart from Amor, she is in love, as Pan points out to her (5.25).

whole. There are terms for the beginning and end of a speech, but none for the middle (266d7–8, 267d3–4); and there are devices, on the one hand, for presenting arguments and evidence, and ways, on the other, for stirring and soothing anger, but none for putting the two of them together. Rhetoric has figured out artlessly the preliminaries to the art, but it knows nothing of the art itself.

For the discovery of those elements Socrates appeals to the arts of medicine and tragedy. These arts split between them the notion of logographic necessity and of whole and part. Phaedrus sees at once that the knowledge of how drugs work does not alone make one a physician; in addition one must know to whom they are to be given and when and how much. He likewise grants that the knowledge of how to make long or short speeches, which either awaken pity or terrify and threaten, does not alone make one a tragic poet; one has to know in addition—and here Phaedrus echoes Socrates in his phrasing—the arrangement of speeches which fit one another and the whole (268a8–d5; cf. 264c5). This double account matches fairly well Socrates' original formulation, but it differs in two decisive respects. Health and strength replace the beautiful, and the perfectly composed speech is, like a tragedy, an imitation. Although it would have been possible for Phaedrus to fault the pharmacist's apprentice for his ignorance of the nature of body as a whole of parts as well as for untimely applications, Phaedrus does not recognize anything but the natural sickliness of body and its artful healing. Accordingly, when the body returns as the model for the soul (just as its bilateral symmetry had served for the articulation of soul in Socrates' two speeches), the drugs and nourishment to be applied to soul prove to be lawful speeches and practices (270b4–9). Justice and law are restored to rhetoric, but it is justice no longer fueled by anger and indignation. Whereas Thrasymachus knew how to arouse pity and was skilled in angering and soothing (267d1), the preliminaries of tragedy include speeches that provoke pity and fear, but the best tragedians are too civilized to express anger (268d6–e2, 269b1–5). In Socrates' myth, the soul was a war chariot as a whole and erotic in all its parts; but now that we are on earth again the soul can be sick or well but neither rivalrous nor beautiful. Harshness and the need for harshness are known to myth and dialectic; they are not known to speech and rhetoric. The white horse now stands alone, and both its origin and what it really is are forgotten. Socrates gives Phaedrus what he wants and unyokes him.

That Pericles dragged Anaxagorean doctrine into the art of speeches introduces an ambiguity into Socrates' assertion that the nature of the soul cannot be grasped adequately "without the nature of the whole"

(270c2). Socrates seems to imply that a strict deduction can be made from Anaxagoras' cosmology to Periclean rhetoric; but Anaxagoras spoke of mind and not soul, and "dragged" certainly suggests that there was something forced in the deduction. If, moreover, one heard the phrase "without the nature of the whole" in a discussion of the soul's nature, one might suppose that the whole referred to was the animal which body and soul make up (cf. *Charmides* 156b6–157d3). Neither Socrates' myth nor Socrates' outline of his second speech lets one forget that body and soul are together; but now Socrates' proposal for a rhetorical science is silent about body as well as about its possible cosmological implications. Socrates leaves it up in the air whether this science will find soul to be polymorphic or not; but if it turns out to have several species, Socrates does not say that one has to discover what makes the soul a whole (270d1–7). For each species the same question is put as for the soul if it were one—what power it has to affect or be affected. There is, moreover, another question about the species of soul. Not only is the structure of soul at issue, but also the number and kinds of souls (271d1–3). In Socrates' myth, souls had shown up as both nine and eleven in number; and though Anaxagorean mind could possibly handle the ninefold division of talents, the eleven types of erotic soul are beyond its grasp. It was, however, the erotic soul that raised the question of the soul as a whole, for the completion of soul was the principal aim of eros. Rhetoric, then, in its independence from dialectic is independent of the erotic science of Socrates, without which the problem of the whole cannot be adequately posed, let alone resolved.

When Socrates is about to summarize the nature of rhetoric, he reminds us of Phaedrus' distinction between words and thought. He cannot, he says, give the words themselves for a written treatise on rhetoric, but he can give the distinctions it must have comprehended (271c6–8). The problem of writing, which had been long held in abeyance, returns on the level of science. It had originally been posed in terms of politics and the framing of a law code. A treatise on rhetoric would be a manual for legislators: given the nature of the citizens, what kind of persuasive speeches can one give to win them over to whatever regime one wants (cf. 270b8). This treatise would be neutral to vice or virtue and could be employed as easily by the corrupter as by the educator of his people. Socrates' first speech by itself is a sample from just such a treatise. One wonders, then, whether there is anything that either checks the development of such an instrument of tyranny or prevents it from being published in a book. It seemed at first that if something was scientific, it could be written; but now we want something scientific to be unpublishable. The solution apparently could not simply be that a rhetorical science is impossible, for Socrates' proposal to match up kinds of souls with kinds of speeches has nothing fantastical about it, however difficult it might be to be truly comprehensive and precise; and to assume, on the other hand, that anyone capable of the task would necessarily be benevolent is altogether wishful. If rhetoric were still tied in with dialectic, as it had been in Socrates' account of what he does, the danger would not exist. Philosophy could not be bothered with the earthly in its pursuit of the hyperuranian.

The possible threat a morally neutral rhetoric poses might seem to be thwarted by a simple consideration. Even though Socrates starts out as if he were outlining a written treatise (271c6–8), in which the causes would be given why certain kinds of men are susceptible or not to certain kinds of speeches (271d2–7), he goes on to say that once one had understood all this, one would have to observe it in actions and be able to recognize someone who was present as a certain type and nature to whom certain speeches would be applicable; and once one had mastered this, the proper occasions for speaking and silence would have to be learned, along with the various kinds of speeches and their appropriateness and inappropriateness on any occasion (271d7–272a8). One could suppose therefore that Socrates' shift from theory to practice, as we would say, obviates the risk, since, it seems, the experience which is needed to make the theory work cannot be in a book. This is certainly Phaedrus' view (268c2–4). The theoretician of speech and soul necessarily stands apart from the wise man on the spot. Socrates, however, does not accept such a distinction; he speaks of the theory and the practice as one finished art, and he seems to be indifferent as to whether it is spoken or written (272b1).

We ourselves, moreover, have to recognize Plato as the one who put together the same combination of theory and practice in his representation of Socrates; indeed, the *Phaedrus* itself exhibits in its two parts the separation and the join of theory and practice. In what way, then, does the Socrates of Plato differ from the treatise Socrates seems to propose? First, as a representation it elevates the circumstantial to the necessary and veils the very measure of the mean it pretends to display. Second, it is geared solely to philosophy and resists its political abuse. Plato's resistance, however, seems an inadequate defense against the more unscrupulous and no less gifted. What necessarily bars the way to Socrates' proposal? After all it seems not too difficult to put in a warning that there is more chance in the world than any treatise can handle adequately. Any science, if it has a practical side, has to issue the same warning; but that would not prevent it from offering samples from real life, however heavily edited they would have to be. The real obstacle to such a rhetoric is its impossibility, for it is a premise of this would-be science that any speech must conform to the kind of soul which is going to hear it (270e3; cf. 269d4); but as written it cannot comply with its own premise unless its speeches discriminate among its readers. A published treatise of this kind would in a decisive sense be unpublished (cf. Aulus Gellius 20.5.9–12). It is possible to straddle philosophy and rhetoric, as Phaedrus has done at least up to now; and it is possible to cut free of philosophy, as Socrates predicts Isocrates may do; but it is impossible to turn a philosophic rhetoric against itself. It is protected by self-knowledge.

Socrates has so far been silent about the beings about which rhetoric speaks. The discussion had begun with the question of writing, and it will soon end with it; and as the second topic had been truth and opinion, so Socrates brings it back again through an objection of Teisias. If, he says, someone weak and manly strikes a strong and cowardly man, and steals his cloak or anything else, neither ought to tell the truth in court; but the coward must say that he was not struck by one man alone, and the brave that they were alone and, "How could I, being the sort I am, have attacked him who is the sort he is?" Teisias' objection is absurd, since he unwittingly assumes that the speaker knows the truth either about himself if he pleads or prosecutes his own case or about the plaintiff or defendant if he is the hired gun. Teisias takes for granted the difference between the appearance of body and the hiddenness of soul; but it could happen that the body hides its weakness or its strength and the soul reveals itself in an expression or a gesture. Teisias, however, does seem to have a point. Granted that the probable (*ta eikota*) are nothing but the manifold of the likenesses of beings crossed with the natures of souls, so that in Teisias' example the weak is a likeness of the cowardly and the strong of the manly, how would one make the just prevail? Teisias' example brings about an impasse between justice and injustice, and Socrates seems to admit that the knowledge of the deformation truth undergoes in opinion includes the knowledge that no rhetoric is powerful enough to have its own way on every occasion. Knowledge of beings and souls limits the Gorgianic dream of a comprehensive rhetorical power. Only if Gorgianic rhetoric restricts itself to speeches apart from beings and souls can it pretend to do what it cannot. Lysias' speech was a test case. It claimed that it could have the same effect as a lover's speech without any knowledge of eros or of soul. As a consequence of this ignorance, the speech could neither be spoken by anyone nor addressed to anyone, and the nonlover could not be distinguished from the lover.

# XVI
## An Egyptian Story

(274b6–278b6)

The fact of written legislation had made writing in itself neutral and left open the question whether writing could ever be beautiful regardless of how beautifully written the laws were. Socrates' second speech decided this issue, insofar as it praised erotic possession as superior to any sobriety and sanity the laws can induce. Socrates' criticism of writing, then, recapitulates this point, but it does so without any evident appeal to eros or even to philosophy, for in his summary of what makes a speech or writing artful, Socrates assumes, as he had throughout the second part, that the beings are fully known (277b5–c6). Indeed, philosophy returns in the summary about writing, where Socrates implies that the truth the philosophic writer knows is his ignorance of the beings (278c4–d6). Although Socrates distinguishes between human and divine concerns, in his preface to the discussion of writing (273e5–274a2, b9–10), the gods he cites are not the beautiful Olympian gods but the Egyptian gods Theuth and Thamoun (or Ammon). These gods are inconceivable as the objects of eros, and Thamoun was ruling over all of Egypt from Thebes. Herodotus tells us that the Egyptians knew of no god in human shape in 11,340 years, but they said gods had ruled in Egypt and dwelt with men before this time, and the last god to rule was Typhon (2.142–144). We are to imagine, then, a time when gods ruled men directly, and there was no need for legislation as memorials of a one-time theocracy; but we are also aware, through the existence of Egyptian writing, that the gods have long since withdrawn from the earth. The forgetfulness and seeming wisdom, which Thamoun realized were unavoidable concomitants of writing, must not have outweighed the advantages of written law. To be reminded of the gods through the law, though all living memory must be lost with their absence and a seeming wisdom about the gods inevitably reign, is radically different from the divine reminders of Greek poetry, which link eros and the beautiful and subvert the law. The withdrawal of the gods or the hiddenness of the gods must accompany the promulgation of the divine law. The presence of the gods in the form of ourselves cannot but prevent the establishment of divine law. The most sacred laws among the Greeks are called unwritten laws (Sophocles *Antigone* 454–55).

Of the seven arts Theuth discovered, four are serious—number, calculation, geometry, and astronomy—and three playful—checkers, dice, and letters. Thamoun found fault with all of them; presumably, he criticized the encouragement to idleness he foresaw in games and the belief in the comprehensive wisdom of mathematics. Socrates tells only the part about letters, and he makes a dialogue between Theuth and Thamoun. We are forcibly reminded that the speech of each god must fit the soul of each god. Thamoun distinguishes between inventiveness and critical judgment. His distinction recalls Socrates' maieutic art, which was good for judging true and false but incapable of generating anything on its own (*Theaetetus* 149a1–151d3). Whatever may be true of Socrates' art, Thamoun denies that self-knowledge is possible. A bias in favor of one's own blinds one to the defects of one's own. A seeming wisdom belongs to the inventor of letters no less than to whoever uses them thereafter. Socrates' story is altogether silent about what led Theuth to the discovery of letters; Thamoun asked him only about their own usefulness. The discovery of letters, according to Socrates, involved the insight that articulate sounds were composed of vocalic and nonvocalic elements (*Philebus* 18b6–d2). What is silent in itself can be isolated from whatever is sounded, and the infinite stream of sound can be reduced to a finite number of kinds. Theuth's discovery, then, has nothing to do with writing and publishing; in itself, it is a paradigm for the kind of analysis Socrates showed he had practiced in his second speech (cf. 277b7). Since, however, letters can be used nonparadigmatically for recording, they are the instrument of all teaching in which one does not articulate the manifold of the beings but rather collects them into one. This had been the way of Socrates' first speech. Letters, then, comprehend the synthetic and analytic ways of Socrates himself; only by thinking them together is writing completely vindicated. In any writing, its didactic character must be its most manifest aspect; but once one attends to what led to its becoming most manifest, it ceases to be didactic and becomes an instrument of ascent. The temporality of instruction is replaced by the spatiality of reflection at the moment when one looks back and puts in its proper place the part that appeared as the whole.

Socrates tells a story, which as a form of instruction prohibits one from asking who is the speaker or speakers and where they are from, but asks only whether Thamoun tells the truth (275b5–c4). Socrates urges Phaedrus to violate the principles of rhetoric, and Phaedrus willingly complies. The moral of the story effaces the story. Phaedrus' compliance illustrates perfectly how easily edification becomes the bottom line. Socrates now has so much authority over Phaedrus that he does not dare ask whether the story is true or how it could be rationalized away. Socrates accepted the official teaching of Athens about Boreas so that he could come to know himself; Phaedrus accepts the official teaching of Socrates because he does not know himself. Phaedrus is a warning of how not to read a Platonic dialogue.

Socrates' two objections to writing are not Thamoun's. The first is that writings are like the offspring of painting; they look alive, but if one asks them a question they remain silent. Far from writings instilling seeming wisdom, they are all too easily dismissed for seeming wisdom, for they always signify one and the same. Socrates' second objection is that writings do not know when to speak, to whom to speak, and when they are to be silent. Just as Socrates' first objection is exemplified in Phaedrus' construing of Socrates' Egyptian story, so his second objection is obviated by the same story. The story is silent if it is not read dialogically, and the story is discriminating and circumstantial if it is so read. Socrates' second objection in itself is a criticism of the law, which by its very generality cannot cover all contingencies (*Statesman* 294a10–c9). The first defect of writing can be a danger only if the writing is authoritative or by chance the soul of the reader has no defenses against the writing. Of these possibilities, the first is nothing but the obstacle the law puts in the way of thinking; the second can arise only if the character of the writing coincides exactly with the reader's soul-type. Such a coincidence is very flattering to the reader and without self-knowledge can be fatal. Flattery is the comprehensive class into which Socrates in the *Gorgias* put sophistry and rhetoric; its effectiveness was obvious to us in Socrates' first speech in the *Phaedrus*. Erotic speech necessarily has this element of flattery in it (cf. *Sophist* 222d7–223a1); only if one corrects for it, as Socrates did in his second speech, can a writing be philosophical. It is remarkable, then, that Socrates' two objections against writing are directed against both the law and its apparent opposite. Socrates, however, implies by his own practice that, of public and private writings, which either order or cajole, only the erotic speech admits of self-correction. The law cannot but be dumb.

A writing cannot think. It cannot possibly answer all the questions one might put to it, and it cannot possibly be adjusted to all souls under all circumstances. No one alive could do it either. The defectiveness of writing seems to be no more or less than the defectiveness of any human being, whose knowledge cannot be as perfect or his prudence as flexible as Socrates imagines. Socrates adds that a writing cannot defend itself if it is unjustly reviled; but Socrates could not defend himself either; and a writing could take the same line as

Socrates did against Callicles, that it is not worthwhile to stop at nothing in one's own defense, and that it is demeaning to conform entirely with the position of the ruling power in order to be safe. If one surveys the four stories of the *Phaedrus*, Boreas, Olympian gods, cicadas, and Theuth, the conventionality of Socrates' beliefs seems more evident in the first half and his inventiveness in the second; but at the same time it is striking that Socrates' innovation—the hyperuranian beings—though it tops the Olympian gods, still depends on them, however stripped they are of everything but their erotic meaning. Socrates is consistently opposed to the law in both parts of the *Phaedrus* (277d7, 278c4, e2); but his extravagance in the first half denies the possibility of wisdom, and his extravagance in the second half is precisely his affirmation of its possibility. The argument of the *Phaedrus* shows why Socrates could not be consistent on this point in both its halves and still argue against the wisdom of the law. The law cannot be argued against unless strictly scientific speaking is possible.

Perhaps the most shocking remark in Socrates' second speech was about the unnaturalness of sexual generation (250e4–5). The perpetuation of one self through another could not but seem unnatural if lover and beloved can be united forever through philosophy (256e1). Socrates' cosmology, moreover, was not up to distinguishing between motion and becoming. Now, however, through a casual mention of writing as having a father who always has to defend it, Socrates allows himself to give a writing a legitimate brother, who is, Phaedrus says, the living and ensouled speech of the knower (275e4–276a9). That a writing is a phantom image of living speech, or a corpse, is one thing; but what exactly is an ensouled speech? Is it hypallage for "a speech of someone alive"? Or does legitimate speech have a soul of its own? Socrates, at any rate, in contrasting the gardens of Adonis with the serious works of the farmer (276b1–c2), manages to transform speech into seed and souls into soils, so that he envisages simultaneously the immortality of the knower's speech and the happiness of each pupil in succession (276e4–277a5; cf. 278a5–b2). The elimination of the hyperuranian allows a return to the earthly and self-perpetuation through asexual generation. Where, however, did the seed come from? Are we to take seriously the possibility than man is neither divine nor bestial but like a plant vegetative (*Timaeus* 90a6)? Socrates had rebuked Phaedrus for not having the faith of his fathers who believed that the first prophetic speeches were of an oak (275b5–c1). Indeed, Socrates stayed in town, he told Phaedrus, because trees refused to teach him (230d4); and at that time only the lure of a book could draw him away from Athens. Now, however, that science is perfect, the country is as good a place as any, and the opinions of men are no longer needed. Now, Socrates says, the legitimate speech is written in the soul of the learner (276a5, 278a3). Now there is growth but not growth of wings.

Socrates closes the gap between speaking and writing by making the transmission of knowledge from teacher to pupil a back-formation from its dissemination by writing. The legitimate brother of scientific speech is legitimated through its bastard. Socrates finally shows us how the knowledge of what is can be used to move gradually through a series of likenesses from what is to what is not and back again so that what began in opposition ends up in an amalgam that suits Phaedrus. Phaedrus can be restored to his beloved Lysias with an image that retains the truth in a fabulous form. We ourselves cannot but think of the Platonic Academy and wonder how Socrates, in looking ahead to Plotinus and beyond, and comparing that succession with the silent and dead image of himself in the Platonic dialogues, would judge the fruits of the first against the beauty of the other. The *Phaedrus* makes it easy, perhaps all too easy, for us to decide.

The ambiguous nature of writing is maintained to the end. Socrates summarizes separately the two issues of the second half of the *Phaedrus*. The first summary concerns what makes written speech artful or not; the second concerns the baseness or nobility of speaking and writing speeches (277a10–278b6). In the first summary, Socrates distinguishes between the species of whatever one speaks or writes about and the natures of soul, and he correlates this distinction with that between knowledge and insight (between *eidenai* or *epistasthai* and *diidein*). The indifference in his summary to the difference between speaking and writing, on the one hand, and instruction and persuasion, on the other, implies that a writer might have to write more than one book about the same thing if he were going to arrange for a fit between species and nature and assign complex speeches to a complex soul and simple to simple. The degree to which something is divided into its species depends on the nature of the soul to which it is addressed. An undivided species is not necessarily indivisible, and an atomic species is not necessarily with its atomic congeners. When Socrates turns to the second issue, dialogic speaking is distinguished from nondialogic speaking and writing, and dialogic speaking is alone recommended as serious if the purpose is learning, but the model for instruction is still speeches written in soul. The first summary suggests that likeness-making is unavoidable even in instruction, and the second points by its silence to the imitation of dialogue.

# XVII
# Lysias and Isocrates

(278b7–279c8)

The final message Phaedrus is to bring to Lysias arms Lysias against any possible reproach from politicians, for he is no worse as logographer than they are as lawgivers; but if Lysias wants to be a philosophic writer, he must be able to defend whatever he writes and prove by deed its inferiority to that defense. Socrates leaves it up in the air how we are to proceed in the case of a writing whose author is dead. Protestations of earnestness or affirmations of playfulness are hardly adequate indexes of what the writer understood or not. To be playful (*prospaizein*) also means to celebrate a god (262d2, 265c1). Socrates' measured praise of Isocrates seems designed to test our ability to judge how well on the basis of his writings Isocrates sustained his philosophic impulse. On the face of it, Isocrates shows how easily rhetoric and philosophy can diverge; but in his speech on Helen, Isocrates tries to exonerate Helen by enhancing her association with Theseus. Theseus was wise and Helen beautiful. The subordination of the beautiful to wisdom is not a bad motto for the *Phaedrus*.

There are two prayers at the end of the *Phaedrus*. The first belongs jointly to Socrates and Phaedrus; the second is Socrates' alone, but, Phaedrus claims, it is common to them both. The first is not formally a prayer; no gods are addressed, and the verb "to pray" is for form's sake (278b3, 5). The second is a prayer to Pan and all the other gods of the place; it seems to be more than a wish and peculiar to Socrates. In the first prayer Socrates and Phaedrus would want each or each other to be a philosopher (278b2–4); in the second prayer, Socrates wants the gods to grant him to be beautiful within and everything he has on the outside to be dear to whatever is within, and Socrates himself to hold the wise man wealthy, and the quantity of his gold to be exempt from plundering except by the moderate (279b8–c3). The structure of the prayer recalls Socrates' first speech, where the nonlover convicted the lover or himself of ruining the soul, the body, and the external goods of the beloved, and the aging lover was unpleasant besides. Socrates asks for a harmony of inside and outside, though one is to be beautiful and the other is ugly; and he asks for a transvaluation of wealth that makes both "gold" and "moderate" into controversial terms (cf. 235e2). Socrates, it seems, asks to be a book; he asks to become Plato's *Phaedrus*. Phaedrus' request, then, that Socrates pray the same for him would in that case be automatically granted, for, as he says, "the things of friends are in common."[1]

---

1. Apuleius in his *Metamorphoses* calls himself as narrator Lucius. *Lucius* is a translation into Latin of *Phaidros* ("Bright"). Lucius tells us that a Chaldaean predicted he would become a book (2.12).

# Epilogue

## On Reading Poetry Platonically

Sappho wrote a poem addressed to Aphrodite. In that poem she imagines Aphrodite's descent from heaven and her asking with a smile, "Who has committed an injustice against you, Sappho?" (fr. 1, 19–20). And after Aphrodite promises to help her as she has in the past, Sappho ends the poem by summoning her as an ally in war (*summakhos*). Sappho understands love in terms of right and Aphrodite as a goddess of revenge. The issues of justice and love are presented together, and there is no suggestion that they could be separated once Sappho asks a god to alleviate her suffering. Socrates has acknowledged the experiential truth of this coupling in his image of the war chariot of the soul, but he also has suggested how it would be possible to uncouple them. The result of such an uncoupling can be seen in the *Gorgias*, where Socrates anatomizes the will to punish and its appearance of rationality. Eros and moral indignation seem to be alternative grounds for what constitutes the nature of man. Which alternative, one could ask more exactly, links up with rationality? The individuality of the will and the wholeness of eros seem to be in competition for the hand of reason. The difficulty in the choice reason has to make can be seen if one considers the relation the white and black horse have to one another, on the one hand, and Socrates' proposal, on the other, that punitive rhetoric can be effective if its patient can be split between a higher and a lower self. There is a structural resemblance between the pair Polus-Callicles and the pair Socrates-Phaedrus, even if Socrates looks more like Callicles than like Polus. The structural resemblance, however, conceals the difference between the self-control punitive rhetoric would achieve and the confrontation with one's own ignorance Socratic rhetoric aims at. Socrates seems to suggest that eros is naturally superior to the will despite the fact that the illusion of the self against the self seems not to differ very much from the illusion of the erotic ideal. Socrates makes the difference turn on the question of self-knowledge, which he denies is possible in the element of political moderation, for there one has to submit blindly to corrective punishment (*Gorgias* 480c6).

Odysseus told the Phaeacians how he had defeated Polyphemus—he of many names—by calling himself Outis—he of no name or no one. Odysseus connected *outis* with *mētis*, which was simultaneously another form of *outis* and a word for wisdom or craft (*Odyssey* 9.403–415). Odysseus identified mind with anonymity. Mind is no one's. Man, however, is not no one. Everybody when he is born, Alcinous told Odysseus, is given a name regardless of whether he is good or bad (8.552–554); and Odysseus initiates his own suffering by telling Polyphemus his real name (9.500–505). Circe turned half of Odysseus' men into swine though their minds remained intact (10.240). Odysseus volunteered to rescue them, and presumably as a reward for his justice Hermes met him on the way and showed him the nature (*phusis*) of the moly: "It was black in its root, and its flower was like milk" (10.304). Since we are not told what Odysseus did with the moly, and yet Circe's magic spell was ineffective against him, we are led to suppose that Odysseus realized that things have natures, and this knowledge alone kept his mind together with his human shape. That Odysseus then went to Hades and saw human shapes without mind tends to confirm that Odysseus was the first to recognize the indissoluble duality of man. Socrates' account of that duality is a reflection on Odysseus' discovery. Eros and mind, or Olympian gods and speech, seem to extend and deepen Hermes' gift.

When Circe finds that she cannot enchant Odysseus' mind (10.328), she proposes that he sleep with her in order to confirm their trust in one another (cf. *Phaedrus* 256d1–2), but Odysseus refuses at first, for Hermes had warned him that she might unman him unless she were bound by a mighty oath. The nature of man—of body and mind together—is not the same as his sexual nature—of male or female— and which the mere knowledge of man's nature cannot either preserve or deduce. Socrates' myth had also failed to account for the sexes. His awareness of the failure emerged in the *Gorgias*, when he associated his own inconstancy with Callicles', with whom he shared a double love, for Alcibiades and philosophy in his own case, for Demos and the Athenian demos in the case of Callicles. The union of Alcibiades and philosophy was also a failure, as we know from the *Symposium*; but had it succeeded it would have been a pairing of the white and the black horses of the *Phaedrus* and due to Socrates' erotic art. Socrates' erotic art was based on the necessity for a double structure to all Socratic dialectic. This structure in the broadest terms is determined by the relation between nonphilosophy and philosophy, or the ascent from the level of opinion to that of knowledge. The appearance of this double structure is not always the same. In the *Gorgias*, it showed up in the moral idealism of Gorgias, Polus, and Callicles that mirrored defectively Socrates' knowledge of his own ignorance. In the *Republic*, as I tried to show in *Socrates' Second Sailing*, the city in speech and the dialogic city are another version of the same structure.

# General Index

Acharnae, 68
Achilles, 71; and Hector 51
Adverbs, 52
Aeschylus, 124, 179n
Agathon in Plato's *Symposium*, 149
Agent and patient, 51
Alcibiades, 62, 64–65, 196; lisp of, 67
Anaxagoras, 56, 182–84
Animal (*zōion*), 90, 137; ambiguity of, 19; and image, 176; rational, 104; writing as, 103
Antisthenes, 166n
Apuleius, 142n, 166, 182n, 193n
Archelaus, 6; Polus' account of, 44, 99
Arginousae, 48
Aristophanes, 151; *Clouds*, 24; *Frogs*,65; *Knights*, 63, 94; speech in Plato's *Symposium*, 66, 68, 149
Art: and experience 37, 82; knowledge of good and cause, 37
Ascent and self-motion, 154
Ass, 166–68
Athens: empire of, 95; statesmen of, 97; suspends right to execute, 41
Audience, 26–27
Aulus Gellius, 57, 186; on *Gorgias*, 93n; on Lysias and Plato, 160

Beast, 144
Beating, 67
Beautiful (*kalon*), 141; and pleasure, 49; pun on, 49, 63; and rationality, 156; and ugly, 49; and wing 144–47
Being and seeming, 34
Beloved. *See* Nonlover
Body (*sōma*), 76; intellectualized, 57; phantom image of, 79; and soul, 56, 88, 99; as tomb, 75. *See also* Soul
Boreas, 111
Boxing, 24
Brachylogy (and macrology), 12

Callicles: afraid of demos, 89; eloquence of, 70; friend of Gorgias, 9; freedom from nature in 82; good will of, 68–69; indulgence of, 83; insincerity of, 94; pleasure for, 26; and Polus, 46; role in *Gorgias*, 80; split between himself and Polus, 86; squeamish, 8; as touchstone, 62; two loves of, 62; two parts of argument of, 61, 64; unknown elsewhere, 7
Chaerephon, 9, 26, 61
Chariot, 136–37; of war, 143, 183
Cicadas, 162
Cicero, 34, 59, 101n
Circe, 196
City: and country, 114; and Eros, 153; justice in, 28; strength of, 67
Cleon, 7n
Compassion, 96
Conscience, 48
Controversial (and noncontroversial), 175
Conversation. *See Dialegesthai*
Cookery, 36
Corpses and burial, 48
Cosmetics, 36
Cosmology, 136–37
Countryside, 114
Courage. *See* Manliness

*Daimonion* of Socrates, 40, 121, 127
Danaids, 75
Darius, 66
Daube, D., 166n; on *iniuria*, 92n
Death: fear of 93–94; as life, 79
Deliberative speech, 120
Democracy and tyranny, 74
Demos, 70, 72; of Athens, 63; ignorant, 27; in plural, 84–85; as scapegoat, 90
Demos, son of Pyrilampes, 62–63
Demosthenes, 93

Dialectic and rhetoric, 13
*Dialegesthai* (conversation), 111, 152, 155, 181; defense against tyranny, 112
*Diamakhesthai*, 84
*Digest*, 93
*Dikē* (justice): pun on, 55. *See also* Punishment
Disloyalty, 94
Divination, 131
Dodds, E. R., 68n
*Doxa* (reputation and opinion), 24–25

Education, neglected in *Gorgias*, 43
Egyptian gods, 156
Enchantment, 163
Entropy, 135
Epideictic speech, 125
*Epiplēttein* (rebuke), 56
Eros: art of 103, 155; definition of, 121; delusion of, 133; etymology of, 140; as god, 121; and Muses, 162; physiology of, 122; and sight, 144; (in *Symposium*, 3; as strength (*rhōmē*), 123; two elements in, 141; and wing, 145
Erotic soul, eleven types of, 144
Erotic speeches: two kinds of, 106; what in common, 155
*Eu prattein*, pun on, 90
Euripides, 67, 75
Evil, greatest, 26, 42
Experience: and knowledge, 32, 104; shared, 108

Fatherland (*patris*), 59
Fear, 147
Flattery, 33, 189; change in understanding of, 83
Force, 98, 137; and persuasion, 96
Forensic speech, 117
Freedom and enslavement, 81

Gods: beautiful and just, 2; of Egypt; as poets, 100
Good(s), 16, 27; and bad, 167; and being, 136, 165; common, 89; and disorder, 140; for Polus, 40; and power, 70; unconditionality of, 78
Gorgias, 89; as ambassador, 7n, 23; brother of, 23; and Callicles, 65; *Helen* of, 12; ignorance of, 24; lesson for, 55; morality of, 27; as rational, 13; rhetoric of, 186; as Socratic type, 26, 30, 36; speech of, 23–25; as spectator, 51
*Gorgias* (Plato's), 122; apparently rhetorical, 5; atmosphere of, 9; difference from Thucydides, 78; relation to *Republic*, 5, 91–92; Socrates' experiment in, 7; unity of, 6
Gratification, 71; Socrates' need for, 32

Hades, 49, 59, 75–76, 88, 100, 138; in *Protagoras*, 3; in *Republic*, 84; no soul in, 100
Health, 122
Heaven, 137
Hedonism, 78
Helen, 192
Heracles, 65
Herodotus, 47n, 67, 94, 111, 137, 168, 187
Hesiod, 131, 162
Hestia, 138
Homer, 51, 112n, 165; Helen of, 130
Hope, not in *Gorgias*, 79
Horse, 137; black and white, 149–51
Human, 74, 114; and hyperuranian, 144
Hyperuranian beings, 130

*Iliad*, 71
Imperialism, 71, 97
Injustice (*adikein*): absolute good for Polus, 43; active and passive, 65; ambiguity of *adikein*, 47; experience of, 92; and happiness, 46
Inside and outside, 38
Insolence (hubris), 121
Insult, 65, 92n, 99
Interiority of soul, 135
Isocrates, 192

Jar (*pithos*), image of, 75–76
Judges (*dikastai*), 56
Justice: as art and knowledge, 6; and beautiful, 30, 49–50; and good, 43; not defined in *Gorgias*, 7; defined, 97–98; and just man, 29; and killing, 41; and moderation, 140; for Polus, 44; and power, 25; and punishment (*dikaiosunē* and *dikastikē*), 36, 47 (*dikē*); in *Republic*, 138; Socrates' understanding of, 29, 97–98
Just murder, 24

Knowledge: of ignorance, 18; and opinion, 143; superiority of, 27
*Kolazein* (to punish), 55

Language, 56
Law, 70–71, 77, 183, 189–90; and beautiful, 49; in *Crito*, 157–58; and gods, 123; divine, 78; and justice, 38
Left and right, 179
Legislator, 156
Lessing, G. E., 71n
Likeness-making, 191
Lion, 71
Literalness, 15, 75–76
Logographic necessity, 117, 176
*Logos*, 89; as cure, 50; diagnostic and therapeutic, 51; meaning of, 15; and myth, 98; and nature, 61; as proportion, 34. *See also* Speech
Love. *See* Eros
Lover: as heretic and idolater, 147; and nonlover, 107, 117; as tyrant, 124
Lust, 122
Lysias, 107, 180; defines Eros, 176; publication of, 116; relevance for Socrates, 117, 175; speech of, 110; as speechwriter (*logographos*), 156; style of, 159n

Macrology, 33
Madness, 121
Manliness (*andreia*), 68, 90, 141–42
Manufacture, 14
Mathematics, proofs in, 13
Medicine, 23; and pain, 57; and tragedy, 183
Meletus 150
Metaphor, 15
Midas, 177
Midwifery, 188
Mind, types of, 144
Mirror-image, 181
Moderation (*sōphrosunē*), 61, 74; as complete virtue, 90; and justice, induction of, 124; and rhetoric, 51
Moral certainty, 58
Moral indignation, 44
Morality, 40, 57, 96, 125, 169
Moral virtue, 77
Mortal and immortal, 132
Mule, 167

Muses, 168n; and Eros 127; Phaedrus and 119
Myth, 11

Natural right, 70
Nature, 102, 196; and law, 122
Nestor, 165, 170
Nietzsche, 60
Nonlover, 107, 116; as beloved, 107; praise of, 126

Oath, 13, 66, 170
Obedience: ambiguity of, 17; replaces emulation, 83
Odysseus, 101; discovers nature (*phusis*), 195–96
*Odyssey*, 100
Olympian gods, 128, 136, 151, 162–63; and pre-Olympian, 140–41
Opinion, 26, 172; and truth, 120. *See also* Knowledge
Order, 85–86
Ovid, 168n

Pain, 55, 76; and benefit, 53; life of, 78
Painting, 11
Pan, 105, 142
Paradigm, 145
Parmenides, 138, 171
*Pathei mathos*, 54
Pausanias in *Symposium*, 131
*Peithetai*, 112
Peloponnesian War, 63; no allusion to in *Gorgias*, 7
Pericles, 85, 95; and Alcibiades, 80n; funeral speech of, 72
Persuasion (*peithō*) 6, 171, 182; ambiguity of, 17; comprehends knowledge and trust, 20–21; "I persuade myself," 18
Phaedrus: no black horse of, 179; character of, 106; defends Lysias, 118; impiety of, 119; in between rhetoric and philosophy, 129; his knowledge of Socrates, 119; and pleasure, 161; as white horse, 150
*Phaedrus*, 155; stories in, 190; and *Symposium*, 106; two parts of, 103
Philosopher-king, 143
Philosophy, 64; and Callicles, 42; injustice of, 26, 42; not known to Zeus, 98; *logos* of 2; and morality, 58

Physiology of desire, 146
Piety, 99
Pindar, 66–67, 71, 177n
Plato, 113, 144; Academy of, 191; art of representation, 11; as makeup artist, 37; and Socrates, 131; writings of, 103, 161
Pleasure, 40, 74; and benefit, 25; and courage, 8; and the good, 51, 82; and pain, 79, 147; science of, 37, 82; and self-knowledge, 25; and virtue, 77
Poetry, 187
*Poiein ti*, 51
Political: for Gorgias, 28; in *Gorgias* and *Republic*, 92; honor, 41; philosophy, 35
Politician, true, 94
Polus: defines rhetoric, 12; favors Socrates' theses, 37; justice of, 31; laughter of, 47; replaces Gorgias, 10; takes from Gorgias, 30
Prayer, 192
Principle and structure of soul, 134
Prometheus, 98–99
Pronouns, personal, 108–9, 118
*Protagoras*, 3, 43, 59–60; Socrates' myth in, 95
Prudence (*phronēsis*), 74
Psychology, 115; two models of, 2–3, 195
*Pterōs*, 146
Pun, 49, 76, 90
Punishment (*dikē*), 47, 75, 195; of Callicles and demos, 89; length of 31–32; phantom image of justice, 58

Randomness and order, 85–86
Rationality, 113, 163; and whimsicality, 39
Religion, 84
*Republic*, 38; class-structure and soul-structure in, 91–92; communism in, 66; Glaucon in, 73, 96, 47; Socrates in, 65; so-called virtues of soul in, 57
Rhetoric, 164; as art, 15; as chief good, 16; and dialectic, 1, 104, 159; as flattery, 36; and force, 17, 96; Gorgias' claim for, 5; Gorgias' definition of, 13–20; kinds of, 12; as phantom image, 21, 33; justice of, 29; in law courts, 20; and morality, 6; power of, 44; as science of speech, 11, 184; scope of 21–22; Socrates' understanding of, 2; structure of, 44–45

Sappho, 118; interpretation of, 195
Science and pleasure, 82
Self-denunciation, 58, 86
Self-identity, 135
Self-ignorance, 52, 151
Self-interest, 119
Self-knowledge, 18, 103, 113–14, 171, 175; and self-control, 195; of Socrates, 133; and writing, 108
Self-motion, 134–35, 154
Self-persuasion, 18
Self-rule, 74
Seneca, 72
Set (god), 168
Sexual: generation, 190; pleasure, 38
Shame, 25, 69
Sincerity, 18–19
Slave (*mastigias*), 99
Snub nose, 150, 167
Socrates: caution of 8; dialogic monologue of, 90; erotic art of, 103; intention in *Gorgias*, 90; justice of, 25; paradoxes of, 6, 48; playfulness of, 62; political art of, 17; questions of, 10; scheme for rhetoric 6, 39; self-knowledge of 112–14; as Silenus, 113; two speeches of in *Phaedrus*, 121, 126, 153–54
Socratic dialogue, 153
*Sophist* (Plato's), 164
Sophists, 97, 158
Sophocles, 188
*Sōphrosunē*, 103; two contraries of, 121; unpraiseworthy, 125
Soul (*psukhē*): being of, 136, 184; and being and speech, 163–64; and body, 33, 100; as breath, 112; form of, 142; and mind, 13, 103; two motions of, 138; as soil, 190; types of, 147–49, 184–86
Spectator, 54
Speech, 144; analytic and synthetic, 129, 179; two kinds of erotic, 103; plan of Socrates' second speech in *Phaedrus*, 132; rational, 15; as seed, 190; science of, 14; and sight, 145; of Socrates, 175; types of, 147–49, 172; and writing, 156. See also *Logos*; Rhetoric

Spiritedness (*to thumoeides*), 166
Stesichorus, 130
Stronger (*kreittōn*), change in meaning of, 67
Suicide, 88
Syllable, 155
*Symposium* (Plato's), 3, 106
Syntax: disorder in, 100, 179n; in *Gorgias*, 17–18

Teaching, 120
Teisias, 186
Telephus, 55
Thamoun (Ammon) and Theuth, 187
Theaetetus, 14n
Theory and practice, 50, 185
Thersites, 71; as scapegoat 100–101
Thirty tyrants, 42–43
Thought (*dianoia*), 144
Thrasymachus, 41, 43, 128
Thucydides, 7n, 13, 59, 75, 80n, 84n, 95–96n; plague in, 22, 77–78; and Plato, 72–73
*Timaeus* (Plato's), 136, 164, 182
Torture, 46–47
Tragedy, 83

Typhon: god 128; in Hesiod, 113–14; in Ovid, 168n
Tyranny: happiness of 50; injustice of 41–42; and philosophy, 125; and rhetoric, 38
Tyrant, 126

Unwritten law, 157

Vowels and consonants, 188. *See also* Syllable

White horse, 150
Whole and part, 34, 184
Will, 18, 29; and fantasy, 77; and meaning (*boulesthai*), 59; and punishment, 54
Wing, 138–41, 145–46
Writing, 104, 184, 189; unity of, 159

Xenophon, 48, 181n
Xerxes, 66

Zeno, 159, 170–71
Zeus, 98, 138, 149
Zeuxis, 19

# Index of Platonic Passages Discussed

*Apology of Socrates*
26a1–7: 57
27d5–28c1: 167
31c4–32a3: 129
31d2–5: 40
32c4–d7: 43
37a5–b2: 22
38d6–2: 96
40a2–3: 97

*Charmides*
156b6–157d3: 184
161c5–6: 151

*Cratylus*
398d1–e3: 140
398a4–6: 175
399d10–e3: 112n
408d2–3: 142
416b6–d11: 49
420b3–4: 133

*Crito*
54b2–c7: 139

*Epistles*
2:314c1–4: 37, 155

*Euthyphro*
2b11: 150

*Gorgias*
447c5: 61
448d9: 10
449a7: 28
451a6–c6: 15
452d5–8: 8, 17
452e1–453a5: 2
453c3: 51
453c4: 59

454c1–5: 19
454e1–8: 21
456a7–457c3: 12
456c2: 30
457c3: 8
458d1–4: 9
459e1: 27
459e6–8: 164
459e8–460e2: 29
460e7: 26
461a7–b2: 5
461c8: 96
461d2: 31
462b4: 97
464c1: 34
465c3–7: 36
466b1–c5: 39
467c3–4: 49
467d1–468a2: 40
469c5–7: 41
470d: 7
470d5: 43
470e6–471a3: 34
470e10: 68
472a7: 7
472e1–2: 46
473d5: 47
473e6: 7
474c2–4: 49
475c2: 50
476a7–8: 47
478a5: 97
478b8–479b5: 57
479b8: 56
480c4: 59
480c5–6: 59, 195
481d5: 7
482a2–5: 1
483a8: 93n
483e3: 66

483e4–484a6: 65
484b7: 96
485b2–c1: 66
485c2–d2: 67
485d3–e2: 125
486c2: 41
488b3: 96
488c2: 71
489c6: 71
494a1: 76
494a7: 8
494b1–5: 55
494c2–3: 78
495b8: 71
496e7–8: 79
499a2–b8: 61
500c8: 82
501a3–b1: 37
501a5–6: 82
503c2–3: 7
503c7–d2: 85
503e1–504a1: 103
503e4–6: 85
504d3: 61
505c1–4: 32
505d1: 177
505d4: 96
506a3–5: 90
507b5–c2: 61
507e6–508c3: 91
508e1: 102
508e6–509a7: 90
510b8: 95
512b2: 66, 88
513c4–6: 93
517b3: 95
517b6: 96
517c2: 8
517d1–2: 96, 97
518a5: 97

204  Index of Platonic Passages Discussed

518e3: 72
519a3: 8
519a8: 7
519d5–e2: 97
520a4: 95
521b4–c2: 60
521d7: 17
522b9–c2: 97
522e1–4: 83
523e1–525d5: 100
524b1–c4: 137
524d8: 101
526c6–7: 101
526d5: 41
527c6–d2: 102
527d2–5: 101
527d5–e1: 102

*Ion*
534c7: 162

*Laws*
860b1–8: 33
864a1–8: 29

*Lysis*
212d8: 64

*Menexenus*
234c2–235c5: 72
243c6: 48

*Parmenides*
12d6–e1: 159

*Phaedo*
58a10–b7: 41
68a3–7: 141
96a6–100b3: 182
115c6–d2: 51

*Phaedrus*
227b9–10: 177n
227c5–8: 110
227c9–d2: 117
229a3–4: 11
229d4: 143
230d4: 190
230d6–e1: 180
231a1: 161
232a8–233d5: 116

234d6: 118
235e2: 193
237d4–5: 121
241c5: 132
241d1: 128
241e5–6: 126
242a5–6: 127
242c3–7: 133
242e1: 118
242e2–3: 131
243d6: 131
244a1: 118
244a3–4: 131
244a4: 119
244b6–c5: 131
245b4: 134
245b5–c1: 132
245d8–e1: 137
245e4–6: 135
246c2: 137
246c6–d3: 173
247e2–3: 141
247e4–6: 137
248b1–5: 140
248b5–c2: 141
248a6: 142
248d7–e2: 133
248e3–5: 126
249c4: 144
249d7: 146
249e3–4: 121
250a7: 135
250b7–c2: 133, 149
250d7–e1: 146
250e4–5: 190
251a2–6: 147
251c6–7: 146
252a4–6: 126
252d3: 148
252e4: 154
252e5–253a5: 148
254a7: 122
254e1–5: 150
255c7: 145
255d3–6: 151
256b6: 133
256b7–c7: 150
256d1–2: 196
256e1: 151, 190
257a3–6: 127
257b5: 129

258d4–5: 156
258e1–5: 161
259e4–260a4: 120
259e4–260d2: 20
260b1–c2: 166
261a3: 169
261a3–5: 170
261a7–b2: 2
261b3–d8: 170
261e6: 171
262c10: 103
262d2: 193
262e4: 176
264a2–3: 176
264c2–5: 1, 176, 183
265a9–11: 177
265c1: 193
265c5–6: 175
265c8–d1: 103
265d3–5: 120
265e1–266b1: 179
265e3–4: 121
266d7–270b9: 183
268c2–4: 185
269d4: 186
270b8–271d3: 184
270e3: 186
271c6–d7: 185
271d5–272a1: 1
271d7–272a4: 22, 185
272b1: 185
273e5–274b10: 187
274b6–7: 156
274c1–4: 151
275b5–c4: 188, 190
275b6: 124
275d4–9: 2
275e4–277a5: 190
276a5: 191
277a10–278b6: 191
277b5–c6: 187
277b7: 188
277d7: 190
278a3: 191
278a5–b2: 190
278b3–5: 192
278c4–d6: 187, 190
279b8–c3: 192

*Philebus*
18b6–d2: 188

Index of Platonic Passages Discussed   205

21c6–8: 9
47a3–b9: 122

*Protagoras*
315b9–c8: 2
342a7–c3: 95
345e6–346b5: 60

*Republic*
341c4–342c7: 40
343b1–c1: 128
360e1–361d3: 11, 38
361e3–362a3: 47
433a1–6: 139
442a8: 36
492a5–b3: 158
496b6–c3: 125
496c3–5: 131
509d3: 137
518d9: 57
527a6–b1: 15

536c4: 1
618c1–e2: 144

*Sophist*
222d7–223a1: 189
228d6–11: 29
230b4–d5: 14
239e1–240a2: 106
241d1–3: 104
259e5–6: 164
262b9–c7: 164

*Statesman*
294a7–8: 131
294a10–c9: 189
296c8–d5: 94
294a10–301e5: 158
299c3–4: 97
303b8–c5: 158
307a1–3: 126

*Symposium*
174a4: 11
177a5–c5: 106
177d8: 103
180a7–b4: 118
180d3–e3: 131
192d5–e4: 68
198d3–7: 164
2165b5: 64

*Theaetetus*
149a1–151d3: 188
172a1–b6: 169
185c4–e2: 14n

*Timaeus*
19b4–c2: 85
29b1–d3: 164
90a6: 190

Printed in Poland
by Amazon Fulfillment
Poland Sp. z o.o., Wrocław